THE CHANGING LAW OF THE SEA
— Western Hemisphere Perspectives —

THE CHANGING LAW OF THE SEA

———

Western Hemisphere Perspectives

———

Edited by RALPH ZACKLIN

CARNEGIE ENDOWMENT FOR INTERNATIONAL PEACE

INTER-AMERICAN STUDY GROUP
OF INTERNATIONAL LAW

SIJTHOFF – LEIDEN – 1974

ISBN 90 286 0084 1

Library of Congress Catalog Card Number: 73-91982

Printed in the Netherlands.

CONTENTS

Page

Acknowledgments   1

Preface   3

Members of the Inter-American Study Group of
    International Law   7

I.   The Quiet Revolution:
      Canadian Approaches to the Law of the Sea   9

II.   Towards a New Law for the Seas:
      the Evolution of United States Policy 33

III.   Latin America and the Development of the
      Law of the Sea: an Overview 57

IV.   Mexico and the Law of the Sea 79

V.   Central America and the Caribbean 105

VI.   Venezuela: the Country in the Caribbean 123

VII.   Brazil 133

VIII.   Uruguay 149

IX.   Argentina and the Law of the Sea 167

X.   Chile 189

XI.   Peru: The Road to the West 205

ANNEXES 223

Annex I   Multilateral Instruments 224

The Geneva Conventions

1. Convention on the Territorial Sea and the Contiguous Zone . 224
2. Convention on the High Seas 231
3. Convention on Fishing and Conservation of the
   Living Resources of the High Seas 239
4. Convention on the Continental Shelf 244

Annex II   Regional Instruments and Declarations 249

1. Declaration of Santiago on the Maritime Zone,
   August 18, 1952 249
2. Agreement Supplementary to the Declaration of
   Santiago 1954 250
3. Montevideo Declaration on the Law of the Sea 1970 251
4. The Lima Declaration of the Latin American States
   on the Law of the Sea 1970 252
5. The Declaration of Santo Domingo 1972 253

Annex III   Bilateral Instruments and Declarations 257

1. Agreement on Fishing between Brazil and Argentina,
   signed at Buenos Aires on 29 December 1967 257
2. Agreement on Fishing and Conservation of Living Resources
   between Brazil and Uruguay, signed at Montevideo on
   12 December 1968 258
3. Agreement between the United States of America and the
   United Mexican States on Traditional Fishing in the
   Exclusive Fishery Zones Contiguous to the Territorial Seas
   of Both Countries. Effected by Exchange of Notes signed
   at Washington on 27 October 1967 259
4. Agreement between the Government of the United States
   of America and the Government of Canada on Reciprocal
   Fishing Privileges in Certain Areas off Their Coasts. Signed
   at Ottawa on 24 April 1970 264
5. Agreement between the Government of the Federative
   Republic of Brazil and the Government of the United
   States of America Concerning Shrimp. Done at Brasilia
   May 9, 1972 266
6. Treaty between the United Kingdom and Venezuela
   Relating to the Submarine Areas of the Gulf of Paria,
   February 26, 1942 270

Acknowledgments

In the preparation of this volume the editor has been fortunate enough to have received the assistance of several members of the Carnegie Endowment's staff. Particular thanks are due to Vivian D. Hewitt and Jane Lowenthal, Librarian and Assistant Librarian respectively of the James T. Shotwell Library, for their unflagging determination in obtaining even the most obscure reference materials.

The painstaking task of typing and retyping successive drafts of the manuscript was ably and cheerfully performed by Jane Flood with the assistance of Catherine Kubiak and Margaret Ameer Cataldo. The final copy editing of the manuscript was diligently carried out by Barbara Harkins.

Preface

The third United Nations Conference on the Law of the Sea, which will begin its deliberations in New York and Santiago in 1973 and 1974, is the culmination of several years of intense multilateral diplomacy. The outcome of the Conference will have profound political, economic, and strategic consequences for all States and all mankind. In the search for the reciprocity which is essential to a viable and lasting agreement on the new law of the sea, the American States are destined to play a crucial role, commensurate with their contribution to the contemporary evolution of the law of the sea.

A generation ago, the United States unleashed a revolution in the oceans when President Truman formulated the continental shelf doctrine, possibly the most revolutionary international legal concept of modern times. In 1952, Chile, Ecuador, and Peru established another milestone with the creation of a 200-mile maritime zone; more recently such powerful States as Argentina and Brazil have asserted claims to a broad territorial sea or maritime zone; and in the apparent culmination of this revolution of continental proportions, the States of Central America and the Caribbean have jointly espoused the concept of the patrimonial sea. Finally, in the northernmost part of the hemisphere, Canada has emerged as a nation profoundly concerned with the preservation of its Arctic heritage and the conservation of the natural wealth of its maritime provinces.

The law and practice of the Western hemisphere nations with their combination of national and ecumenical concerns are both symptomatic of the problems and revelatory of the choices facing the members of the international community generally. This volume addresses itself to what is perceived to be the central issue of the Conference, the question of zones within national jurisdiction. It is a matter of historical record that all previous attempts to reach agreement on the breadth of the territorial sea — in 1930, 1958, and 1960 — failed. Since 1960, both the complexity of the issues and the urgency of reaching agreement have increased. The war for the seas is openly discussed and in some parts of the globe is actually taking place. By comparison with the situation prevailing today, 1960 in retrospect appears positively simplistic. Not only does the breadth of the territorial sea remain to be determined but, in the intervening years, new concepts, such as the patrimonial sea, have been developed and dissatisfaction with some of the rules established in 1958, such as the outer limit of the continental shelf, has surfaced.

It is against this background of a crisis in the law of the sea that the present volume has been prepared. Its objectives and audiences are twofold. Firstly, by analyzing the law and practice of States in a scientific yet pragmatic manner, the authors have attempted to demystify the scope and content of the diverse claims

3

advanced by individual States or group of States of the hemisphere. For it is only on the basis of a reciprocal knowledge and understanding of such claims that a viable international agreement can be achieved. To the extent that this volume attains this end, hopefully it will have made a modest contribution to the evolution of a new law of the sea. Secondly, the volume is addressed to all those engaged in the study and teaching of international law. It has been apparent for some time that despite an abundant literature in this field a gap exists between the specialized works such as Colombos' *International Law of the Sea* and articles which deal with very specific aspects of the law of the sea. The omnibus character of the former rules out anything but the most perfunctory summary of national legislation and practice, while the specificity of the latter rests on the frequently unwarranted assumption that the reader is well-versed in the intricacies of, say, Peruvian legislation and practice. The contributions to this volume and the selected documents appended to the text are designed to provide students and teachers with the materials by which they may study and comprehend the practice of an important group of States.

The Changing Law of the Sea: Western Hemisphere Perspectives is the product of an Inter-American research group sponsored by the Carnegie Endowment. The group was created specifically to provide a forum for the examination of and research into contemporary international legal problems of a regional character, and to prepare teaching materials, based particularly on the practice of the Latin American and Caribbean States, for use in the universities of the region. The Inter-American Study Group of International Law became operational in January 1971 when it held its first meeting at the Institute of International Relations in Trinidad. Between January 1971 and May 1973, the Group held a total of four week-long meetings, culminating in a meeting held in Rome in May 1973 at the invitation of the Italian/Latin American Institute at which the Study Group's conclusions were discussed with a group of European international law specialists.

The Study Group has concentrated its research in two principal areas: the law of the sea and international economic law. The present volume is the first collective publication of the Group on the law of the sea, although a number of the contributions have been published previously in international law journals on three continents. A Spanish language edition of the present volume will be published by Fondo de Cultura Economica in Mexico early in 1974.

With regard to international economic law, the members of the Study Group have devoted themselves to an analysis of the theories and realities of international economic relations in terms of the Latin American perspective. The first stage of the Group's work was devoted to the most-favored-nation clause, the traditional basis of international economic law. A preliminary edition of a volume entitled *América Latina y la clausula de la nación mas favorecida* was published in Santiago in 1972. The subsequent research of the Group in this field has been concerned with an examination of alternatives to the most-favored-nation clause including such institutions as State trading, commodity agreements, and producers' agreements. The entire body of research conducted by the Study Group in the international economic law field will be published by Fondo de Cultura Economica in 1974.

Although the contributions contained in the present volume are the responsibility of each individual author, the authors have benefited from the discussion of their studies by the Group as a whole. It should be stressed, however, that the conclusions reached in individual chapters are those of the author and do not represent a consensus of the Group. .

Editing an English language edition of this volume has presented a number of linguistic difficulties. Although the administrative language of the Group was, of necessity, English, the Group itself was multilingual to a marked degree, conducting its meetings in Spanish, English, French, and Portuguese. The contributions to the present volume were written in the individual author's mother tongue and translated where necessary into English. The chapters originally written in Spanish and Portuguese were translated by Francisco Orrego; the chapter on Canada was translated from the French by the editor.

Ralph Zacklin
New York, August 1973

Members of the Inter-American Study Group of International Law

Frida M. Pfirter de Armas is a professor of international law, Universidad Nacional de Rosario, Rosario, Argentina. She is the author of two chapters in the present volume and also contributed to the preliminary edition of *Latin America and the Most-Favored-Nation Clause.*

Tom J. Farer is professor of law at Rutgers University, Camden, New Jersey, U.S.A. He is a frequent contributor to journals and is the author of a chapter entitled "Law and War" in *The Future of the International Legal Order* (Princeton, 1971).

Celso Lafer teaches international law and relations at the Law School of the University of São Paulo, São Paulo, Brazil. Author of a number of studies, including "El convenio internacional del cafe" in *Derecho de la Integración,* No. 12 (1973) and a contributor to *Latin America and the Most-Favored-Nation Clause,* he is co-author with Felix Peña of *Argentina y Brasil en el sistema internacional* (Buenos Aires, 1973).

Vicente Marotta Rangel is professor of international law and Chairman of the Department of International Law at the University of São Paulo, São Paulo, Brazil. He is the author of *Natureza Juridica e Delimitacao do Mar Territorial* (São Paulo, 1970, 2nd ed.) and *Direito e Relacoes Internacionais* (São Paulo, 1971).

Isidro Morales Paul is head of the Department of Economic Integration of the Instituto de Derecho Publico of the Universidad Central de Venezuela, Caracas, Venezuela. He contributed to *Latin America and the Most-Favored-Nation Clause* and is the author of a number of articles in the field of economics.

Jacques-Yvan Morin is Professor of Public International Law at the University of Montreal, Montreal, Canada. He is the author of a number of articles on the law of the sea including "Le progrès technique, la pollution et l'évolution récente du droit de la mer au Canada, particulièrement à l'égard de l'Arctique," in the *Canadian Yearbook of International Law* (1970).

Francisco Orrego Vicuña is in the Department of Legal Affairs of the Organization of American States, on leave from the School of Law, University of Chile, Santiago, Chile. The author of numerous articles and books, he is the editor of *Latin America and the Most-Favored-Nation Clause* and the author of *Chile y el Derecho del Mar* (Santiago, 1972).

Felipe H. Paolillo is professor of international law in the Faculty of Law of the University of Montevideo, Montevideo, Uruguay. The author of numerous articles on the law of the sea and international economic law, he is a contributor to the present volume and *Latin America and the Most-Favored-Nation Clause*. His most recent publication is "Revolucion en los oceanos" in *Revista Uruguaya de Derecho Internacional* (1972).

Felix Peña is head of the legal section of the Instituto para la Integración de America Latina and Professor of Latin American political systems in the Faculty of Social Sciences of the University of Salvador, Buenos Aires, Argentina. The author of numerous publications in the field of economic integration, he is co-author with Celso Lafer of *Argentina y Brasil en el sistema internacional* (Buenos Aires, 1973). Felix Peña is the editor of *Derecho de la Integración*, a review published by INTAL.

Bernardo Sepúlveda is professor of public international law in the Colegio de México and also teaches at the Universidad Nacional de México. In addition to his contributions to the present volume and *Latin America and the Most-Favored-Nation Clause,* he is co-editor of *La O.N.U.: Dilema a los Veinticinco Anos* (Mexico, 1970), author of *La Inversion Extranjera en el Mexico de Hoy* (Mexico, 1973), and has collaborated in the preparation of the Spanish edition of Sorensen's *Manual of Public International Law* (Mexico, 1973).

Francisco Villagrán Kramer is professor of international law and Head of the Department of Economic Integration Law at the University of San Carlos, Guatamala. In addition to numerous articles on the law of the sea and international economic law, he is also the author of *Casos y Documentos de Derecho Internacional* (Guatemala, 1960), *Integración Economica Centroamericana,* (Guatemala, 1967), *Teoria General del Derecho de la Integración* (Costa Rica, 1969), and the forthcoming *Estrategias para una politica de desarrollo equilibrado en el proceso de integración economica centroamericana* (Guatemala, 1973).

Ralph Zacklin is the Director of the International Law Program, Carnegie Endowment for International Peace. He joined the Carnegie Endowment in 1967 after collaborating with Professor Max Sorensen in the preparation of the *Manual of Public International Law.* He is the author of *The Amendment of the Constitutive Instruments of the United Nations and Specialized Agencies* (Leiden: Sijthoff, 1968) and a number of articles. His latest book is *State of Siege: Rhodesia, the United Nations and International Law* to be published later this year.

Chapter I

The Quiet Revolution:
Canadian Approaches to the Law of the Sea

Chapter I

THE QUIET REVOLUTION:
CANADIAN APPROACHES TO THE LAW OF THE SEA

Jacques-Yvan Morin

INTRODUCTION

With the approach of the 1973 and 1974 conferences, the Canadian positions with regard to certain important aspects of the law of the sea are worth considering. Not only has Canada played an active part in the negotiations which have led to the organization of the conference, particularly in the United Nations Seabed Committee, but the compromise solutions submitted by Canada have frequently broken deadlocked discussions and enabled the work of the committee to advance.

This active role is not surprising given the importance of the sea in Canada. Bathed by three oceans, Canada ranks second in the world in the length of its coasts and the size of its continental shelf, which represents approximately 40 percent of its land territory. Thus, the problems related to the exploitation of the biological and mineral wealth of the seas, navigation, and the protection of the marine environment are in the forefront of Canada's preoccupations. Before participating in the multilateral discussions which have taken place in the United Nations since 1967, Canada acted unilaterally to protect its coasts from the dangers of excessive exploitation of living resources and of pollution.

With regard to most of the major issues of the law of the sea, a distinctive Canadian position exists which, to a certain extent, has undoubtedly influenced other countries, developed and developing. These issues will be examined in the following order:

(1) The Territorial Sea,
(2) The Contiguous Zone,
(3) Straits,
(4) The Continental Shelf,
(5) Fishery Zones,
(6) Pollution Prevention Zones.

THE TERRITORIAL SEA

The traditional breadth of Canada's territorial waters was three nautical miles.[1] A legacy of British law, this rule had been incorporated in the Anglo-

American treaty of 1818 before being assimilated into domestic legislation. The 1936 Customs Act, which defined the breadth of the territorial sea, was based upon the three-mile rule "in accordance with international law." Even though the government moved away from this classical principle, subsequently at the second Geneva Conference in the search for a compromise (a six-mile territorial sea), it did not modify its own legislation. Thus, when Parliament was called upon in 1964 to vote on this issue, the breadth of Canada's territorial jurisdiction on the seas was still limited to three miles, though care was taken to add a nine-mile fishery zone and to authorize the adoption of straight baselines where applicable.

In June 1970 a new Act modified the classical rule. Henceforth, the Canadian territorial sea comprises: "those areas of the sea having, as their inner limits, the baselines [whether straight or following the low-water mark according to the particular case] and, as their outer limits, lines measured seaward and equidistant from such baselines so that each point of the outer limit line of the territorial sea is distant twelve nautical miles from the nearest point of the baseline."[2]

The maritime belt so defined includes the fishery zone created by the 1964 Act, since this zone extends exactly twelve miles from the baseline. The essential objective of Parliament at that time was the protection of coastal fishing and the exclusive fishery zone provided the best solution. However, from the moment when Canada decided to use this zone for other purposes, particularly pollution control, it became necessary to extend to this zone all the rights and powers of territorial jurisdiction. One of the important effects of the 1970 Act was, therefore, the elimination of the "contiguous" fishing zone, as defined in 1964, but a new fishing zone has taken its place which extends to "areas of the sea adjacent to the coast of Canada." This will be discussed in further detail below.

If the territorial sea has been enlarged, the baselines provided for in 1964 and defined by decree remain the same, with the exception of modifications resulting from new legislative provisions concerning low-tide elevations. In effect, Section 5 of the law now reads as follows:

"(1) The Governor in Council may, by order, issue one or more lists of geographical co-ordinates of points from which baselines may be determined and may, as he deems necessary, amend such lists.

"(2) In respect of any area for which geographical co-ordinates of points have been listed in a list issued pursuant to subsection (1) and subject to any exceptions in the list for the use of the low water line along the coast between given points *and the use of the low water lines of low tide, elevations situated wholly or partly at a distance not exceeding the breadth of the territorial sea from the coast,* baselines are straight lines joining the consecutive geographical co-ordinates of points so listed."

This somewhat ambiguous text appears to mean that, as a general rule, the baselines are formed by a straight line connecting headlands; however the government may in exceptional cases resort to the low-water mark. It should be noted that these provisions would seem to run counter to Article 3 of the Convention on the Territorial Sea, according to which the low-water line is the "normal" baseline for the measurement of the territorial sea. However, the Canadian coastline meets all the requirements of Article 4 of the Convention concerning the utilization of the straight baseline method. Because of the broken network of bays and fjords of all sizes, similar to the Norwegian coast, the low-water line can be employed in only a small number of places. Wherever the straight baseline method cannot be applied, the traditional limits are used: either the low-water line, or in the case of internationally recognized historic waters, their outer limit.

The earlier decrees of 1967 and 1969 governing the baselines on the coasts of Labrador, Newfoundland, Nova Scotia, Vancouver Island, and Queen Charlotte Strait remain in force, since the 1970 Act envisages the extension of the territorial sea and not the modification of the baselines from which it is to be measured. Baselines on those coasts which have not been regulated by a decree since the 1964 Act remain unchanged. Reference here must be made to the decree (Order in Council) of December 18, 1937, and to the charts (Customs Act Maps) provided for by the 1936 Customs Act which were published between 1938 and 1942.[3] Even though these charts remained incomplete, probably due to the war, and in fact only cover a portion of the Atlantic coast, the decree, on the other hand, established the breadth of territorial waters with respect to the entire Canadian coastline, including Hudson Bay but with the exception of the Arctic coast.[4]

Because of the disharmony of the sources and the ambiguous nature of the status of certain maritime areas adjacent to the Canadian coast, such as the Gulf of St. Lawrence or Queen Charlotte Sound, it is necessary to examine more closely the application of the new law and its impact on the territorial sea in each of the major maritime provinces; firstly the Atlantic and Pacific coasts, and finally the special case of the Arctic archipelago.

The Territorial Sea on the Atlantic Coast

The decree of October 26, 1967, divided the Atlantic coast into three regions: Labrador, southeast and east Newfoundland, and southwest Newfoundland. The baseline consists of 113 straight lines and a small number of low-water marks. The decree, therefore, simplifies considerably the configuration of the maritime frontier of Newfoundland, which had previously been a source of controversy. The broken line of this frontier encloses in one tracing the huge bays opening onto the Atlantic, certain of which were claimed by Great Britain as historic bays.[5] The simple fact of having increased the breadth of the territorial sea to twelve miles has resolved several conflicts, because the mouth of Conception Bay as well as those of St. Mary's Bay and Hare Bay is less than twenty-four miles wide; moreover, Article 7 of the Convention on the Territorial Sea provides for the possibility of tracing a demarcation line between the natural points of entry of a bay, when the distance between them is less than twenty-four miles.

With regard to bays which exceed the distance provided for by the Convention and other stretches of water which cannot qualify as bays, because their area is smaller than the semi-circle the diameter of which is formed by the line drawn between the points of entry, the decree applies the straight baseline method. In the great majority of cases, the government has not departed from the "reasonable" criteria defined by the International Court of Justice in the Anglo-Norwegian Fisheries Case[6] and restated in Article 4 of the Convention on the Territorial Sea—in other words, the line does not diverge from the general direction of the coastline, even on large-scale maps, and the stretches of sea enclosed by these baselines are linked to the land territory closely enough to be governed by the regime of internal waters. Only in the case of Confusion Bay and Notre-Dame Bay are there grounds for doubt. The "bay" of Confusion scarcely forms an inflexion in the coastline, but it is true that a more tightly drawn baseline would not have greatly altered the outer limit of the territorial waters, because of the proximity of the Sainte-Barbe Islands. A more doubtful case is that of the line of demarcation off Notre-Dame Bay, the configuration of which required a more subtly drawn line of enclosure.[7] It should be noted that a government spokesman recently admitted to the House of Commons Permanent Committee on Foreign Affairs that certain straight lines have not been "universally accepted" by other States.[8] It would appear, however, that these States (United States, Japan, and certain European States) have not objected to any particular baselines but rather to the method of tracing in general.

On the Labrador coast, innumerable isles and rocks which dot the coastline, itself deeply indented by fjords, bear a close similarity to the Norwegian *skjaergaard*.[9] Thus, quite correctly, the 1967 decree traced a series of straight lines which from cape to rock link Double Island, situated at the entrance to the Hudson Strait, to Cabot Island near the entrance to the Strait of Belle-Isle.

The 1967 decree constituted only the first stage in the application of the 1964 Act. The second stage began with the Order in Council of May 29, 1969, which establishes the geographic coordinates on the basis of which the baseline of the Nova Scotia coast is to be traced (Region 4). From Brier Island, situated at the entrance to the Bay of Fundy, to Cape North, which marks the entrance to the Gulf of St. Lawrence, the baseline consists of fifty-one straight lines, half of which are linked to headlands and half to offshore islands.[10] The decree refers to the detailed marine charts published by the Canadian Hydrographic

14

Service, and the government has published a small-scale chart showing the waters of Nova Scotia.[11]

The Special Case of the Gulf of St. Lawrence

It was generally expected that the 1969 decree, after having fixed the baselines on the Nova Scotia coastline, would clarify the status of the Gulf of St. Lawrence. In its previous decree, the government had stopped the baselines at the entrances to the Straits of Belle-Isle and Cabot. The time was ripe, therefore, to endorse the numerous official declarations in which Canada had claimed the waters of the Gulf. To accomplish this, it would have been necessary to draw straight closing lines across the two straits so that this maritime space, so important for the neighboring provinces, would become internal waters according to the terms of Article 5 of the Convention on the Territorial Sea. The government did not do so, however, and it is a moot question whether it has abandoned these claims or whether it is merely deferring a decision which might raise international difficulties.

To a large extent, the question is related to the rights and interests, whether of a conventional or customary nature, claimed by certain foreign States over the Gulf and the territorial waters of Newfoundland, Quebec, and the Magdalen Islands. France and the United States acquired by treaty, in 1713 and 1783 respectively, rights for their fishermen to continue to fish certain parts of the Atlantic coast. The rights of the United States were later renewed[12] while those of France slowly eroded as the Newfoundland coast became increasingly populated by British subjects. At the present time, following the treaty of 1818, the United States has freedom of fishing in the territorial waters of Newfoundland, from Quirpon Island to the Ramea Islands (passing by Cape Ray) as well as on a part of the southern coast of the Gulf, in the waters of the Magdalen Islands and Labrador. France has kept its "French Shore" from Cape St. John to Cape Ray, passing by the Strait of Belle-Isle, in other words over the whole of Newfoundland opposite the Gulf, until the recent treaty concluded between Paris and Ottawa. Following this agreement, which came into force on March 27, 1972, a restricted number of fishermen of the two countries may fish the waters of Newfoundland and St. Pierre and Miquelon; but France has renounced its former rights.[13]

Another treaty on reciprocal fishing rights entered into force on April 24, 1970, between the United States and Canada. According to this agreement, the nationals of the two countries may continue their traditional fishing activities up to three miles from the coast. American fishing vessels will continue to fish the waters of the Gulf.[14] A more complex problem was that of the customary or historic fishing rights of eight countries whose fishermen have been active in the waters of the Gulf since time immemorial. These States were not disposed to abandon their rights without conditions and Canada proposed a gradual with-drawal of their vessels (a "phasing out") to enable them to reorganize their activities without excessive loss. Agreements of this kind have been signed with Britain, Denmark, Portugal, Norway, and Spain. The activities of vessels of these countries will not continue beyond 1980.

The foregoing may help to explain the Canadian Government's decision to go no further than the delimitation of the fishery closing lines across the Straits of Cabot and Belle-Isle. The Minister of External Affairs, in a speech before the permanent fisheries and forests commission on the scope of the draft territorial sea act, stated that the waters of the Gulf did not form part of "Canadian territorial waters." If that had been the government's intention, he added, "we would have presented different legislation." The government subsequently de-clared its intention of transforming the Gulf into a fishing zone rather than an internal sea, and the new Act grants the government the necessary powers.

If the waters of the Gulf of St. Lawrence are not considered "Canadian territorial waters," neither are they, at the present time, internal waters. For this reason, when the time comes for charting the territorial waters limits in this area, it will be necessary to refer to the 1937 decree and to the customs charts of the Gulf referred to above.[15]

The only criteria incorporated in Article 4 of the Convention on the Terri-torial Sea are the nature of the coastline, the general direction of the coast, and the close relationship of the land and the waters around it. In addition, "account may be taken, in determining particular baselines, of economic interests peculiar to the region concerned, the reality and the importance of which are clearly evidenced by a long usage." But the herring and cod catch on the banks and gulf and off the coast of West Newfoundland are essential for the needs of the neighboring population, for whom it is the principal resource.[16] According to some, the foreign trawlers have contributed to the depressed state of the econ-omy of the region.

In conclusion it may be said that it would not be unreasonable for Canada, taking into account the conventional or customary rights claimed by ten foreign States, to assert its jurisdiction over this arm of the sea which is so intimately linked to its physical and economic geography, especially considering that the Straits of Belle-Isle and Cabot are only used by vessels proceeding to the St. Lawrence and Great Lakes ports. It remains to be seen if the transformation of the Gulf into an internal sea will result in the abolition of the right of innocent passage through the Straits of Cabot and Belle-Isle (see below).

Hudson Bay and Hudson Strait

Before leaving the Atlantic coast, a brief examination of Hudson Bay and Hudson Strait, unilaterally closed by the 1937 decree on territorial waters and the customs zone, is necessary. Part IV of the decree ordered the preparation of a chart showing a baseline drawn across the entrance to Hudson Strait, from Button Islands off Cape Chidley in Labrador to Hatton Headland on Resolution Island. This chart has never been published, but the decree is still in force.[17]

The Canadian territorial waters extend therefore to twelve miles from a straight baseline thirty-seven miles in length drawn between the natural points of entry of Hudson Strait.

The Territorial Sea on the Pacific Coast

The Order in Council decree of May 29, 1969, applies to Vancouver Island (Region 5) and to the Queen Charlotte Islands (Region 6). The former covers the whole of the west coast of Vancouver Island, from Bonilla Point in the south to Winifred Island, and consists of an unbroken series of twenty-two straight baselines drawn between the headlands and the many islands which dot the coastline.[18]

On the other side of the island, the sea penetrates the rocky coastline through narrow passages which form part of Canadian internal waters. In the north these straits are known under the collective name of the "Inside Passage." In the south the Canadian-American frontier, delimited by a series of treaties concluded since 1846, is established by a broken line beginning at the entrance of the Strait of Juan de Fuca on the Pacific and following, *grosso modo,* the median line between the Canadian and American islands which dot the access to the Strait of Georgia.[19] All the stretches of water north of the median line are also part of Canadian internal waters.

Region 6 includes the whole of the coastline of the Queen Charlotte Islands, from Kunghit Island in the south to Langara Island in the north. The baseline consists of twenty-three straight lines drawn between the islands and headlands.[20] As is the case with the Atlantic coast, the decrees do not deal with all the outstanding questions. In particular the maritime frontier of Hecate Strait and Dixon Entrance, to which Canada claims historic rights, remains to be fixed, as well as the status of Queen Charlotte Sound.

These questions are not yet ripe for solution. From the practical point of view, it is impossible to fix the frontier between Hecate Strait and Queen Charlotte Sound without obtaining the consent of the interested States, particularly the United States. This is the reason for which the government has contented itself for the moment with transforming the region into an exclusive fishery zone.

While maintaining its positions with regard to the historic character of Hecate Strait, Canada considers it inopportune, having regard to the present state of the law of the sea, to risk its claims over Queen Charlotte Sound — which remains part of the high seas. The government has been authorized by Parliament, however, to convert this space into an exclusive fishing zone.

THE CONTIGUOUS ZONE

According to Article 24 of the Convention on the Territorial Sea and the Contiguous Zone, the coastal State may exercise control in a zone contiguous to its territorial waters necessary to prevent or punish the infringement of its customs, fiscal, immigration, or sanitary regulations committed *within its territory or territorial sea.*

This does not amount to an extension of the State's territorial jurisdiction but is rather an exceptional right mutually recognized by States on the high seas in order to safeguard their jurisdiction on the territorial sea and on their territory. The commentary of the International Law Commission on the right of hot pursuit was quite explicit on this point: "Acts committed in the contiguous zone do not give rise to a right of hot pursuit on the part of the coastal State."[21]

By reference to this definition, Canada does not have a contiguous zone. Prior to 1920 the Customs Act provided that "Canadian waters" for customs purposes comprised the territorial sea, at that time three miles wide, and the country's internal waters. To this were added "Canadian customs waters" extending nine miles beyond the "Canadian waters." At first sight this appears to be a contiguous zone since the combination of the territorial and customs waters produces a twelve-mile zone.

This geographic similarity must not obscure the legal difference between the Canadian zone and the zone defined in the Convention. In effect, in the "Canadian customs waters" Canada exercises its jurisdiction over Canadian vessels or vessels owned by a person residing or domiciled in Canada, as well as over any other category of vessel designated by the government. It appears from the Act that the jurisdiction exercised over those vessels (which creates no problem for vessels flying the British flag) includes the punishment of infractions committed in the zone. This jurisdiction originates in the "hovering laws" of Great Britain and the British colonies. It has been recognized by other States for many years but does not constitute a "contiguous zone" in the sense of the 1958 Convention.

Since 1970 the territorial sea has been enlarged to twelve miles and therefore includes the former zone of "Canadian customs waters." However the Act maintains a similar zone of nine miles beyond the new territorial sea so that the customs jurisdiction now extends twenty-one miles from the baseline. Any Canadian vessel, or a vessel owned by a person residing or domiciled in Canada navigating in this zone, may be boarded, stopped, brought into port, and confiscated if circumstances warrant it.

In other areas which may be the object of a contiguous zone (fiscal, health, immigration), the Canadian Parliament has not deemed it appropriate to intervene beyond the outer limit of the territorial sea.

18

STRAITS

Most of the Canadian straits are in internal waters, that is to say within the baselines marking the interior boundary of territorial waters. This is the case, for example, of the long channel which separates Vancouver Island from the mainland, the Inside Passage, the breadth of which varies from one to three miles. The same is true of the Strait of Juan de Fuca situated between the United States and Vancouver Island and which is divided by the Canadian-American frontier of 1846. This maritime space is within the internal waters of the two countries, even though its breadth varies from nine to seventeen miles. The historic title of the two countries has never been questioned.

The Hudson Strait has been closed since 1937 by a straight line drawn between Button Islands and Hatton Headland on Resolution Island. In fact, Canada has considered Hudson Bay and Hudson Strait as forming part of its internal waters, since at least the beginning of the century. The relatively inaccessible position of Hudson Bay, the fact that it is completely surrounded by Canadian territory and that its navigation is only possible between August and October may explain the general tolerance towards the Canadian claim.

The Belle-Isle and Cabot Straits which provide access to the Gulf of St. Lawrence are a minimum of ten and fifty-six miles wide respectively. If the Canadian claims to the waters of the Gulf are well founded, these straits are part of the country's internal waters and territorial sea. To the extent that it can maintain that these waters have for a very long time been considered internal waters, Canada would not be required to respect the right of innocent passage of foreign vessels. Since the status of these waters was revised for the first time in 1949, upon the entry of Newfoundland into the Canadian Federation, it is somewhat questionable whether it may be asserted that these were internal waters *ab initio*.

If, on the other hand, the Canadian claims (which at the present time seem to be in suspense since the government has contented itself with transforming the Gulf into an "adjacent fishing zone") result in transforming into internal waters areas which previously formed part of the high seas, must the right of passage in the Gulf be maintained in accordance with Article 5 of the Convention on the Territorial Sea? It seems clear that the answer is yes.

Moreover, in this hypothesis, it may be asked whether Canada is bound to maintain or whether it can abolish a right of passage in straits which join two parts of the high seas? In the *Corfu Channel Case* the International Court of Justice defined an international strait as one "used for purposes of international navigation."[22] Now the Belle-Isle and Cabot Straits are only used by vessels sailing to the St. Lawrence and Great Lakes ports in Canada and the United States; they are not used by vessels sailing between one part of the Atlantic and

19

another. It is possible therefore to maintain that Canada, if it closed the Gulf, could prohibit passage in the straits or require prior authorization. However such restrictions would be rather theoretical since Canada may regulate passage in the Strait of Belle-Isle in any event, following the extension of the territorial sea to twelve miles.

A more complex situation is present in the Canadian Arctic. The celebrated Northwest Passage, the object of fascination for explorers since the sixteenth century, consists of a multitude of straits the breadths of which vary from a few miles to several dozen miles.[2 3]

Explorations carried out since the beginning of the century (it was not until 1903 that the Norwegian explorer Amundsen succeeded in navigating the passage for the first time) have uncovered four practicable routes through the Arctic islands, all of which are subject to Canadian territorial jurisdiction. These four routes begin on the Atlantic coast, at the Lancaster Sound, and terminate in the west in the Beaufort Sea.

Since 1950, the Canadian Hydrographic Service has mapped the underwater topography of practically the entire archipelago, with the exception of McClintock Channel, the southern portion of Viscount Melville Sound, and further north the area of Norwegian Bay; these soundings will be completed in the next few years. In the meantime, Canadian and American ice-breakers are becoming increasingly familiar with the glacial conditions, which vary considerably according to the place and the year. Gradually there is being developed the possibility of utilizing this maritime route for commercial purposes, even though it is possible, at the present time, to do so only during a few summer months. Furthermore, until quite recently the economic advantages to be derived from exploiting the Northwest Passage were not immediately apparent.

This question assumed a new importance with the discovery in 1968 of petroleum deposits in northern Alaska around Prudhoe Bay. It would appear that the Alaska oil fields are the largest ever discovered in North America. Furthermore it is predicted that the needs of the Atlantic coast cities of the United States alone will reach two million barrels a day in the course of the next decade. The petroleum industry has quickly seized upon this market as a natural outlet for the Alaskan deposits, provided that a permanent maritime link through the Northwest Passage between Prudhoe Bay and the Atlantic Seaboard conurbation can be established.

The *Manhattan* project was developed by the Humble Oil Company with a view to exploring the problems created by the opening of a new commercial route in the Arctic. The S.S. *Manhattan,* an American oil tanker, was specially reinforced and provided with a hull designed to slide over the ice and to crush it under the weight of the vessel. Thus, transformed into a giant ice-breaker, the *Manhattan* entered the Northwest Passage escorted by the Canadian ice-breaker

John A. Macdonald on September 5, 1969. Ten days later, having been freed from the ice on several occasions by the Canadian vessel, the *Manhattan* reached Sachs Harbour by way of Barrow Strait, Viscount Melville Sound, and Prince of Wales Strait. It returned by the same route to the Atlantic.

The economic importance of this enterprise tends to overshadow its legal and political implications.[24] What exactly are Canada's rights in these waters which it has claimed belong to its "polar region"? Did the voyage of the *Manhattan* transform the Northwest Passage into a series of *international* straits joining two parts of the high seas? Can the Canadian Government regulate passage in the straits for the purpose of preventing pollution?

The breadth of the territorial sea in the Arctic has been twelve miles since 1970, as elsewhere in Canada. However, in the absence of a decree establishing the baselines, the outer limit must be calculated from the low-water mark.

The previous outer limit of the territorial sea of three miles allowed the high seas to reach from the Atlantic to Beaufort Sea via the Parry Channel and McClure Strait. In other words, one of the routes of the Northwest Passage consisted entirely of high seas. This situation has been substantially modified by the increased breadth of the territorial sea. In the Barrow Strait, in the center of the Parry Channel, three islands enable the territorial sea to span the two banks of the strait and to produce a twenty-five mile long break in the continuity of the high seas. This means, as the Canadian legal adviser has said, that Canada's territorial jurisdiction extends unquestionably to the Northwest Passage, whatever may be the status of other waters of the archipelago. It is henceforth impossible to traverse the straits without submitting to the sovereignty of the coastal State.[25]

It is true that all vessels have the right of innocent passage in the territorial sea, in accordance with Article 14 of the 1958 Convention; moreover, even if the government decided to transform these straits into internal waters, by drawing straight closing lines across the entrance, the right of innocent passage would still apply. In fact, nothing in the Canadian attitude indicates that there is any intention to prevent innocent passage, witness the *Manhattan* project.

The government, however, has let it be known that "it cannot accept a right of innocent passage if the right is defined in such a manner as to prevent the coastal States from exercising control over pollution of the waters."[26] In other words, the passage of a vessel which might cause pollution is not considered innocent, because it "constitutes a menace to the security" of the coastal State. Is Canada therefore authorized, in accordance with Article 16 of the Convention on the Territorial Sea, to "take all necessary measures to prevent passage which is not innocent"? May it go as far as to suspend, temporarily, in specified areas of its territorial sea, the exercise of the right of innocent passage, if this suspension is necessary for the protection of its security?

In the first place, it may be asked whether pollution constitutes a true danger to the "security" of the coastal State. To military and navigational security should there not be added security from material damage and "ecological security"? Given the present state of the law, there is no unequivocal response to this question. Nevertheless, it may be presumed that the risk of pollution of the cold waters and the frozen coastline of the northern regions does constitute a grave menace for the States concerned. According to Article 1 of the Convention Relating to Intervention on the High Seas in Cases of Oil Pollution Casualties, signed in Brussels on November 29, 1969, the parties are authorized to take "such measures on the high seas as may be necessary to prevent, mitigate, or eliminate grave and imminent danger to their coastline or related interests from pollution or threat of pollution of the sea by oil, following upon a maritime casualty...." If such measures may be adopted on the high seas, it is not unreasonable to suggest that certain forms of pollution are henceforth to be considered a menace to the security of States.

Secondly, if Canada should suspend the exercise of the right of innocent passage in its territorial waters, may it do so in straits which join two parts of the high seas, for example, the Atlantic Ocean and the Beaufort Sea?

Since the International Court of Justice's judgment in the *Corfu Channel Case,* it is clear that broader rules than those dealing with innocent passage alone may be relied upon in favor of navigation through straits. The Court, in effect, confirmed the right of passage of warships, in peacetime, without prior authorization, through straits which are "used for international navigation."[27] The Convention on the Territorial Sea extended this right to all vessels: "There shall be no suspension of the innocent passage of foreign ships through straits which are used for international navigation between one part of the high seas and another part of the high seas ..." (Article 16, par. 4).

The Canadian Government is of the opinion that the straits of the Arctic archipelago are not of an international character because, prior to the *Manhattan* voyage, they have never been used by foreign vessels and, in addition, cannot be navigated without the assistance of Canadian ice-breakers. Before a Committee of the House of Commons, the Legal Adviser of the Department of External Affairs declared that the status of international strait can be acquired only by the evolution of customary law or by treaty. He pointed out that with respect to customary law, there has been no passage, or utilization, which could confer the status of international strait on this zone, due to the great quantity of ice. Nor did he feel that conventional law settled the question, since it deals with the passage between two parts of the high seas, and one would have to give a very wide interpretation to the definition of the high seas to include therein the Beaufort Sea or the Arctic Ocean since they are ice-bound during most of the year.[28]

Although the argument according to which the Beaufort Sea should not be considered forming part of the high seas is not entirely convincing, it does not seem to be unreasonable to have recourse to a criterion of *utilization,* since this appears both in the judgment of the Court and the Convention. Because of the climactic conditions prevalent in these latitudes, the straits have not been used for international navigation; and the first commercial vessel to attempt to do so, the *Manhattan,* did so as an experiment and with Canadian assistance. Without even relying on the historic title claimed by Canada over the straits, it seems possible to conclude that the Northwest Passage is not a strait within the meaning of international law. Therefore, the government may take the necessary measures to prevent any passage which is not innocent in the territorial waters of the Northwest Passage, going so far as to temporarily suspend the exercise of the right of innocent passage, where necessary for the protection of its coasts.

THE CONTINENTAL SHELF

Canada's continental shelf is the second largest in the world, amounting to approximately 40 percent of its land territory or two million square miles.[29]

The country's "sovereign rights" over these immense submarine areas have not been the object of any special proclamation, but the government fully intends to assume all the benefits accruing to it on the basis of the 1958 Convention on the Continental Shelf to which it is a party, particularly in regard to the "exploitability" criterion. It has been estimated that the reserves of the Canadian shelf surpass fifty-six billion barrels (the corresponding figure for the land reserves is sixty-five billion).[30]

The federal law concerning the production and conservation of petroleum and gas is based on the double criterion of depth and exploitability; it grants the government the power to establish regulations concerning the exploring, drilling, production, and conservation as well as the refining (or treatment) and transportation of petroleum and gas.[31]

There is no published chart showing the precise extent of the Canadian claims over the continental shelf, but there are several governmental documents indicating the position of concessions for the exploration of gas and petroleum.[32] Off Newfoundland these concessions are to be found in the Great Banks region, up to 425 miles to the east of the coast and up to 320 miles to the south. In Nova Scotia licenses may be obtained up to 150 miles from the coast. In the Sea of Labrador licenses are granted in an area between 100 and 200 miles off the coast. On the Pacific coast the concession area comprises the whole of Hecate Strait and Queen Charlotte Sound and extends from twenty to fifty miles from the coast of Vancouver Island and the Queen Charlotte archipelago.[33]

In a number of places, the Canadian continental shelf meets the shelf of neighboring states: the United States, Denmark (Greenland), and France (St. Pierre and Miquelon Islands). According to Article 6 of the Convention on the Continental Shelf, in the absence of an agreement, the delimitation of adjacent shelves should be established by means of a median line, all the points of which are equidistant from the nearest point of the baseline. In the majority of cases affecting Canada, the equidistance principle does not provide a satisfactory solution. Negotiations are under way therefore with the countries mentioned above in an attempt to fix by agreement the dividing line in the straits which separate Ellesmere Island and Greenland, in Juan de Fuca Strait, Dixon Entrance, the Beaufort Sea, George Bank (between Nova Scotia and Maine), and in the arm of the sea between Newfoundland and the French islands.

In accordance with the 1958 Convention, Canada recognizes that the "sovereign rights" which it exercises over the continental shelf do not extend to the superjacent waters, which remain part of the high seas (beyond the twelve-mile territorial sea).

With regard to the delimitation between the continental shelf and the seabed beyond national jurisdiction, Canada believes that this should coincide with the end of the continental margin, everything within that limit forming part of the "geological shelf." According to a chart published in the tenth report of the Canadian Science Council, this limit would generally correspond to the 1000 fathom isobath (1830 meters).[34]

FISHERY ZONES

Between 1966 and 1970 Canada had established "contiguous" fishing zones on all of its coasts with the exception of its Arctic regions.

These exclusive zones extended nine miles beyond the territorial sea, so that the maritime zone reserved to Canadian fishermen was twelve miles wide measured from the baselines. Since for the most part these were straight lines drawn from headland to headland, the area enclosed by these zones was quite considerable in many cases. Allusion has already been made to the *phasing out* arrangements concluded with foreign States having historic rights in Canadian waters.[35]

In 1970, these fishing zones were incorporated into the new twelve-mile territorial sea whose outer limit coincided with the former fishing zone. New "adjacent fishing zones" were created by Parliament and fisheries closing lines fixed by decree.[36] There separate zones are covered by the new regime, and it has not been necessary to extend either the internal waters or the territorial sea of the country.

Zone 1 is in the Gulf of St. Lawrence, the entrances of which are closed by two series of straight lines. The first series crosses Cabot Strait from Money Point to Cape Ray via St. Paul Island, while the second crosses the mouth of Belle-Isle Strait from Eastern White Island to Double Island via Northeast Ledge off Belle-Isle. These lines join, therefore, the extremities of the Labrador and Nova Scotia baselines to those of Newfoundland, but it should be noted that they are not real baselines but "closing lines"; they do not serve to establish the position or the breadth of the territorial sea.

Zone 2 comprises the Bay of Fundy, whose two entrances are closed by a series of eleven straight lines. The line begins at Whipple Point (on Brier Island off the southern coast of the Bay) and crosses the principal entrance as far as Gannet Rock. From there, the line heads seaward to meet Yellow Ledge and Machias Seal Island, which it skirts to return towards Great Manan Island via North Rock. After following the coast of Great Manan Island, it rejoins the Canadian-American frontier in the middle of Great Manan Channel.

Zone 3 comprises Queen Charlotte Sound, Hecate Strait, and Dixon Entrance. The two arms of the sea which provide access to this zone have been closed by straight lines. The first closes Queen Charlotte Sound from Winifred Island to Kunghit Island; the second goes from Langara Island to Cape Muzon.

If these three "adjacent" zones differ geographically from the earlier fishing zones, are they also legally different? The 1964 Act has not been modified on this point and it follows that "the laws of Canada respecting fishing and the exploitation of the living resources of the sea apply to the fishing zones of Canada in the same way and to the same extent as they apply to the territorial sea of Canada."[37]

The Minister of External Affairs has made clear that the maritime areas transformed into "adjacent" fishing zones are not territorial waters. Are they then a part of the high seas in the same way as the "contiguous zone" as defined by the Convention on the Territorial Sea? According to the Minister, the closing lines "will establish regions similar to fishing zones" which until now extended beyond the territorial sea. The effect, he added, "will be identical."[38]

The legal definition of the earlier fishery zones as explained by the government was not always very clear. The 1964 Act itself described them as "areas of the sea contiguous to the territorial sea," and they were frequently designated by the official representatives of the government as "contiguous fishery zones."[39]

It is true that the geographic area covered by the zones coincided with that of the contiguous zone recognized by Article 24 of the 1958 Convention on the Territorial Sea, since it extended seaward from the territorial sea and never exceeded more than twelve miles from the baseline. Nevertheless, a geographic identity does not necessarily mean that the fishery zones in question are legally the same as contiguous zones.

If the fishery zones decreed by States were legally undistinguishable from the contiguous zone, then States could not extend their legislation on fisheries to these zones; *a fortiori* they would not be permitted to exclude foreign fishermen. But these are precisely the objectives of such zones. In Canada, as we have seen, the laws concerning fisheries apply to the fishery zone, whether contiguous or adjacent, in the same way as in the territorial sea.

The conclusion to be drawn from this would seem to be that the fishery zones are not "contiguous zones" in the sense of the 1958 Convention, but rather zones subject to the territorial jurisdiction of coastal States for the limited purpose of fishing. They are "exclusive zones," in the words of Mr. S. Hsu of the International Law Commission, but not territorial waters, since the coastal State does not presume to exercise the totality of its jurisdiction in these zones, which remain subject to the regime of the high seas for the purpose of navigation. It should be pointed out, however, that the fact that they encompass Hecate Strait and Dixon Entrance in no way modifies the status of these waters in Canada's eyes — they are also historic waters.

Canada, therefore, extends its jurisdiction beyond its territorial waters in the Gulf of St. Lawrence, Queen Charlotte Sound, and the other areas mentioned above. In order to define the legal nature of the powers so claimed, an analogy might be drawn with the "sovereign rights" exercised by States over the continental shelf. Such rights should not be confused with full or complete sovereignty, and fishery zones are not territorial waters. In the areas subject to these fishery rights, however, the traditional freedom of other States is restricted; it is no longer the high seas of classical international law.

Consequently, the Canadian Government has entered into negotiations with States whose fishermen had acquired conventional or historic rights in these maritime areas, from which an attempt is being made to expel them. As noted above, agreements have been reached with the United States and France (conventional rights) as well as with certain other countries claiming historic rights. The phasing out principle has been applied to the latter.

The future of the Canadian claims in the new "adjacent" zones is not tied to these agreements only. The unilateral act of the Canadian Government is not without precedents. The Icelandic fishery limits of 1958 comprise large reaches of sea up to sixty-two miles wide in some areas.[40] Furthermore, several Latin American countries have asserted claims over maritime zones called "territorial sea," "patrimonial sea," or "national fishery zones" up to 200 miles wide which, in reality, are extensions of limited jurisdiction for the purpose generally of preserving the biological resources of the area. These claims may differ from Canada's geographically, but legally there is a certain resemblance.[41]

POLLUTION PREVENTION ZONES

The shipwrecks of the *Torrey Canyon* off the coast of Britain and the *Arrow* in Chedabucto Bay, Nova Scotia, served to warn the Canadian lawmakers of the dangers to the marine environment posed by the increasing number of oil tankers. Moreover, in September 1970 Canada opened the first deep-water tanker port in the Western hemisphere; and two more ports for giant tankers have been opened since then. In addition, there is the proximity of the great urban centers of the East Coast of the United States with their ever increasing energy demands.

26

In its report to the Canadian Government in 1970, the group of experts on the prevention of pollution which was set up following the *Arrow* disaster urged the government to go beyond the measures provided for in the 1954 Inter-Governmental Maritime Consultative Organization (IMCO) Convention concerning oil pollution (as amended in 1962 and 1969). This Convention establishes "prohibited zones" for the discharge and ballasting of oil tankers, but refers to the flag State for the suppression of unlawful acts committed beyond the territorial waters of coastal States. The *Arrow* report recommended the establishment of broad pollution control zones, 100 miles wide, for the entire Canadian coast, over which Canada would exercise its jurisdiction.[42]

The government did not go as far as the recommendations of the report, except in the Arctic where special circumstances obliged it to adopt innovative measures of pollution control. Before turning to this, a brief examination of pollution control in territorial waters and fishery zones may be useful.

The Merchant Marine Act was amended in 1969 for the purpose of prohibiting the discharge by vessels of polluting substances without authorization.[43] This and its ensuing regulations are applicable in all Canadian waters (whether territorial or internal) situated south of the 60th parallel. This includes the entire Pacific coast and the Atlantic coast from Cape Kakkiviak (Labrador) to the Bay of Fundy. The Act is also applicable to all the adjacent fishing zones fixed by governmental decree. To the "sovereign right" to regulate fishing in the Gulf of St. Lawrence, Hecate Strait, and Queen Charlotte Sound is added therefore the right to prevent and punish pollution. This jurisdiction is ancillary to the conservation of fisheries and may be justified on similar grounds. It may also be argued that in the Gulf of St. Lawrence or Hecate Strait any pollution is bound to reach the coast, thereby necessitating a strict control on the part of the coastal State.

Finally, the Act applies to all Canadian waters above the 60th parallel, that is, to the islands of the Arctic archipelago, within the territorial waters but excluding waters within "shipping safety control zones" (see below).

The Act authorizes the Executive to establish regulations concerning different categories of pollutants, methods of loading, shipboard registers, compulsory navigation routes, and any other measures designed to ensure shipping safety. The Act also allows the government to regulate and to prevent the discharge of pollutants beyond the territorial sea, but without giving precise indications as to the area covered. Inspectors with broad powers may turn away or exclude vessels from Canadian waters (or fishing zones) if they do not comply with the law. The Transport Ministry is empowered to destroy any vessel in distress, shipwrecked, or abandoned which threatens to pollute the waters. Civil liability resulting from pollution is "absolute and not dependent upon proof of fault or negligence"; the ship owner, and in certain cases the cargo owner, is liable.

In the Arctic, ecological considerations have led the government to create a special pollution prevention zone, 100 miles wide and extending to the whole of the archipelago. The voyage of the *Manhattan* was clearly related to the adoption of the Arctic Waters Pollution Prevention Act of 1970, because it was thought at the time that tankers would use with increasing frequency the Northwest Passage.[44] The Act, however, is not confined to hydrocarbons; it applies to "waste" which is defined very broadly in Article 2.

Parliament grants the Executive the power to regulate the discharge or storage of polluting substances and the construction of works which might cause water pollution. The government may also require proof of solvency from any person engaged in prospecting or exploiting the natural resources of the zone. It may appoint inspectors and levy fines up to $5,000 in the case of a vessel. The pollution prevention officers may seize, with the agreement of the Governor in Council, any vessel and its cargo which has infringed the law *anywhere in the prevention zone;* in the case of a vessel in distress, shipwrecked, or abandoned, the government is empowered to destroy it or tow it away if there is a risk of pollution.

Within the prevention zone the government may establish, by decree, *shipping safety control zones* which are open only to vessels complying with standards prescribed by the regulations relating to:

"(i) hull and fuel tank construction, including the strength of materials used therein, the use of double hulls and the subdivision thereof into watertight compartments,

(ii) the construction of machinery and equipment and the electronic and other navigational aids and equipment and telecommunications equipment to be carried and the manner and frequency of maintenance thereof,

(iii) the nature and construction of propelling power and appliances and fittings for steering and stabilizing,

(iv) the manning of the ship, including the number of navigating and look-out personnel to be carried who are qualified in a manner prescribed by the regulations,

(v) with respect to any type of cargo to be carried, the maximum quantity thereof that may be carried, the method of stowage thereof and the nature or type and quantity of supplies and equipment to be carried for use in repairing or remedying any condition that may result from the deposit of any such cargo in the Arctic waters,

(vi) the freeboard to be allowed and the marking of load lines,

(vii) quantities of fuel, water and other supplies to be carried, and

(viii) the maps, charts, tide tables and any other documents or publications relating to navigation in the Arctic waters to be carried."

Further, the regulations may establish criteria for pilots navigating in ice or impose the use of an ice-breaker. These provisions leave nothing to chance, and the government intends to restrict navigation altogether in certain places and at certain times which are considered to be particularly dangerous.

The United States has seen in these measures a threat to the freedom of the seas. In a press release on April 15, 1970, the American Government declared that it could "neither accept nor acquiesce" in the establishment of such a zone, for fear that the Canadian Act may serve as a precedent in other parts of the world.[45] Washington is "acutely aware" of the peculiar ecological nature of the Arctic region, a region which is important to all nations because of "its increasing significance as a world trade route."

Canada replied to this criticism by observing that the United States had never hesitated to extend its own jurisdiction over the seas when deemed necessary and that the new Act was "a lawful extension of a limited form of jurisdiction to meet particular dangers and is of a different order from unilateral interferences with the freedom of the high seas such as, for example, the atomic testing carried out by the United States and other States. . . ."[46]

The Canadian Government agrees that there are relatively few rules of international law relating to pollution. The Legal Adviser of the Department of External Affairs goes so far as to say that there exists a sort of impasse, even anarchy, in this field. The law of the sea has been influenced too much by the interests of "conservative States which are important maritime States" and, for this reason does not take into account the point of view of States faced with the problems of pollution. The IMCO Convention does not deal adequately with these needs, especially in a region such as the Arctic where *preventive* measures must be taken. According to this view, *"an area of non-law"* exists where the law overtaken by technical progress has become obsolete.[47]

The new Canadian Act is on the frontier of international law but the government believed that it had a duty to act and to contribute to the development of the new law of the sea. It did so, not by proclaiming its sovereignty over the high seas, but by claiming "limited jurisdiction for a precise and vital goal." A distinction must be made between limited jurisdiction and the totality of jurisdiction which constitutes sovereignty; the Arctic Waters Act is analogous to measures for the conservation of living resources and must be seen as "a constructive and functional measure for the protection of the environment."[48]

References

1. See J.-Y. Morin, "Les eaux territoriales du Canada au regard du Droit international," *Canadian Yearbook of International Law* (hereinafter cited as *C.Y.I.L.*), (1963), pp. 86, 98, 100.
2. Statutes of Canada, 1969-1970, 18-19 Eliz. II, C. 68, s. 1. An Act to Amend the Territorial Sea and Fishing Zones Act, International Legal Materials, Vol. IX (May 1970), No. 3.
3. Eleven maps were published covering the Bay of Fundy, Nova Scotia, New Brunswick, Prince Edward Island, and certain areas of the Quebec coast. See article referred to in note 1 above, p. 99.
4. Order in Council P.C. 1937-3139. The regions covered by the decree are as follows: (1) Estuary of the St. Lawrence; (2) Bays and straits of the Maritime Provinces; (3) Bays and straits of the Pacific Coast; (4) Hudson Bay and Strait; (5) Other areas. Newfoundland and Labrador were not part of Canada at the time.
5. See article referred to in note 1 above, p. 114.
6. International Court of Justice Reports, 1951, p. 141.
7. For a detailed analysis, see J.-Y. Morin, "Les zones de pêche de Terre-Neuve et du Labrador," *C.Y.I.L.* (1968), p. 91.
8. House of Commons, 1969-1970, Permanent Committee on External Affairs, No. 25 (April 29, 1970), p. 41.
9. See map in article referred to in note 7 above, p. 94.
10. Order in Council P.C. 1969-1109, SOR No. 278, *Canada Gazette,* Pt. II, Vol. 103, p. 823.
11. Map No. 401 (South and East Coasts of Nova Scotia).
12. Convention of Commerce (Great Britain-United States) of October 20, 1818, Article 1. See map showing extent of these rights in *C.Y.I.L.* (1964), p. 80.
13. Accord relatif aux relations réciproques entre le Canada et la France en matière de pêche, March 27, 1972.
14. Agreement of April 24, 1970, Articles 2 and 3.
15. Customs Act Maps, Nos. 5 and 6, approved by P.C. 3725 and 3726 of August 6, 1940; No. 8 approved by P.C. 1446 of February 27, 1941; No. 9 approved by P.C. 75/6885 of November 26, 1940; No. 10 approved by P.C. 27 of January 7, 1941; No. 11 approved by P.C. 5168 of July 15, 1941.
16. See note 1 above, p. 113.
17. See T.W. Balch, "La baie d'Hudson est une grande mer ouverte," *Revue Droit International,* Vol. 15 (1913), p. 153; also in *American Journal of International Law,* Vol. 7 (1930), p. 546.
18. Order in Council, cit. in note 10 above, p. 824. See Map No. 391 issued by the Canadian Hydrographic Service.
19. Order in Council, cit. in note 4 above, Pt. 3.
20. Order in Council, cit. in note 10 above, p. 825. See Map. No. 392 issued by the Canadian Hydrographic Service.
21. *International Law Commission Yearbook,* Vol. II (1956), p. 285.
22. International Court of Justice Reports, 1949, p. 28.
23. See *Pilot of Arctic Canada,* Vol. I (1959), pp. 107 and 113.
24. See C. E. Forget, "The Arctic: Economic Development, Pollution Control, and Sovereignty," Canadian-American Committee, Memorandum M-98, pp. 11-15 (February 1970).

25. House of Commons, 1969-1970, Permanent Committee on External Affairs, No. 25, p. 18. See also the speech of the Secretary of State for External Affairs in House of Commons Debates, 1969-1970, Vol. 114 (April 17, 1970), p. 6015.
26. House of Commons Debates, 1969-1970, Vol. 114, p. 6015 (speech by the Secretary of State for External Affairs, April 17, 1970).
27. International Court of Justice Reports, 1949, p. 28.
28. Statement of the Legal Adviser, Department of External Affairs, before the Committee, cit. in note 25 above, pp. 19 and 20.
29. See A. J. Beesley, "The Law of the Sea Conference: Factors Behind Canada's Stance," *International Perspectives* (July-August 1972), p. 28; G. Hawkins, "The Pressing Implications of Canada as a Seabed Power," ibid., p. 35.
30. *Oilweek,* May 12, 1969, p. 121.
31. R.S.C., 1970, C. 0-4, Art. 3 (6), as amended in 1st Supplement, C. 30.
32. See maps published by the Department of Energy, Mines, and Resources (August 1970).
33. As of January 1972, no exploration permit had been transformed into a concession. See A. Legault, "Problèmes de souveraineté et de défense," *Notes de Recherches* (1972), No. 3, p. 55 (Centre Québécois de Relations Internationales).
34. *Canada, Science, and the Sea* (1971).
35. See J.-Y. Morin, "La zone de pêche exclusive du Canada," *C.Y.I.L.* (1964), p. 77; "Les zones de pêche de Terre-Neuve et du Labrador à la lumière de l'évolution du droit international," *C.Y.I.L.* (1968), p. 91.
36. Order in Council, *Canada Gazette,* Pt. I, Vol. 104 (December 26, 1970), No. 52, p. 3036.
37. Statutes of Canada, 1964, C. 22, Art. 4, par. 2.
38. Permanent Committee on Fisheries and Forests, 1969-1970, No. 16 (April 21, 1970), p. 12.
39. See, for example, the comment accompanying Bill C-203 (1969-1970), Art. 2.
40. See J.-Y. Morin, "Le progrès technique, la pollution, et l'évolution récente du droit de la mer au Canada, particulièrement à l'égard de l'Arctique," *C.Y.I.L.* (1970), pp. 158 ff. See also *Fisheries Jurisdiction in Iceland* (1972), p. 19.
41. Cf. the legislation of Argentina, Chile, Costa Rica, El Salvador, Nicaragua, Peru, and Uruguay, which recognizes expressly or implicitly the freedoms of navigation and over-flight. See F. V. García Amador, "La Jurisdicción Especial sobre las Pesquerías, Legislaciones Nacionales y Propuestas de los Gobiernos" (mimeo paper), Provisional Edition (Washington, D.C.: Pan American Union, 1972), p. 70.
42. Royal Commission on the Pollution of Canadian Waters, etc. (July 1970).
43. An Act to Amend the Canada Shipping Act, Statutes of Canada, 1968-1969, C. 53.
44. Statutes of Canada, 1969-1970, C. 47.
45. U.S. Press Release, in House of Commons Debates, 1969-1970, Vol. 114 (April 18, 1970), p. 5923.
46. Summary of Note sent by the Government of Canada to the Government of the United States, in House of Commons Debates, 1969-1970, Vol. 114, p. 6027.
47. Permanent Committee on External Affairs, cit. in note 25 above, p. 43 (April 29, 1970); Permanent Committee on Indian Affairs, 1969-1970, No. 15 (April 30, 1970), pp. 7 and 29.
48. House of Commons Debates, 1969-1970, Vol. 114 (April 16, 1970), p. 5951.

Chapter II
Towards a New Law for the Seas:
The Evolution of United States Policy

Chapter II

TOWARDS A NEW LAW FOR THE SEAS:
THE EVOLUTION OF UNITED STATES POLICY

Tom J. Farer and Paulann Caplovitz*

INTRODUCTION

The import of any change in the definition of the territorial sea cannot be overestimated. Its consequentiality may be gauged from the following facts: planes may not overfly the territorial sea without permission; submersible vessels, whether scientific or military, must traverse it on the surface with flag showing; merchant ships may pass without notice or authorization but they may not anchor except for purposes strictly incidental to the passage; the rights of foreign warships are both controversial and contingent; and the mineral and living resources in the subsoil, seabed, and superjacent waters are subject to the exclusive jurisdiction of the coastal State.

Had a single State voted differently at the 1960 Geneva Conference on the Law of the Sea,[1] the United States today would recognize a six-mile territorial sea bounded by a six-mile contiguous zone.[2] As it was, the joint U.S.-Canadian "six-plus-six" proposal[3] fell one vote short of the two-thirds majority necessary for its adoption;[4] thereupon, the United States' chief delegate, Arthur H. Dean, announced his country's continued adherence to its traditional policy of a three-mile territorial sea.[5]

The United States claims to observe and enforce a three-mile limit for its marginal sea and, for the most part, its executive proclamations, legislation, and administrative regulations support this claim. There are, however, certain inconsistencies in its position which, because they afford some basis for other countries to claim wider territorial seas, have contributed to the contemporary movement away from the three-mile limit. A primary inconsistency stems from the entire package of "continental shelf" authorizations dating from the end of World War II. A second one inheres in the Submerged Lands Act[6] of 1953, while a third was generated by the unilateral creation of a twelve-mile exclusive fishing zone in 1966.[7]

---

*Paulann Caplovitz is an Associate at Weil, Gotshal and Manges, New York City.

35

THE U.S. AND THE THREE-MILE LIMIT: NIBBLING AT THE BARRIER

In 1945 President Truman issued a proclamation characterizing

> "the natural resources of the subsoil and seabed of the continental shelf beneath the high seas but contiguous to the coasts of the United States as appertaining to the United States, subject to its jurisdiction and control."[8]

While no outer boundary for this shelf was specified in the executive declaration, an accompanying White House press release[9] indicated that a limit out to a depth of one hundred fathoms (200 meters or 600 feet) was contemplated. In 1953, Executive Order No. 10426, placing continental shelf claims under the Secretary of the Navy, described the scope of these claims as extending "to the furthermost limits of the paramount rights . . . and power of the United States over lands of the continental shelf." President Truman's initiative acquired statutory form in 1953 with the passage of the Outer Continental Shelf Lands Act.[10] Subsequently, an influential administrative memorandum[11] argued that when the U.S. adopted the 1958 Convention on the Continental Shelf[12] the extent of its statutory claim became defined by the Convention's formulation:

> ". . . the seabed and subsoil of the submarine areas adjacent to the coast but outside the area of the territorial sea, to a depth of 200 metres or, beyond that limit, to where the depth of the superjacent waters admits of the exploitation of the natural resources of the said areas. . . ."[13]

This same memorandum, relying on the above definition, justified a lease by the Department of the Interior for exploitation of phosphate deposits discovered forty miles off the California coast. Most of the deposits lie in more than 100 fathoms of water and are seaward of an ocean trench nearly a mile deep. The sea chasm itself is some distance from the shoreline.[14]

Other countries have construed the Truman Proclamation and the Outer Continental Shelf Lands Act to be implicit extensions of the U.S. territorial sea all the way out to the limits of the continental shelf. More important, they have justified express expansions of their own territorial limits to 200 miles on the basis of this interpretation.[15] Section 3 (b) of the statute explicitly admonishes against any such construction declaring that:

> "This Act shall be construed in such a manner that the character as high seas of the waters above the outer continental shelf and the right to navigation and fishing therein shall not be affected."

Strictly speaking, the text does not warrant the implication which several countries have drawn from it. At the same time, the phenomenon of "creeping jurisdiction," described recently by Professor Louis Henkin,[16] is a reality that cannot be ignored. The "creeping" is as much a "seepage upward" (i.e., from the subsoil, seabed, superjacent waters, to the surface) as it is a lateral movement from the coastline. Of course, the process involves both movements simultaneously. Significantly, the 1958 Convention on the Continental Shelf authorizes controls by the coastal State that go beyond what the U.S. claimed for itself. Sedentary fish are brought within its terms, and substantial regulation of navigation and scientific exploration relating to shelf resources is permitted. The U.S., as was noted above, has seemingly incorporated the Convention's expansive definition of the shelf. Concurrently, it has authorized the Coast Guard to place navigational aids[17] anywhere on the superjacent waters to mark shipping lanes circumventing the surface installations.[18]

The Submerged Lands Act of 1953, a second source of at least phenomenological inconsistence in U.S. policy, established the titles of the states to the land and resources beneath navigable waters within state boundaries. "Boundaries" are defined to extend no more than three geographical miles into the Atlantic and Pacific oceans, but a limit of *three marine leagues* (nine miles) is set for the states bordering the Gulf of Mexico. Section 4 declared the seaward boundaries of the states to be a line three geographical miles from shore but expressly preserved state claims exceeding that line if the constitution or laws of the state prior to or upon admission to the Union so provided.

Litigation of this statute eventually produced a complex, six-opinion decision by the U.S. Supreme Court.[19] Finding the statutory language to be inconclusive, the Court decided the case on the basis of legislative history and documents attesting the states' boundaries at the date of admission. The judges declared seaward boundaries of *nine miles* into the Gulf of Mexico for both Texas and Florida while rejecting similar claimed territorial lines for Louisiana, Mississippi, and Alabama. The State Department had vigorously resisted a result that would extend state boundaries beyond the national border of three miles.[20] But, in order to support the congressional conferral of exploitation rights on the states, the Department had argued that the Act granted only a limited, special jurisdiction that did not alter the traditional United States position on its territorial waters. Specifically, the Department was concerned that the existence of state boundaries seaward of claimed national boundaries would prejudice U.S. efforts to avoid a broader rule of the territorial sea becoming established in international law. The Court found no conflict between the Government's diplomatic objectives and the issue of the case on the grounds that the Submerged Lands Act had purely domestic application.

The decision giving Texas a nine-mile seaward border is especially interesting because Mexico's distinguished jurist, Dr. Alfonso García Robles, has relied on certain language in the opinion to support his country's claim for a nine-mile territorial sea.[21] Interpreting the Treaty of Guadalupe Hidalgo,[22] on which Mexico directly rests its claim, the Court concluded that "the obvious and common sense meaning of the... treaty provision is that it separates the maritime territory of the United States and Mexico."[23] This conclusion was decisive in the Court's determination of whether Texas came within the saving clause of Section 4 and thus had three mile or three league seaward boundaries.

To support his view that the Submerged Lands Act did not affect the width of the national territorial sea, Mr. Dean, in rebuttal, quoted his own verse from the opinion:

> We conclude that ... a state territorial boundary beyond three miles is established for purposes of the Submerged Lands Act by congressional action so fixing it, irrespective of the limit of territorial waters.[24]

A fair implication of this statement is that a state can enjoy a border that extends beyond the national boundary. The soundness of the implication is another matter. In any event, the Court expressed no opinion on the precise issue here, that is, whether the boundary was valid vis-à-vis other nations. Dr. Robles dismissed the contention, first advanced by Secretary of State Buchanan,[25] that a border recognized by two countries as between themselves was a nullity with respect to third parties. Certainly at one time the State Department considered any state line drawn beyond the three-mile limit to be inconsonant with a national assertion of a three-mile territorial sea. That the Department has subsequently changed its mind is apparent from the arguments offered by Mr. Dean.

A third feature of U.S. behavior susceptible to the charge of inconsistency is its unilateral establishment of an exclusive fishing zone extending nine miles from the territorial sea.[26] It is probably impossible to harmonize this enactment in terms of the Convention on the Territorial Sea and the Contiguous Zone. Article 24 of the Convention, which provides for a contiguous zone, limits its operation to the enforcement of customs, fiscal, immigration, or sanitary regulations. Even if conservation of living resources were read into the purposes of this zone, it is doubtful that this U.S. prohibition of foreign fishermen *only* would qualify as a good faith conservation measure, since it bears no marked rational relationship to its objective. The mere fact of being described as a conservation measure can hardly suffice to establish *bona fides*. Article 2 of the 1958 Convention on the High Seas[27] declares freedom of fishing to be one of the elements of freedom of the high seas. Since Article 1 defines the high seas as "all parts of the sea that are not included in the territorial sea or in the internal waters of a State," the exclusive fishing law must effect some erosion of the psychic and juridical barrier which the U.S. has sought to maintain three miles from the continental baseline.

It should be added that there is nothing theoretical about this extension of sovereign authority. It is backed by effective power, as the seizure of Cuban fishing vessels that proceeded within this limit so concretely evidenced.

The State Department raised no objection to this legislation. Indeed, it observed in a letter[28] to the committee considering the legislation that there was a

"... trend toward establishment of a 12-mile fisheries rule in international practice. Many states acting individually or in concert with other states have extended or are in the process of extending their fisheries limits to 12 miles. Such actions have no doubt been accelerated by the support for the proposals made at the Geneva Law of the Sea Conferences in 1958 and 1960 of a fisheries zone totalling 12 miles as part of a package designed to achieve international agreement on the territorial sea."

Noting these developments, the letter continued:

"... action by the United States at this time to establish an exclusive fisheries zone extending 9 miles beyond the territorial sea would not be contrary to international law. *It should be emphasized that such action would not extend the territorial sea beyond our traditional 3 mile limit"* (emphasis added).

The letter concluded that since the proposed legislation would contribute to the worldwide trend, it would be more difficult in the future to assert an exclusive fishing right *beyond* twelve miles.

There is nothing, of course, in the history of the law of the sea which requires the whole panoply of sovereign rights to accompany any thrust of authority beyond the territorial sea boundary previously accepted by the acting State. In a precise juridical sense, verbal categories such as "territorial sea," "contiguous zone," or "high seas" are mere forms of summary reference to bundles of rights and obligations the substance of which will vary over time.

Even the territorial sea has not been an area subject to the exercise by the coastal State of an unrestricted discretion; in modern times at least, it has been qualified by a servitude for the benefit of innocent commerce. Conversely, the high seas have never been entirely immune to coastal State jurisdiction. Until recently, however, extensions of jurisdiction into the high seas have almost invariably been incident to the protection of territorial interests such as self-defense, the minimization of pollution damage, and the enforcement of fiscal laws.[29]

Two particular rights have determined the distinctive character of the territorial sea. One is the right of exclusive jurisdiction over resources. Beyond the territorial sea, free competition prevailed — ownership followed appropriation. Within the territorial sea, the coastal State had authority to determine both the identity of the appropriator and the means and terms of his appropriation. Discrimination in favor of coastal interests was entirely legitimate.

The second right, related to national defense, was the right to exclude submarines (unless surfaced and identified), aircraft (seeking to pass through the air above the territorial sea), and warships not in transit or whose passage was not "innocent."

Translated into operational terms, the State Department's assertion that an exclusive fisheries zone "would not extend the territorial sea beyond our traditional three-mile limit" communicated little more than our determination to continue to acquiesce in overflight and unidentified submersion; etc., up to a point three miles from our coast and, perhaps, that we would insist upon comparable acquiescence by other States, at least to the extent they too claim a mere three-mile territorial sea. In addition, it may have implied the belief that other States would generally accept this division of the territorial-sea bundle rather than insisting on towing the whole thing farther out from shore and erecting there a new integrated barrier.

If most States were willing to accept the disintegration of the original bundle and to impose on their self-defense rights the severe geographical restrictions which the U.S. so exigently prefers, then the State Department's reassurance would not be misleading and the allegation of inconsistency would be emptied of real content. But if they were not, if the acceptance of a straitened defense area were perceived by them as an integral element of a compromise, a compromise rendered attractive only by the associated element of non-discriminatory access to marine resources, then the extension of national jurisdiction over marine resources would be a threat to the three-mile limit and perhaps to modestly broader alternatives as well.

When national jurisdiction over the continental shelf was proclaimed, the world was assured that the living resources of the sea were unaffected. But States lacking the blessings of a broad shelf were unprepared to accept limply the Divine dispensation. If the U.S., the U.S.S.R., and certain other happily endowed States could appropriate chauvinistically the resources of the ground off their coasts, then other States were determined to appropriate the resources of the water above their far deeper and hence inaccessible (and in any event possibly barren) coastal grounds. They were unpersuaded by the insistence that geological realities required new conceptions of the national domain.

Like any juridical barrier, the three-mile limit is ultimately phenomenological in nature. It could exist only as long as it survived in the minds of men. The U.S. has played a significant role in arranging its demise.[30]

VECTORS OF U.S. POLICY

At present a majority of States proclaim territorial seas with a breadth in excess of three miles.[31] If these claims related only to the appropriation of living resources, apparently the U.S. would be unconcerned, as long as the claims did not exceed twelve miles. Indeed, as implied above, the creation of an exclusive fisheries zone by the U.S. can be construed as an implicit acceptance of a twelve-mile limit for that purpose. What does intensely concern the U.S., however, is the security threat apprehended in the conversion of a host of hitherto international straits into portions of one or more States' territorial seas.

The U.S. is unequivocal in its determination to retain the incidence of high seas passage through all straits that would be "territorialized" by a twelve-mile limit. In so doing it has enhanced, of course, the bargaining positions of States which border the relevant straits to the extent they are more concerned about resource than defense interests. As long as the U.S. is unyielding on the issue of free passage, yet eager to achieve wide agreement on the full range of marine law issues, it clearly must diminish its intransigence by yielding on other issues, assuming that its parochial interest with respect to various resource issues is not served optimally by proposals likely to enjoy the support of the straits States.

Accepting the primacy in intra-governmental (i.e., bureaucratic) negotiations of what one might call the Mahan perspective (in other words that the U.S. must be free to deploy massive power — particularly naval power — throughout the world for purposes of nuclear defense, the deterrence and conduct of conventional wars with other powerful States, and for purposes of imperial sorties into the Third World), why, one may ask, is the U.S. unwilling to settle for the right of "innocent passage" which it claims warships enjoy within the territorial sea and, *a fortiori,* through national straits "which are used for international navigation between one part of the high seas and another part of the high seas or the territorial sea of a foreign State"?[32]

The answer is obvious. Firstly, there is the absence of overflight rights. Innocent passage relates only to the surface of the sea; the air above it is closed. Free passage over straits somewhat reduces reliance on successful overflight negotiations.

Secondly, there is the Polaris submarine, the core of the U.S.'s nuclear deterrent. Fear is expressed that its invulnerability, by moving in a medium inhospitable to sustained surveillance, would be compromised seriously by the necessity of surfacing whenever passing through straits — such as Gibraltar — with a width less than twenty-four miles. It is implied that the alleged risk of a successful trailing operation initiated during a surface passage through straits might deter utilization of the Mediterranean, which is within such easy lobbing distance of European Russia.

Why, even assuming the reality of this risk, it should be seen as affecting the American deterrent by even a scintilla is a riddle wrapped in an enigma. After all, it would still leave vast reaches of the Atlantic, Pacific, and Indian oceans available to the Polaris fleet, the bulk of which is now armed with Poseidon missiles with a range in the vicinity of three thousand miles.[33] Moreover, work proceeds apace on the Undersea Long-Range Missile System (ULMS), the next generation of undersea missiles which will enjoy a range of at least four thousand miles.[34] And when one recalls that each of the approximately forty-eight U.S. submarines carries sufficient warheads to obliterate several dozen Hiroshimas, the Polaris "problem" assumes the form of a neurotic syndrome, especially when one considers that even if the Soviet Union does not already possess a sophisticated antisubmarine warfare (ASW) tracking and detection system operative in key straits and capable of identifying *submerged* vessels, it is quite probable that they will develop one in the near future.[35]

One suspects that it is not so much the deterrent as the imperial (so-called "peacekeeping") mission which is seen to be threatened by nationalization of the straits. It is the increased difficulty of getting the Marines to Lebanon rather than the "nukes" to Kiev which may best explain U.S. priorities in law of the sea negotiations.

Since the Marines are moved primarily by surface ships, one might suppose that "innocent passage" would suffice to allay the fear of insufficient mobility.[36] It does not, however, in part because of a soupçon of uncertainty about the applicability of the innocent passage doctrine to warships, but in large measure out of fear that even if its applicability were universally conceded, under a variety of circumstances innocence might be contested. The U.S. itself independently recognizes the right of innocent passage for military vessels and neither requires notice from foreign warships in its territorial sea nor *gives* notice when entering the national waters of other States.[37] This policy represents a substantial change in little more than sixty years. Speaking for the U.S. in 1910 Elihu Root declared:

> "Warships may not pass without consent into this territorial sea zone, because they threaten. Merchantships may pass and repass because they do not threaten."[38]

In 1930 at the Hague Codification Conference, the United States espoused the view that warships may pass as a matter of courtesy, but not as of right, through territorial waters. By 1965, the U.S. had begun to regard passage of military ships as a right *per se* without requiring notice or authorization to and from the coastal State.

It is perhaps a moot issue whether the declared U.S. policy of affording innocent passage for warships in *its* territorial sea is reserved only for friendly countries, since it does not appear that any State has ever been tempted to test U.S. delicacy about its national sea.[40] One possible though oblique indication of official attitudes emerges in the Navy and Coast Guard responses to Soviet fishing trawler activity within three miles of the eastern seaboard. Sightings by local fishermen generated some alarm in the neighboring communities which led in turn to congressional hearings. The hearings revealed that the Soviet ships were merely following a navigational routing that the U.S. Coast Guard publicly advises to be tne most advantageous lane for Atlantic traffic bound for Cuba.

With the advent of Soviet influence in Cuba, the movement of Soviet vessels from the North Atlantic fisheries southward was to be expected of course. The indifference by the Coast Guard and Navy to this traffic within the territorial sea was striking,[41] particularly in light of an earlier Coast Guard proposal for a policy of stopping and boarding *all* foreign fishing ships in the U.S. territorial sea, whenever they were sighted, regardless of the apparent "innocence" of their passage.[42]

Despite U.S. theory and practice, the "right" of innocent passage by warships through territorial waters, including those which comprise straits, is not universally acknowledged.[43] Nevertheless, a serious open challenge to its exercise by U.S. warships, at least when in transit through straits connecting two parts of the high seas, seems unlikely in the near future. This prediction is based on suppositions broader than the military power and political influence which are insufficient to allay U.S. anxiety.

In the first place, the contemporary "right" enjoys a venerable lineage highlighted by the opinion of the International Court of Justice in the *Corfu Channel Case:*

> "It is, in the opinion of the Court, generally recognized and in accordance with international custom that States in time of peace have a right to send their warships through straits used for international navigation between two parts of the high seas without the previous authorization of a coastal State, provided that the passage is *innocent.* Unless otherwise prescribed in an international convention, there is no right for a coastal State to prohibit such passage through straits in time of peace."[44]

The practice reflected and re-enforced by the I.C.J. may have been codified in the 1958 Geneva Convention on the Territorial Sea and the Contiguous Zone. Section III thereof, which is entitled "Right of Innocent Passage," is subdivided into a set of "Rules Applicable to All Ships" and three sets of rules applicable respectively to "Merchant Ships," "Government Ships Other Than Warships," and "Warships." One of the "Rules Applicable to *All Ships"* (emphasis added) is that:

> "There shall be no suspension of the innocent passage of foreign ships through straits which are used for international navigation between one part of the high seas and another part of the high seas or the territorial sea of a foreign State."[45]

Thus, straits are distinguished from other parts of the territorial sea wherein innocent passage may be suspended temporarily "if such suspension is essential for the protection of its [the territorial sovereign's] security."[46]

The only "Rule Applicable to Warships" is Article 23's declaration:

> "If any warship does not comply with the regulations of the coastal State concerning passage through the territorial sea and disregards any request for compliance which is made to it, the coastal State may require the warship to leave the territorial sea."

By its very existence, this rule fills out a textual structure which seems to compel the conclusion that the reference to "ships" in Article 14 (right of innocent passage in ordinary territorial waters) and Article 16 includes warships. This structural evidence is reinforced by the Article's mandate in that it appears to assume participation by warships in the general authorization of innocent passage. At any rate, that certainly is the U.S. view.[47]

One may still speculate, however, as to whether what has been granted by Articles 14 and 16 has not in large measure been revoked by the infelicities of Article 23. In view of what precedes it, Article 23 is infuriatingly ambiguous. Does the reference to territorial sea include the straits described in Article 16? Presumably yes. If it does, then precisely what kinds of regulations may the coastal State enforce to qualify Article 16's mandate? Unless the whole mess is attributable to a consciously incoherent essay in compromise, one must assume that the "regulations" relate to matters which will not seriously impede passage —matters such as navigational channels, priorities, and pollution control. Perhaps the strongest evidence supporting the U.S. interpretation was the reservation of certain signatories (including all members of the Soviet Bloc except Poland) concerning the right of the coastal State to determine whether and how warships may pass through the territorial sea.[48]

Whatever the intentions of the various signatories, the fact is that today the practice of a majority of States reflects implicit adherence to the U.S. view that the innocent passage of warships requires no authorization.[49] Especially significant for U.S. interests is its apparent acceptance by States that sit astride the great international straits such as Gibraltar. In arguing against "high seas passage" through territorialized straits, the Spanish Government, for instance, has found in the right of innocent passage a sufficient guarantee of all legitimate superpower security interests.

The cardinal reason why a frontal collision is unlikely is the ability of straits States to protect their security (including ecological) interests not by challenging the very concept of innocent passage as it relates to warships but rather by finding culpable a passage perceived to be threatening. And surely it is just this — the flexibility of the concept and the prospect of genuine conflicts of security interests between coastal States and the great maritime powers — which fuels U.S. concern.[50] Suppose, for instance, a conflict erupted in the Middle East or on the southern flank of NATO and the U.S. decided to reinforce the Sixth Fleet. If Spain and Morocco had mutual security treaties with a direct or indirect participant in the conflict, who was likely to regard with hostility U.S. involvement, might they not contend that under the circumstances passage by U.S. naval contingents could not be deemed innocent? Indeed, even if any alliance relationship was absent, might they not find the passage of an imminent belligerent to be "prejudicial to peace," since it might convert their territory into a target for a preemptive strike? Even if passage were finally authorized, there might be some delay while its innocence was debated; and this contingency alone is sufficient to evoke a sense of revulsion in U.S. naval circles.

Controversies over the alleged innocence of a given passage are not foreseen solely in the context of armed conflict. There is, in addition, fear that nuclear-powered or nuclear-armed warships might be denied passage on grounds of an unacceptable risk of pollution or accidental holocaust.

U.S. officials have been consistent in their demands for "free" passage through and over straits which would be nationalized by extension of the territorial sea to twelve miles. In the bland yet ingenuous words of Leigh Ratiner, former Chairman of the Department of Defense Advisory Group on the Law of the Sea:

> "Nations which depend on their merchant marine and navies for economic and national security — nations such as the United States, the United Kingdom, and the Soviet Union amongst others — can be strangled by having access to oceans limited or delayed when passing through narrow international straits. Submerged passage of submarines, overflight of aircraft, and freedom from restriction generally would disappear. To the extent they would continue to exist, these rights would depend on the good graces of the coastal State or States bordering on the strait in question. Such a result would be unacceptable to any country with global interests, a global foreign policy, a large merchant marine, and a large navy and air force. It is principally for this reason that the United States has opposed territorial sea extensions beyond three miles."[51]

From the willingness of the U.S. delegation to the 1960 Geneva Conference to accept the "six-plus-six" compromise mentioned earlier, territorial sea extensions appear to strike a strategic nerve when they probe beyond six miles. The reason is probably both qualitative and quantitative. Qualitative consequences are epitomized by the example of Gibraltar's pinching the umbilical cord of the Sixth Fleet.[52] Quantitative differences are equally striking. Under the three-mile rule, high seas can be found within more than 100 commercially or militarily significant straits. A six-mile limit shrinks them to less than fifty. And when the limit inflates to twelve miles, the number of high seas straits totters toward zero.[53]

The second most influential interest which has shaped U.S. policy with respect to the marine environment is the petroleum industry.[54] Its concerns are focused on the continental shelves of the U.S. and other generously endowed nations. Its bias is toward the maximum extension of coastal State jurisdiction conceivable under Article I of the Geneva Convention on the Continental Shelf. To that end it has, according to Ratiner, "adopted highly nationalistic rhetoric not only in the United States but in countries where nationalism and pro-Americanism are far from synonymous."[55] In this connection, one industry spokesman has justified its position as follows:

> "...it is far better for the American consumer that the terms on which American industry explores and develops the resources of a foreign continental margin be stated in the varied terms of the laws of a large number of coastal States competing with one another for the investor's capital than that all continental margins be controlled by a single governmental monopoly; that is, by a single international agency which is created by treaty and is dominated by the objective of extracting from the consumer all that the traffic will bear in the form of costs added as taxes, royalties, production sharing, and direct free-ride participation in profits but not risks."[56]

Other forces which shape the U.S. negotiating position are various fishing interests and hard-mineral mining companies preparing to exploit mineral-rich nodules on the seabed. Fishing interests are divided because those who operate off the U.S. coast naturally prefer a broad exclusion of foreign competition, while those who work the coastal waters of foreign States — primarily Latin American — inevitably prefer the classic three-mile limit or something very close thereto.[57] Mining companies seem concerned primarily about attempts by developing States to enjoin exploitation activities beyond the limits of national jurisdiction pending agreement both as to the definition of those limits and the character of the international regime for the residue of the marine environment.[58]

THE U.S. COMPROMISE

The U.S. proposals for new conventional law to govern the external marine environment provide straitsniks with a reasonably full meal while assuring decently meaty, if not entirely satiating, bones for the rest.[59] Article II of its "Draft Articles on the Breadth of the Territorial Sea, Straits, and Fisheries" provides that:

> "1. In straits used for international navigation between one part of the high seas and another part of the high seas or the territorial sea of a foreign State, all ships and aircraft in transit shall enjoy the same freedom of navigation and overflight, for the purpose of transit through and over such straits, as they have on the high seas. Coastal States may designate

corridors suitable for transit by all ships and aircraft through and over such straits. In the case of straits where particular channels of navigation are customarily employed by ships in transit, the corridors, so far as ships are concerned, shall include such channels.

"2. The provisions of this Article shall not affect conventions or other international agreements already in force specifically relating to particular straits."

This is, to be sure, a little less than unqualified high seas passage. As John Stevenson put it in congressional testimony delivered when he was still State Department Legal Adviser and Chairman of the Interagency Law of the Sea Task Force:

"Under our Draft Articles we are talking about freedom solely for the limited purpose of transit, so that you would not be able to do anything that was not for the purpose of transit, whereas on the high seas generally a State can do what it wishes as long as it does not unreasonably interfere with other uses of the high seas by other countries. For example, you can conduct military maneuvers or exercises on the high seas but you could not do so when you are simply exercising a limited right of transit through a strait."[60]

Nor, he added, could you conduct scientific research while transiting. Lingering in a strait is another high seas right which would not obtain under Article II.

In his statement accompanying the U.S. Draft Articles, Mr. Stevenson affirmed an indissoluble relationship between this free transit provision and Article I's authorization of a twelve-mile territorial sea,[61] an authorization which, for States that had already claimed more, was coincidentally a restraint. It was, undoubtedly, this negative feature of Article I to which Mr. Stevenson referred when he announced that the U.S. Government "would be unable to conceive of a successful Law of the Sea Conference that did not accommodate the objectives of these Articles [I and II]."[62]

Since Article I allows States claiming a territorial sea of less than twelve miles to fill the gap between their claims and twelve miles with an exclusive fishing zone, it is apparent that one of the primary consequences of the U.S. proposal, if it were accepted, would be to cut back on burgeoning jurisdictional claims to living resources swimming more than twelve miles from the coast. Its other main functional consequence is to assure the continued availability of all the world's seas for the deployment of U.S. naval power "which must be relied on to implement those [global] responsibilities"[63] which the U.S. has seen fit to define for itself.

One cannot readily tell whether the jurisdictional restraint on exclusive fishing zones inherent in Article I is among the non-negotiable "objectives," since the Article's thrust in this dimension is softened significantly by Article III's preference arrangements. The arrangements are based on an initial division of the fish world into the three categories: "coastal" (e.g., the anchovy); "anadromous" (e.g., salmon); and "highly migratory oceanic stock" (e.g., tuna). In the case of the last-named, which constitutes something under twenty-five percent of the world's fish catch, there is no coastal State preference. With respect to species which normally inhabit waters adjacent to the coast (therefore, "coastal"), the coastal State would be allocated that percentage of the allowable catch[65] that it can harvest.[66] "States in whose fresh waters anadromous stock spawn" receive a comparable allocation.[67] Both preferences are, however, subject to so-called "historic fishing rights" expressed in the following terms:

> "The percentage of the allowable catch of a stock traditionally taken by the fishermen of other States shall not be allocated to the coastal State. This provision does not apply to any new fishing or expansion of existing fishing by other States that occurs after this Convention enters into force for the coastal State."[68]

Where waters are optimally exploited or already overexploited, so that there is no immediate prospect for overall expansion of the catch, the U.S. proposal is not calculated to evoke a warm reception from coastal State governments, particularly if the comparatively recent Japanese and Russian industrialized flotillas would stand among its beneficiaries. The caveat that the historic rights provision "does not apply to any new fishing or expansion of existing fishing by other States *that occurs after this Convention enters into force for the coastal State"* (emphasis added) certainly implies that they would. It is possible that the edge of this provision may be slightly dulled by a footnote stating "the view of the United States Government is that an appropriate text with respect to traditional fishing should be negotiated between coastal and distant-water fishing States." For there is some intimation here that the historic rights standard would be a point of departure, rather than an inflexible parameter, for bilateral negotiations. Its function may not be so much to bind the coastal State as to balance the negotiating power it derives from proximity, the relatively greater intensity of its interest,[69] and the power bestowed on it by other provisions of the U.S. Draft Articles to initiate the precise system of conservation and regulation.

TOWARDS A HEMISPHERIC POSITION ON A
NEW LAW OF THE SEA

Latin American States will have difficulty not only with the traditional fishing proviso and the exclusion of migratory species from the preferential arrangements, but also with the second qualification to the coastal and anadromous preference, namely its restriction to the percentage "that it can harvest." This would preclude the kind of potentially lucrative licensing operations which are available to shelf-rich States in connection with the exploitation of mineral resources. At least it would tend to work that deprivation if the most obvious means for its avoidance — fishing by locally incorporated and licensed subsidiaries of foreign enterprises — were deemed to be Convention-breaking.

Control over the mineral resources of the coastal seabed has not occasioned serious disputes between the U.S. and Latin American States because both have pressed for recognition of a broad measure of national autonomy. For shelf-poor States, such as Peru and Ecuador, the issue of mineral-extraction jurisdiction has only analogical significance.[70] But in east coast States, such as Argentina and Brazil, that have large and presumably rich shelves, it necessarily enjoys the high priority one notes in the U.S.

The position of the U.S. as an enormously powerful developed State with worldwide interests does promote a certain divergence in method. Having only marginal extra-hemispheric political interests, lacking the means to exploit extra-hemispheric resources, and being themselves underdeveloped, the Latin States appear interested only in the most meager allocation of resources for inter-national-community development which may be required to insure respect for their national claims. While some influential forces within the U.S., particularly the petroleum industry, obviously share this perspective, for reasons limned above the U.S. Government associates the national interest with the achievement of worldwide consensus. That requires certain concessions to landlocked and shelf-poor States and other States that wish to promote international control over a considerable bulk of ocean resources.

The U.S. concessions assume the form of a tri-sectored seabed. The first sector, the zone of national jurisdiction, would extend at least to the 200 meter depth line. Although the distance from shore of this point varies from several miles to several hundred miles, in the average case it would be less than fifty miles.[71]

The second sector, the so-called "international trusteeship area,"

"would begin at the 200-meter depth, or in cases where the waters reach a greater depth within twelve miles, at the edge of a twelve-mile territorial sea, were agreement achieved on a twelve-mile territorial sea. The U.S. proposed that the intermediate zone extend seaward to embrace the continental margin, but it also indicated at the most recent session of the U.N. committee its willingness to consider several criteria, including a mileage distance from shore, for the outer limit of the intermediate zone. Within the intermediate zone, coastal States would regulate exploration and exploitation, but there would also be international standards and compulsory dispute settlement designed, for example, to assure protection of other uses of the area, global protection of the marine environment from

49

seabeds pollution, and some sharing of revenues with the international community."[72]

While no State could "claim or exercise sovereign rights" in the intermediate zone or, *a fortiori*, beyond it,[73] the coastal State would, in the formal role of trustee for the international community, exercise effective economic control over the area, subject to certain international standards and review by the International Seabed Authority. Translated into functional rights, this means that coastal States may discriminate in favor of their nationals, may determine the timing of exploitation, and may retain a disproportionate share of all revenues (between one-third and one-half is proposed). The revenue retention provision, Ratiner writes, "clearly accommodates those developed countries with substantial resources off their coasts who would not benefit from a revenue-sharing formula (distributable only to developing countries), and makes easier the decision of developing coastal States with sizeable continental margins who could not be sure which system was more in their net financial interest."[74]

Since both the trusteeship and national jurisdiction beyond the twelve-mile territorial sea insofar as it affects the seabed relate only to the exploitation of natural resources, non-coastal States are free to use the seabed for other purposes, including the implantation of antisubmarine warfare tracking devices. In other words, all the nuances of the strategic interests defined by the U.S. Government enjoy full protection.

Beyond the area of trusteeship jurisdiction, the international regime would exercise exclusive control over mineral exploitation. The only minerals likely to be exploited in the deep-sea environment in the near future are found in seabed ocean nodules.[75] One authority estimates that commercial-scale exploitation is unlikely before 1985.[76] For the time being, then, the commercial action is on the shelves. With or without an effectively universal agreement, the U.S. and its shelf-rich Latin counterparts can anticipate a prosperous future in the coastal marine environment.

If, as one gathers, the Latin American States are not particularly concerned with the kinds of strategic interests which dominate U.S. policy, then at least for once it is possible to identify a significant convergence of U.S. and Latin American interests. While the concrete expressions of their respective interests do not yet coincide, they do appear to be within successful negotiating distance of each other. Or so one could conclude not only from an examination of their underlying interests, but also from the more immediate evidence of an emerging regional consensus contained in the joint statement of the Inter-American Juridical Committee[77] signed by the U.S. member, among others, on February 9, 1973. While he is nominally independent, it would be hard to find many people who would anticipate important divergence between the formally-expressed views of the U.S. member and those of the U.S. Government.

The statement is sufficiently broad to conceal modest differences of approach, yet is sufficiently specific to have exposed fundamental disagreement had it existed. The outline of a hemispheric compromise is there. For the U.S. there is free overflight and navigation beyond the twelve-mile limit. For the romantic nationalists there is the bold assertion that the "sovereignty or jurisdiction of a coastal State extends beyond its territory and its internal waters to an area of the sea adjacent to its coasts up to a maximum distance of 200 nautical miles, as well as to the air space above and the bed and subsoil of that sea,"[78] subject, of course, to the aforementioned freedom of overflight and navigation. For the mineral interests there is an assertion of national jurisdiction all the way to the abyssal depths even where the resulting outer boundary of national jurisdiction would be in excess of 200 miles from the coast. For coastal fishermen there is the assurance that within the 200-mile zone the coastal State has the power to reserve exploitation of living resources for its nationals, while for distant-water fishermen there is the aspirin of a regional preference the terms of which will be developed by bilateral, multilateral, or regional agreements. And for the rest of the world there is the proposal – or is it an ultimatum? – that the "future legal system governing the high seas and the exploitation of their resources should be organized on regional and not on worldwide bases."[79]

Given the extra-hemispheric interests of the U.S., one cannot believe that this statement foreshadows definitive repudiation by the U.S. of the rather more universalistic approach expressed in its draft proposals. But it does suggest that the U.S. is determined to shape a compromise acceptable to the Latin American States and that it solicits their close cooperation in efforts seeking to structure a new legal regime for the sea.

References

1. For an account of the elaborate U.S. negotiations to induce Ecuador to abstain, see Arthur H. Dean, "The Second Geneva Conference on the Law of the Sea," *American Journal of International Law*, Vol. 54 (1960), pp. 751, 780-782. Dean obtained State Department permission to offer Ecuador the assurance that the U.S. would never take the initial evidentiary step necessary to demonstrate its historic fishing practice off Ecuador's shores. This omission would stop the U.S. from claiming to be within the exception to the "six-plus-six" proposal that allowed qualifying States to continue fishing in the contiguous zone, from which all foreign fishing was excluded, for a period of ten years. At first, Ecuador accepted this offer and agreed to abstain. But, then, during the voting itself, it demanded immediate release of all past U.S. claims for reimbursement of fines paid to Ecuador by U.S. ships seized within its claimed 200-mile territorial sea. The U.S. delegation, of course, lacked authority to waive congressional or private claims and, therefore, could not comply with this last-minute demand. Ecuador voted against the proposal.
2. The territorial sea comprises the waters immediately adjacent to the coastal State, the territorial extension of which it is considered to be. Before the 1930 League of Nations Conference on the Sea (which failed to reach agreement on the width of territorial waters) there was considerable support for the view that coastal prerogatives were more like "servitudes" than creatures of sovereignty. See J. Andrassy, *International Law and the Resources of the Sea* (New York: Columbia University Press, 1970), p. 45, for a capsule statement of the evolving rationale of the concept.

The contiguous zone is that area beyond the territorial sea within which the coastal State may exercise limited controls for special purposes, for example, enforcement of fiscal, immigration, sanitation, and customs regulations. The 1958 Convention on the Territorial Sea and the Contiguous Zone, 15 *United States Treaties (in Force)* (hereinafter cited as *U.S.T.*) 1607, *United States Treaties and Other International Acts Series* (hereinafter cited as *T.I.A.S.*) No. 5639, effective September 10, 1964, did not specify a width for the territorial sea but it did limit the contiguous zone to twelve miles measured from the baseline from which the territorial sea is measured.

In the absence of a rule limiting the breadth of the territorial sea, the provision for a contiguous zone that did not confer the right to exclude foreign fishermen seems anomalous until one reviews the negotiating history of the 1958 and 1960 Conferences. The concept of a contiguous zone with exclusive fishing rights was common ground between those delegations that were holding out for an exclusive fishing zone (traditionally considered an incident of the territorial sea) at least twelve miles broad and other delegations, primarily the U.S. and Great Britain, that insisted on a territorial sea less than twelve miles wide. When the compromise failed, the conferees were left with a largely superfluous contiguous zone.

3. This proposal was first advanced at the 1958 Conference by the United Kingdom on April 1, 1958 (United Nations Doc. A/CONF.13/C.1/L/134). The U.S. adopted it on April 15, 1958, with revisions (United Nations Doc. A/CONF.13/C.1/L/159, Rev. 1.) It was proposed anew by the U.S. and Canada at the 1960 Conference called especially to reach agreement, not achieved at the previous conference, on the width of the territorial sea and an exclusive fishing zone (United Nations Doc. A/CONF.19/SR.13, p. 8).

4. The final vote was 54 in favor, 28 opposed, 5 abstaining. Cited in S. Oda, *International Control of Sea Resources* (Leyden: Sijthoff, 1963), p. 104.

5. United Nations Doc. A/CONF.19/SR.14 (1960), p. 6. Interestingly, the first known expression of a United States view on territorial limits at sea involved fishing rights and the distance involved was nine, not three miles. It came in a congressional report in 1782 on the rights of U.S. fishermen in which it was declared that U.S. peace negotiators were instructed that the United States "did not claim the right of fishing within three leagues of the British shores," P. C. Jessup, *The Law of Territorial Waters and Maritime Jurisdiction* (New York: Jennings, Inc., 1927), pp. 49-50. In notes to British and French foreign ministers, dated November 8, 1793, on the subject of neutral zones, Secretary of State Jefferson observed that "the greatest distance to which any respectable assent among nations has been at any time given, has been the extent of the human sight, estimated at upwards of twenty miles, and the smallest distance, I believe, claimed by any nation whatever, is the utmost range of a cannon ball, usually stated at one sea league," J. B. Moore, *A Digest of International Law* (Washington, D.C.: Government Printing Office, 1906), Vol. I, p. 702; also appearing in P. C. Jessup, op. cit., p. 6. Continuing, Jefferson noted that although the "ultimate extent" of the marginal sea was reserved "for future deliberations," the President had instructed American officials to restrain the enforcement of their orders "for the present to the distance of one sea league, or three geographical miles from the seashores," J. B. Moore, op. cit., Vol. I, p. 702; also appearing in P. C. Jessup, op. cit., p. 50. This policy was codified by Congress in legislation that gave federal district courts "cognizance of complaints … in cases of captures made within the waters of the United States or within a marine league of the coast or shores thereof," Section 6, Act of June 5, 1794, I Stat. 384.

6. United States Code (hereinafter cited as U.S.C.), Vol. 43, pp. 1301-1315.

7. U.S.C., Vol. 16, pp. 1091-1092 (Supp. IV, 1969).

8. Proclamation No. 2667, 59 Stat. 884 (1945).

9. *Department of State Bulletin,* Vol. 13, p. 484 (1945).

10. U.S.C., Vol. 43, pp. 1331-1343.

11. Cavanaugh (Associate Solicitor, U.S. Department of the Interior), Gower Federal Service – Continental Shelf O.C.S. 1961-25.

12. Ratified March 24, 1960. 15 *U.S.T.* 471, *T.I.A.S.* No. 5578, effective June 10, 1964.

13. Article 1, United Nations Doc. A/CONF.13/L.55.

14. O. L. Stone, "U.S. Legislation Relating to the Continental Shelf," *International and Comparative Law Quarterly Review,* Vol. 17 (1968), p. 103. In fact, exploitation never commenced and the lease was eventually relinquished. Since then, no lease appears to have been granted under comparable circumstances; we do not know whether this reflects a change in government policy or the absence of offers.
15. For an account of this development, see T. A. Garaicoa, "The Continental Shelf and the Extension of the Territorial Sea," *Miami Law Quarterly,* Vol. 10 (1956), p. 490.
16. Testimony before Special Subcommittee on Outer Continental Shelf, Senate Committee on Interior and Insular Affairs, 91st Congress, 1st and 2nd Sessions, January 22, 1970.
17. U.S.C., Vol. 14, p. 81, as amended, 1966.
18. 14 C.F.R. 209/135 (1)–(46) sets forth markings for Shipping Safety Fairways and Anchorage Areas, Gulf of Mexico, "to provide safe approaches through oil fields ... to the entrances to the major ports along the Gulf Coast." 209/170 (g) (1) and (2) specify similarly extensive regulations for the Pacific Ocean at Port Hueneme, California.
19. *United States v. Louisiana, et. al.* 363 U.S. 1 (1960). For a thorough discussion of the circumstances of the litigation and the opinion, see A. Shalowitz, *Shore and Sea Boundaries,* Pub. 10-1, Department of Commerce (Washington, D.C.: Government Printing Office, 1962), Vol. I, pp. 132-154.
20. Testimony before 1949 Senate Hearings, 1953 Senate Hearings, and the *Congressional Record,* all cited by the Supreme Court. See *United States v. Louisiana, et. al.,* loc. cit., note 19 above, pp. 31-32.
21. Comment, *American Journal of International Law,* Vol. 55 (1961), p. 669, in response to Dean's article, cited in note 1 above.
22. 9 Stat. 922 (1848). Article V of the Treaty provides: "The boundary line between the two republics shall commence in the Gulf of Mexico, three leagues from land, opposite the mouth of the Rio Grande ... or opposite the mouth of its deepest branch if it should have more than one branch emptying directly into the sea."
23. 363 U.S. 1, p. 62 (1960).
24. 363 U.S. 1, pp. 35-36, quoted by Dean, *American Journal of International Law,* Vol. 55 (1961), p. 679.
25. P. C. Jessup, op. cit., note 5 above, p. 52. Secretary Buchanan was replying to a British Note protesting this very provision of the Treaty on the theory that it, indeed, extended U.S. territorial waters beyond the three-mile limit.
26. U.S.C., Vol. 16, pp. 1091-1092 (Supp. IV, 1969).
27. Ratified March 24, 1960, 13 *U.S.T.* 2313, *T.I.A.S.* No. 5200, effective September 30, 1962.
28. Letter of Douglas McArthur II for the Secretary of State, to Senate Subcommittee on Merchant Marine and Fisheries of the Committee on Commerce, 89th Congress, 2nd Session, Hearings, May 18-20, 1966, pp. 1-2.
29. Almost from its inception the United States asserted its right to control activities on the high seas adjacent to its coasts for the latter's protection. 1 Stat. 668 (1799) authorized customs officers to board and search all vessels bound *to* U.S. ports, including foreign ships, when they were within four leagues (12 nautical miles) of the U.S. coast to enforce custom regulations. The power to search and arrest was conferred. The Tariff Act of 1922, 42 Stat. 989, expanded this authorization to include *all* ships within the twelve-mile zone whether or not headed for U.S. ports.

   Contemporary authorization for Coast Guard enforcement powers is found in U.S.C., Vol. 14, p. 89. Enforcement of the navigation laws appears in U.S.C., Vol. 19, p. 1581 (b) and (e); the customs laws in U.S.C., Vol. 19, p. 1581 (e) and (f), pp. 1701 and 1703; the oil pollution laws (now covering discharge "into or upon the waters of the contiguous zone") in U.S.C., Vol. 33, p. 1161 (Supp. 1969); the conservation laws (actually exclusive fishing zones) in U.S.C., Vol. 16, p. 1081 (1964) establishing a three-mile zone and in U.S.C., Vol. 16, pp. 1091-1092 (1966) setting a twelve-mile zone.

   Policing of the territorial sea itself appears somewhat casual. In the words of the General Counsel for the Treasury Department, Fred Smith, "Present operating practices of the Coast Guard do not normally demand intensive surveillance of all existing territorial limits. If [the twelve-mile fishery zone is enacted] it is anticipated that present levels of patrol and enforcement activity would continue unless there is evidence of widespread violations of prohibitions contained in [the statute]." Testimony for Hearings on a Twelve-Mile Fishery Zone, before the Senate Subcommittee on Merchant Marine and Fisheries, Committee on Commerce, 89th Congress, 2nd Session, pp. 5-6 (hereinafter cited as Hearings on Twelve-Mile Fishery Zone).

For a detailed discussion of Coast Guard enforcement practices, see Testimony of Captain Reynolds, Hearings on Russian Trawler Traffic in U.S. Territorial Waters, before the House Subcommittee for Special Investigations, Committee on Armed Services, 88th Congress, 1st Session, pp. 23-72.

30. Compare Leigh Ratiner, "United States Oceans Policy: An Analysis," *Journal of Maritime Law and Commerce,* Vol. 2 (1971), pp. 225, 227-228. One cannot say now whether United States Government decision makers should have known then that a unilateral claim, whether territorial or not, was going to touch off in later years a race by others to grab and hold vast areas of the sea and seabeds. There can, however, be no question that decision makers knew that the risk existed. For if that risk had not been foreseen, the Proclamation, if only for the sake of simplicity, would have claimed the seabed itself and not the resources. Instead, the Proclamation was carefully circumscribed so as not to give any country a basis for claiming more rights in areas adjacent to their coasts than the United States had claimed in the area adjacent to its coasts.

What the United States Government did not know then, but what it has since learned, is that when an important nation asserts the unilateral right to take certain action, what may be copied by other nations is not necessarily the action itself but rather the basis upon which the action was taken. Thus, Chile, Ecuador, and Peru did not believe themselves to be constrained by the text of the Truman Proclamation when they agreed on the Declaration of Santiago which proclaimed their sole jurisdiction and sovereignty over an area of the sea, the sea floor and subsoil extending 200 nautical miles adjacent to their coasts. Since the 1952 Declaration of Santiago, these three countries have many times set forth various legal rationales for their claim. One of their arguments is that if the United States had a unilateral right to claim the resources of the seabed adjacent to its coasts to the exclusion of all other countries, they, too, had a similar unilateral right to make claims consistent with their own national interests.

31. As long ago as 1969, forty-six States claimed a twelve-mile territorial sea, an additional thirty-one States asserted claims from four to 200 miles (excluding those claiming twelve-mile limits), while only thirty-three observed a three-mile national sea. U.S. Naval Oceanographic Office List of Territorial Waters Claims as of June 1969 (R.S. 9060/69, 1969), cited by M. R. Deddish, Jr., "The Right of Passage by Warships Through International Straits," *JAG J.,* Vol. 24 (1969-1970), p. 81.

32. The quotation is from paragraph 4 of Article 16 of the Geneva Convention of 1958 on the Territorial Sea and the Contiguous Zone (see note 2 above). For discussion see pp. 43-44.

33. Hedrick Smith, *New York Times,* January 12, 1972.

34. Ibid. See also Drew Middleton, *New York Times,* March 4, 1972.

35. See the penetrating testimony of Professor H. Gary Knight in Hearings before the Subcommittee on International Organizations and Movements of the Committee on Foreign Affairs of the House of Representatives, 92nd Congress, 2nd Session, April 10 and 11, 1972: "Law of the Sea and Peaceful Uses of the Seabeds" (Washington, D.C.: Government Printing Office, 1972), pp. 71, 74, and 75. Hereinafter cited as *Hearings.*

36. For an overview of the subject, see Note, "Peacetime Passage by Warships Through the Territorial Sea," *Columbia Law Review,* Vol. 50 (1950), p. 221, and more recently, S. Slonim, "The Right of Innocent Passage," *Columbia Journal of Transnational Law,* Vol. 5 (1966), p. 96.

37. Testimony of Dr. Robert Frosch, Assistant Secretary of the Navy (Research and Development), Hearings on National Marine Sciences Program before the Subcommittee on Oceanography, House Committee on Merchant Marine and Fisheries, 90th Congress, 1st Session, p. 345 (1967), cited in M. R. Deddish, Jr., op. cit., note 31 above, p. 85.

38. XI Proceedings, North Atlantic Coast Fisheries Arbitration, Senate Document No. 870, 61st Congress, 3rd Session (1910), p. 2007, quoted in K. D. Lawrence, "Military-Legal Considerations in the Extension of the Territorial Sea," *Military Law Review*, Vol. 29 (1965), pp. 47, 75 and 76.
39. K. D. Lawrence, op. cit., note 38 above, pp. 75 and 76.
40. The writers did not find evidence of sightings of foreign military vessels within U.S. territorial waters.
41. See especially the lengthy testimony of Captain Reynolds, Chief of Port Security and Law Enforcement, Coast Guard Headquarters, Hearings on Russian Trawler Traffic in U.S. Territorial Waters before the House Subcommittee for Special Investigations, Committee on Armed Services, 88th Congress, 1st Session, pp. 23-72.
42. In December 1962, almost a year after the proposal first surfaced, the State Department replied with a qualified rejection, approving instead a general Coast Guard policy of stopping all foreign fishing ships *not* in innocent passage. Report on Russian Trawler Traffic in U.S. Territorial Waters by House Subcommittee for Special Investigations, Committee on Armed Services, 88th Congress, 1st Session, p. 5.
43. M. R. Deddish, Jr., op. cit., note 31 above, p. 82.
44. *Annual Digest and Reports of Public International Law Cases,* 1949, p. 161.
45. Paragraph 4 of Article 16.
46. Paragraph 3 of Article 16.
47. See, for example, A. Shalowitz, op. cit., note 19 above, p. 237. For a different conclusion based on inferences extractable from the record of the Conference proceedings, see Sorenson, *Law of the Sea,* No. 520, International Conciliation 235 (November 1958). For a broad review and analysis of the Conference's work in this area, see G. Fitzmaurice, "Some Results of the Geneva Conference on the Law of the Sea," *International Comparative Law Quarterly*, Vol. 8 (January 1959), pp. 73, 90-108.
48. M. R. Deddish, Jr., op. cit., note 31 above, p. 85, footnote 50.
49. Ibid., p. 83.
50. Cf. Stevenson in *Hearings* (cit. in note 35 above), p. 4: "Moreover, some coastal States have interpreted innocent passage subjectively, arguing, for example, that the flag, cargo, or destination of a vessel is a relevant consideration."
51. Op. cit., note 30 above, p. 263.
52. The lifeline narrows to as little as 7.75 miles and widens at most to 23.75 miles.
53. See Kennedy, *A Brief Geographical Hydrographical Study of Straits Which Constitute Routes for International Traffic;* United Nations Doc. A/CONF.13/6/Add.1 (1957); and K. D. Lawrence, op. cit., note 38 above, p. 67.
54. See L. Ratiner, op. cit., note 30 above, p. 236. See also the statement of Northcutt Ely in *Hearings* (cit. in note 35 above), pp. 36-58.
55. Ibid., p. 237.
56. Northcutt Ely in *Hearings* (cit. in note 35 above), p. 44.
57. In his report on the 1960 Geneva Conference (see note 1 above), Arthur H. Dean expressly cited the interests of American distant-water fishermen as obstacles to extension of the U.S. territorial sea, explaining their position in terms of their need to exploit fisheries lying off South American countries that claim 200-mile territorial seas precisely to exclude these U.S. fishermen. For detailed presentations of their viewpoints, see Hearings on Twelve-Mile Fishery Zone (cit. in note 29 above), statements by Dr. W. M. Chapman, Van Camp Seafood Company, p. 69; W. R. Neblett, National Shrimp Congress, p. 119; A. Felando, American Tunaboat Association, p. 103. Both the West Coast and Northeast Coast fishing trades have vigorously sought congressional protection. Their principal villain, of course, is the Russian trawler fleets that expanded enormously in the sixties. The West Coast also singles out Japanese fleets as a threat both from the standpoint of conservation and its own more parochial well-being. See testimony of J. Ostensen, New Bedford Fishermen's Union, p. 164, Hearings on Twelve-Mile Fishery Zone, for a comprehensive statement of the northeasterners' position. For a review of West Coast interests, see testimony of F. Phebus, Fishermen's Marketing Association, pp. 61 and 68 of Hearings on Twelve-Mile Fishery Zone.

58. See Statement of John G. Laylin, in *Hearings* (cit. in note 35 above), pp. 31-36.
59. For the seabed proposal, see *International Legal Materials*, Vol. IX (1970), p. 1046. For the "Draft Articles on the Breadth of the Territorial Sea, Straits, and Fisheries," see *Report of the Committee on the Peaceful Uses of the Seabed and the Ocean Floor Beyond the Limits of National Jurisdiction*, Annex IV, 241, General Assembly Official Records, 26th Session, Supp. No. 21 (A/8421).
60. *Hearings* (cit. in note 35 above), p. 11.
61. Ibid., p. 4.
62. Cited by H. Gary Knight, in *Hearings* (cit. in note 35 above).
63. L. Ratiner, op. cit., note 30 above, p. 238.
64. Stevenson, *Hearings* (cit. in note 35 above), p. 5.
65. "Conservation measures shall be adopted that do not discriminate in form or in fact against any fishermen. For this purpose, the allowable catch shall be determined, on the basis of the best evidence available, at a level which is designed to maintain the maximum sustainable yield or restore it as soon as practicable, taking into account relevant environmental and economic factors."
66. Sub-paragraph 2 C.
67. Sub-paragraph 2 D.
68. Sub-paragraph 2 E (1).
69. See Leigh Ratiner, op. cit., note 30 above, p. 232: "It has been argued by well-intentioned Americans that a civilized nation cannot in 1970 use force to establish or protect its rights on the high seas. These same people, however, would in all likelihood support military action in defense of our land boundaries. Our territory then becomes a more important objective than the rights which our nation, and all other nations, have beyond its borders. When a coastal State extends its boundary into the sea, it acquires a strong motivation to defend its new territory. At the same time, however, objecting or user nations are put at a substantial psychological disadvantage. For they are claiming no territory – only rights. Their citizens are not likely to rally in defense of obscure legal rights. As only one example of this state of affairs, one may point to United States reluctance, over the years, to protect U.S. tuna boats off the coast of South America. Yet, the citizens of the *coastal* State will and have quickly rallied in defense of their newly acquired territorial waters just as they would and have rallied to the defense of their territorial lands. As an example of *this* state of affairs, one may point to the persistent and regular seizures of these same U.S. tuna boats."
70. See note 30 above.
71. Stevenson, *Hearings* (cit. in note 35 above), p. 5.
72. Ibid.
73. Article 2, Chapter I of U.S. Seabed Proposal, loc. cit., note 59 above, p. 1048.
74. L. Ratiner, op. cit., note 30 above, pp. 247-248.
75. See Statement of F. L. LaQue, Senior Lecturer, Scripps Institute of Oceanography, *Hearings* (cit. in note 35 above), pp. 59-60.
76. Ibid., p. 66.
77. Resolution on the Law of the Sea approved by the Inter-American Juridical Committee on February 9, 1973. OAS Doc. AG-Doc. 345-73, March 26, 1973.
78. Ibid.
79. Ibid.

Chapter III

Latin America and the Development of the Law of the Sea: An Overview

Chapter III

LATIN AMERICA AND THE
DEVELOPMENT OF THE LAW OF THE SEA:
AN OVERVIEW

Ralph Zacklin *

INTRODUCTION

The expanding nature and changing structure of international law have been dominant themes in international legal doctrine for the past quarter of a century.[1] In practice, however, the evidence suggests that the much-heralded "quantitative and qualitative renovation of international law"[2] has thus far been confined largely to the more formal aspects of inter-State relations such as diplomatic and consular immunities or the law of treaties, and has not produced any substantial realignment in economic or political terms.

The law of the sea, despite major codification conferences in 1930, 1958, and 1960, remains in a state of turmoil because it represents a political and economic reality for all States. Any change in the law of the sea will have major repercussions on the existing allocation of economic, and consequently political, resources of States. The renovation of the law of the sea, therefore, constitutes the first genuinely substantive international legal confrontation of the post-1945 international community. It is, furthermore, a confrontation in which there is an unusual degree of real as opposed to formal equality among States by virtue of the fact that the sea is one frontier on which territorial or jurisdictional claims may be asserted without necessarily possessing the power normally required for territorial aggrandizements.[3] This peculiarity of the sea in international relations is of fundamental importance to an understanding of the emerging law of the sea since it permits and encourages a free play of national interests expressed through unilateral acts. As Charles Chaumont has so lucidly expressed this phenomenon:

> "Certaines questions maritimes telles que celle de la largeur de la mer territoriale et celle du plateau continental ont une spécificité concrète qui les différencie d'autant plus des autres problèmes territoriaux que, pour les Etats riverains de la mer, la frontière maritime est la seule dont l'extension

---

*The views expressed in this chapter, as in all the chapters, are the personal views of the author and do not reflect a consensus of the Study Group.

ne se heurte pas à des compétences territoriales déja acquises. Le plus souvent elle peut donc se faire sans agression ni impérialisme."[4]

Latin American attitudes toward the development of the law of the sea cannot be correctly perceived unless placed in this politico-economic perspective. Historically speaking, the drama of Latin America has been its chronic inability, individually or collectively, to assert an effective political, economic, and legal independence. From Bolívar's despairing and anguished cry ("I have plowed the seas") to the faltering exercises in economic integration of the Latin American Free Trade Association, the Central American Common Market, and the Andean Group, the centrifugal forces of political, economic, and cultural diversity have persistently frustrated all attempts to create a viable Latin American identity.[5]

In the legal field, Latin American initiatives in the late nineteenth and early twentieth centuries to modify the status quo, such as the Drago doctrine and the Calvo clause, were effectively isolated and stifled by the European powers and the United States, while the elaborate inter-American legal system is considered by some to be overly abstract and bearing little or no relationship to the political, economic, and sociological realities of contemporary Latin America.[6]

The renovation of the law of the sea, with its broad political, economic, and strategic ramifications, provides the Latin American States with the ideal terrain on which to challenge the old order, for it is an issue with respect to which they can combine political independence and economic nationalism in the broader context of the dialectic between developed and developing nations.

An important attribute of the Latin American States as they approach the new law of the sea conference is that they possess, more than any other group of States, a history of cooperative endeavor in this field and a keen sense of purpose. Since 1945, the Latin American States have created a considerable body of practice and doctrine on all aspects of the law of the sea. The most important, and controversial, source of this Latin American doctrine consists of unilateral acts – legislation, decrees, declarations – which have been consistently enforced by Latin American States, frequently in the face of protests by foreign governments. These unilateral acts are supplemented and buttressed by a variety of bilateral declarations and agreements, sub-regional institutions, resolutions, and agreements such as the Permanent Commission of South Pacific States (Chile, Ecuador, and Peru), declarations and resolutions of regional organizations and organs, and a multitude of statements by Latin American representatives in international conferences and United Nations organs.

The cornerstone of the Latin American approach to the law of the sea is the nexus between the sea and the land. In geographic or economic terms, this is most easily understood by reference to the immense coastlines of many Latin American States[7] or to the living and mineral resources of the sea.[8] What is less frequently appreciated by outside observers is the psychological aspect of this nexus, familiar to island nations such as the United Kingdom and Iceland but not normally associated with large land-mass States such as Argentina, Chile, or Peru.[9] This psychological factor has an important bearing on Latin American attitudes giving rise to what many Latin American States regard as the essential unity of the zones within national jurisdiction: the territorial sea, zones of special jurisdiction, and the continental shelf. The translation of this essential unity into a new legal concept is one of the principal Latin American objectives in the forthcoming law of the sea conference.

The present chapter is an attempt to present to the reader a general overview of the developments in Latin America, to identify the positions adopted, and to delineate the emerging Latin American consensus – a consensus which will exert an important influence on the final outcome of the third law of the sea conference.

THE TERRITORIAL SEA

Historically, the fundamental problem of the law of the sea has been the delimitation of the frontier between the territorial sea and the high seas. After the historic doctrinal clash between Grotius and Selden in the seventeenth century, international law gradually evolved toward a customary rule based on the range of a canon which, at the time, was approximately one marine league or three miles.[10] This rule enjoyed a lengthy period of stability until 1930, when the League of Nations' attempt to codify it failed. Since then, there has in effect been no generally accepted rule of customary or conventional law regulating the breadth of the territorial sea, although the 1958 Geneva Convention on the Territorial Sea and the Contiguous Zone provides, by implication, that the territorial sea shall not exceed twelve miles.[11] The successful development of the law of the sea contemplated by United Nations General Assembly Resolution 2750 C (XXV) of December 17, 1970, will depend, to a large extent, on agreement concerning the territorial sea, the two most important elements of which are its legal nature and its breadth.

At first sight, the legal nature of the territorial sea would not appear to be in any doubt. The 1958 Convention codified the customary international law principle according to which "the sovereignty of the State extends, beyond its land territory and its internal waters, to a belt of sea adjacent to its coast, described as the territorial sea" (Article 1). Within the territorial sea, the coastal State retains most of its sovereign powers, subject to the right of innocent passage by foreign ships (Articles 14 to 23).

The clear-cut distinction, however, which once existed between the territorial sea and the high seas was blurred by the introduction of the contiguous zone concept in the 1958 Convention, and has been further emasculated by the policies of several Latin American States whose interpretations of the territorial sea have not always corresponded to the definition of the 1958 Convention. This attachment of different meanings to the same label is a source of considerable confusion which can be eliminated only through the common acceptance of a precise definition of the legal nature of the territorial sea. Although Article I of the 1958 Convention unquestionably reflects *opinio juris* with respect to the legal nature of the territorial sea, as the post-1958 practice has demonstrated, it is essential that this be accompanied by agreement on the breadth of the territorial sea, the two elements being intrinsically interrelated, if common acceptance is to be achieved.

The problem, then, with regard to the territorial sea is reduced to the question of its breadth, an issue which has proved elusive, at least in modern times, since 1930.

The most distinctive position with regard to the breadth of the territorial sea is that which is generally identified with Latin America. Dissatisfaction with the classical three-mile rule was first manifested by a number of Latin American States at the 1930 Hague Conference for the Codification of International Law, but it was not until the early 1950s that the first outlines of a regional position began to emerge. In the Declaration on the Maritime Zone signed in Santiago on August 18, 1952, Chile, Ecuador, and Peru proclaimed "... as a principle of their international maritime policy [exclusive] sovereignty and jurisdiction ... " over their coastal waters to a distance of 200 miles.[12]

The Santiago Declaration was reinforced by the establishment of a Permanent Commission, and in 1954, the three States signed a Supplementary Agreement by which, *inter alia,* they agreed to act jointly "in the legal defense of the principle of sovereignty over the 200-mile maritime zone."[13]

The importance of the Santiago Declaration in the evolution of the Latin American position cannot be over-emphasized. Despite the fact that it represented the views of only three States, the Declaration has had a pervasive regional influence; and the final vindication of its principles will possibly be witnessed in the global context.

Two aspects of the Declaration, in particular, must be stressed. The first is its underlying economic and social rationale, expressed in terms of economic development and the conservation and protection of natural resources.[14] In this respect, the Declaration was the precursor of two of the principal moving forces of the contemporary international community. The second, and from the legal point of view more important, aspect is that the Declaration is concerned with a *maritime zone* rather than the territorial sea.[15]

It is true that the Declaration makes repeated use of the phrase "sovereignty and jurisdiction," but it is also true that it refrains from attaching the label "territorial sea" to the area. Thus, while the language of the Declaration lends itself to a certain ambiguity, it would seem nevertheless to have more in common with special zones than with a territorial sea *stricto sensu*. This ambiguity in the language is reflected in the implementation of the Declaration by each of the three States which has been far from uniform in content.

The broader impact of the Santiago Declaration was virtually immediate as it rapidly filtered through the inter-American system, drawing support from regional organs and conferences such as the Inter-American Council of Jurists, the Hispano-Luso-American Congress of International Law, and the Tenth Inter-American Conference.[16]

Yet, despite these expressions of support, the South Pacific States remained isolated both regionally and internationally. The majority of Latin American States continued to adhere to the traditional concept of a territorial sea and, at the 1958 and 1960 Geneva Conferences, adopted a middle of the road position with respect to the breadth of the territorial sea.[17] But partly because of the confusion surrounding the practice of the South Pacific States and partly because of the spectacular nature of some of the incidents arising from the enforcement of the Santiago Declaration,[18] the 200-mile claim has been frequently misrepresented as *the* Latin American position. In fact, notwithstanding a major realignment of the claims by Latin American States in recent years, Latin America continues to exhibit a high degree of asymmetry with respect to the breadth and even the nature of the territorial sea. Broadly speaking, contemporary Latin American legislation and practice may be grouped under three main heads: (1) claims to a territorial sea *stricto sensu* not exceeding twelve miles; (2) claims to a 200-mile maritime zone of limited sovereignty; and (3) claims to a 200-mile territorial sea *stricto sensu*. The different claims of Latin American States are set forth in the table on page 64.

The first group is a combination of twelve States, geographically circumscribing the Caribbean, whose territorial sea claims, varying in breadth from three to twelve miles, correspond to the definition contained in Article 1 of the 1958 Geneva Convention. Five of these States have ratified the Convention or acceded to it.[19]

The third group consists of four States which have enacted legislation or promulgated decrees extending the territorial sea to 200 miles, subject only to the right of innocent passage. The Ecuadorian Decree No. 1542 of November 10, 1966, Panamanian Law No. 31 of February 2, 1967, and the Brazilian Decree-Law No. 1.098 of March 25, 1970, expressly employ the term "territorial sea" and, in addition, explicitly or implicitly, reject any rights within the zone other than innocent passage.[20] The position of the fourth member of this group, Peru, is somewhat ambiguous. Supreme Decree No. 781 of August 1, 1947, establishes Peruvian sovereignty and jurisdiction over the adjacent sea to a distance of 200 miles but expressly grants freedom of navigation to vessels of all nations.[21] On the one hand, this provision is incompatible with the traditional concept of the territorial sea as expressed in the 1958 Convention and, furthermore, both the

Territorial Sea and Jurisdictional Claims
of Latin American Countries
(distances in marine miles)

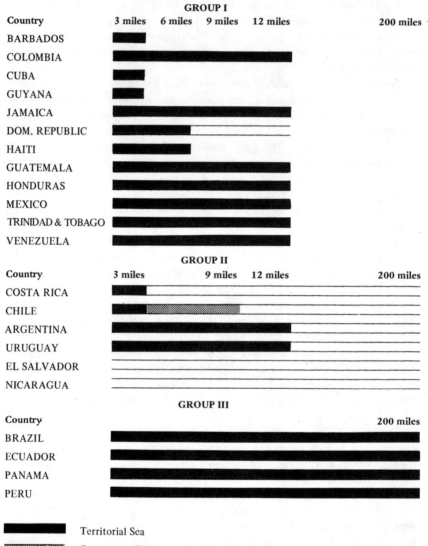

GROUP I

| Country | 3 miles | 6 miles | 9 miles | 12 miles | | 200 miles |

GROUP II

| Country | 3 miles | | 9 miles | 12 miles | 200 miles |

GROUP III

| Country | | 200 miles |

Territorial Sea

Contiguous Zone

Maritime Zone of Limited Sovereignty

Source: United Nations Doc. A/AC.138/50, "Limits and Status of the Territorial Sea, Exclusive Fishing Zones, Fishery Conservation Zones, and the Continental Shelf," and *América latina y la extension del mar territorial* (Montevideo, 1971), updated to January 1973.

preambular considerations in the decree and the omission of the term "territorial sea" would seem to suggest that the decree is aimed at the establishment of a maritime zone of limited sovereignty rather than a territorial sea.[22] On the other hand, there is evidence to suggest that the Peruvian maritime zone is a *de facto* territorial sea in which Peru exercises exclusive sovereignty and jurisdiction subject only to innocent passage. International agreements entered into by Peru subsequent to the 1947 Decree, posterior Peruvian legislation regulating such matters as fishing rights, navigation, and overflight, and particularly the manner in which Peruvian authorities have consistently enforced their sovereignty, point more readily to a territorial sea claim than to one of limited sovereignty.[23] Thus, although Peru does not expressly claim a territorial sea of any breadth, the characteristics of its 200-mile maritime zone appear to be assimilable to a territorial sea *stricto sensu.*

In between these two groups representing opposite ends of the territorial sea spectrum, there has evolved a median position which is something of a composite of the two. Six States − Argentina, Chile, Costa Rica, El Salvador, Nicaragua, and Uruguay − claim a 200-mile maritime zone of limited sovereignty within which the territorial sea *stricto sensu* does not exceed twelve miles. Although the relevant decrees or legislation are couched in language which suggests the exercise of sovereignty, this is in fact limited through the express or tacit acknowledgment of freedom of navigation and overflight within designated areas of the zone, characteristics which are of course incompatible with the traditional concept of the territorial sea.[24]

This overview of the Latin American territorial sea claims demonstrates quite clearly both the quantitative and qualitative asymmetry in contemporary Latin American practice. Quantitatively, these claims cover the entire spectrum of territorial limits from the classical three miles to the more extensive 200 miles; qualitatively, some of the claims correspond to the classical conception of the territorial sea as reflected in the Geneva Convention, others redefine this conception in more flexible terms, and yet others abandon the concept of the territorial sea altogether in favor of a system of maritime zones. Against this background of manifest heterogeneity, the product of almost three decades of national political, economic, and legal adjustments, Latin American chancelleries are engaged in a regional attempt to forge a consensus position that would embrace the three principal Latin American tendencies.

At first sight, the achievement of a consensus would appear beyond reach. But, as the table on page 64 graphically demonstrates, despite the considerable substantive differences which continue to prevail in the individual legislation and practice of Latin American States, by 1970 a realignment of considerable geopolitical importance had already taken place. A combination of groups 2 and 3, leaving aside the qualitative difference in the precise legal nature of the claims, results in the creation of a massive bloc extending from the Equator to Tierra del Fuego with a 200-mile marginal sea. The once isolated South Pacific States now find themselves progressively integrated into a system of continental rather than sub-regional proportions.

This pronounced trend towards continentalism has been encouraged and developed in a series of regional meetings, the first of which took place in Montevideo in May 1970 at the invitation of the Uruguayan Government and which was to be attended by the ten Latin American States claiming a 200-mile marginal sea.[25] This was followed three months later by a meeting in Lima of twenty Latin American States.[26] Finally, in June 1972, there took place in Santo Domingo a specialized conference of Caribbean States. Each of these meetings has resulted in a declaration embodying certain basic principles or rights from which it is possible to extrapolate the embryonic elements of a common Latin American position.[27]

Broadly speaking, the Declarations contain three basic principles or rights: (1) the right of every nation to exercise control over its natural maritime resources;[28] (2) the right to delimit maritime sovereignty and jurisdiction in accordance with reasonable criteria having regard to each State's geographical, geological, and biological characteristics;[29] and (3) the right of every State to enact regulatory measures of an economic nature in areas of maritime sovereignty and jurisdiction without prejudice to freedom of navigation and overflight.[30] These principles are based on considerations deriving from the special economic and social requirements of less-developed States and from the necessity to conserve the natural resources of the sea for the benefit of mankind as a whole.[31] It should be observed that neither the Montevideo nor Lima Declarations expressly refer to the "territorial sea," preferring instead the formula "maritime sovereignty and jurisdiction." The Santo Domingo Declaration, however, specifically addresses itself to the "territorial sea" as defined by the Geneva Convention and, furthermore, endorses a twelve-mile limit.

With the exception of those States claiming a territorial sea *stricto sensu* in excess of twelve miles (Brazil, Ecuador, Panama, and, possibly, Peru), the positions adopted by the Montevideo-Lima meetings and the Santo Domingo meeting are not necessarily incompatible.

The three regional declarations would appear to point the Latin American States in two possible directions. The first, and least satisfactory, direction, in essence, would incorporate the existing divergencies rather than dissolve them. The Latin American States, for example, could divide along sub-regional lines with one group composed of the States in the Montevideo bloc and a second sub-regional group composed of the Santo Domingo bloc. The second, and more constructive, direction lies in the development of a new formula, a juridical construct for the legitimation of extended jurisdictional claims for specific economic and social purposes which, while leaving intact the concept of a narrow territorial sea, would bridge the gap separating States with traditional claims from those with more extensive claims. The development and emergence of such a formula will be examined below.

ZONES OF SPECIAL JURISDICTION

Historically, States have from time to time established and enforced zones of special jurisdiction in areas that normally form part of the high seas. The creation of such zones in connection with fishing and the conservation of marine resources or with the enforcement of municipal legislation, such as the United States National Prohibition Act of 1920, has normally been effected by means of unilateral acts, though it was frequently subject to subsequent bilateral agreements.[32]

The 1958 Geneva Convention on the Territorial Sea and Contiguous Zone introduced, for the first time, the concept of special zones into positive international law. Article 24 of the Convention provides for a zone of the high seas contiguous to the territorial sea in which the State may exercise control over foreign vessels for the specific purposes of the prevention and punishment of infringement of customs, fiscal, immigration, and sanitary regulations. Since the outer limit of the contiguous zone established by the Convention is twelve miles and the territorial sea margin in any future international agreement will certainly be not less than twelve miles, the contiguous zone could well be a casualty of the new convention.

The lesson to be drawn from the creation of the contiguous zone is that zones of special jurisdiction are essential if a uniform territorial sea is to be established. The 1958 and 1960 Geneva Conferences rejected Latin American proposals for the establishment of exclusive fishery zones but paid a heavy price in the failure to reach agreement on the breadth of the territorial sea. Since then an increasing number of Latin American States have established exclusive or semi-exclusive zones for the purposes of fishing or conservation. More recently, the Montevideo, Lima, and Santo Domingo meetings have reaffirmed the right of coastal States to explore, conserve, and exploit the natural resources of the sea adjacent to their coasts as a basic principle of the new law of the sea.

A concerted effort, therefore, would once more appear to be under way among the Latin American States with respect to the development of a new formula for zones of special jurisdiction adjacent to the territorial sea.

In enunciating the basic principles of the law of the sea, the Montevideo and Lima Declarations attached no specific labels to the maritime zone over which coastal States should exercise their sovereignty and jurisdiction. By contrast, the Santo Domingo Declaration deals specifically with precise areas of the sea — the territorial sea, the continental shelf, the high seas — including an area described as the "patrimonial sea." The patrimonial sea is "a zone adjacent to the territorial sea" in which the coastal State would exercise "sovereign rights" over the living and mineral resources found therein, whether they be in the waters, sea-bed, or subsoil.[33] The breadth of this zone would be determined by agreement, preferably multilateral, among States, but in any event the combined breadth of the territorial and patrimonial seas would not exceed 200 miles. The zone would not interfere with freedom of navigation and overflight and the laying of pipe-lines and cables except insofar as these activities might conflict with the exercise of the coastal State's patrimonial rights (Article 5). The principal purpose of the zone is economic, although the coastal State would also have a duty to promote and the right to regulate scientific research and to adopt anti-pollution measures (Article 2).

The formulation of the patrimonial sea concept in the Santo Domingo Decla-ration bears a close resemblance to a proposal advanced by Edmundo Vargas in his Preliminary Report on the Territorial Sea and Patrimonial Sea presented to the Inter-American Juridical Committee.[34]

The patrimonial sea is conceived as a zone distinct from, but adjacent to, the territorial sea in which the coastal State would exercise sovereign rights but not sovereignty. The distinction is important. In other words, the coastal State would possess a usufruct over the "patrimonial" area which would permit it to exploit the economic potential of the zone directly or through the granting of concessions and licenses. To some extent, a system of this type is already in *de facto* operation in Brazil and Uruguay and has been for some time in the 1952 Santiago Maritime Zone.

Historically, the lineage of the patrimonial sea may be traced to two specifi-cally Latin American concepts — the epicontinental sea and the comple-mentary sea — neither of which achieved a generalized degree of acceptance.[35] In addition, special zones for a variety of purposes have from time to time been established in the Americas. For example, the 1939 Declaration of Panama established a wide "collective security" zone extending up to 300 miles on both the Atlantic and Pacific coasts. More recently, the Treaty of Tlatelolco[36] pro-vided for a nuclear-free zone and the Canadian Arctic Waters Pollution Preven-tion Act creates a 100-mile anti-pollution zone.

Thus, the patrimonial sea can hardly be described as a new concept but rather as a case of old wine in new bottles. The departure from the past, however, lies in the potential degree of support for the concept in Latin America and else-where. It is significant that the proposal emerges from the Santo Domingo group of Caribbean States and not, as might have been expected, from the Montevideo group of 200-mile States. Outside Latin America, the concept has already been substantially endorsed by a group of African States.[37]

The concept is undoubtedly attractive to many States from the economic point of view but this cannot obscure the fact that there are also many States which for geographic reasons cannot share in the benefits of such a formula.

There will also be opposition from the major maritime powers on both strategic and economic grounds. It is doubtful, therefore, whether the patrimonial sea is really a "transcendental" concept, in the words of Mr. Vargas, but it is nevertheless an important point of departure in the search for a compromise solution to the problem of the territorial sea.

Finally, two recent proposals should be mentioned. In February 1973, the Inter-American Juridical Committee adopted a series of principles and standards which "represent the common elements of the position of the American States." This latest Inter-American Juridical Committee draft is noteworthy for a number of substantive and political reasons.

From the substantive point of view, the draft does not refer expressly to either the territorial sea or the patrimonial sea. Instead, paragraph 1 establishes that the sovereignty or jurisdiction of the coastal State extends beyond its territory up to a maximum distance of 200 nautical miles as well as to the air space above and the bed and subsoil of that sea. Paragraph 2 distinguishes two zones within the 200-mile area: one that extends to twelve miles and a second from twelve miles up to a maximum of 200 miles. This distinction is made for a number of specific purposes: (1) within the twelve-mile zone, the right of innocent passage shall prevail; (2) within the outer zone, between twelve and 200 miles, ships and aircraft shall enjoy free navigation and overflight subject to coastal State regulations with regard to the preservation of the marine environment, activities of exploration, exploitation, and scientific research and safety of maritime navigation and transportation; (3) the powers of the coastal State within the outer zone shall extend to the exploration of the sea, its bed and its subsoil, and exploitation of the living and non-living resources that are found therein; it may reserve these activities for itself or its nationals, or allow them also to third parties in accordance with provisions of its domestic legislation or any international agreements it may conclude in this regard; the coastal State may also regulate and develop measures necessary for the purpose of preventing, reducing, or eliminating the damage and risks of pollution, promote scientific research, and establish specific regulations for the purposes of exploration and economic exploitation with respect to the various realms of the sea that it may believe advisable to establish in the area up to the limit of 200 miles; (4) within the outer zone, the coastal State shall authorize the laying of underwater cables subject to the domestic regulations of that State for the regulation of navigation, scientific research, and preservation of the marine environment.

The political nature of the transaction embodied in the Inter-American Juridical Committee's latest proposal appears in paragraph 5 which states that ships and aircraft that transit through or over international straits that are customarily used for international navigation and that join two free seas enjoy the freedom of navigation and overflight established for the outer zone. This provision is clearly an attempt to deal with the strategic concerns of the United States.

Further political transaction is contained in paragraph 9 which grants to non-coastal States preferential rights in relation to third States for the exploitation of living resources within the outer zone.

The second recent development is a draft circulated by Colombia, Mexico, and Venezuela, dated April 2, 1973, which was submitted to the United Nations Seabed Committee.[38] This draft contains provisions concerning the territorial sea up to twelve miles and a patrimonial sea up to a maximum of 200 miles. The tripartite draft substantially embodies the provisions contained in the Inter-American Juridical Committee principles of February 1973.

THE CONTINENTAL SHELF

The third area which completes the unity of zones within national jurisdiction is the continental shelf.

The Latin American preoccupation with the legal regime of the continental shelf may be traced to the bilateral agreement between Venezuela and the United Kingdom in 1942, which regulated the respective rights of the parties over the submarine areas of the Gulf of Paria.[39] But it was the Truman Declaration of 1945 which drew attention to the economic potential of the shelf and provided the impetus for a rapid succession of shelf claims by Latin American States.

The geographic and geological characteristics of the Latin American continent have played an important role in determining the continental shelf policies of Latin American States. The Pacific coast of Latin America drops abruptly into the ocean, depriving countries with long coastlines, such as Chile and Peru, of all but a very narrow shelf, while the Atlantic and Caribbean coast countries are endowed with a broad shelf. Because of the economic benefits to be derived from the resources of the shelf, the nature and scope of the sovereign rights of coastal States over the shelf area is of considerable practical importance to Latin America.

From the Latin American perspective, the principal shelf issues are the definition of the outer limit of the continental shelf, the delimitation of the shelf between adjacent or opposing States, the definition of natural resources of the shelf, and finally the legal regime for the superjacent waters. These are all issues over which Latin American States have long been at odds with the major maritime powers.

The definition of the outer limit of the shelf is a *sine qua non* of a regime for the area beyond national jurisdiction. It is today generally accepted that Article 1 of the 1958 Convention on the Continental Shelf is inadequate for the purpose of drawing a line between national and international jurisdiction since the criteria of depth and/or exploitability under contemporary technological conditions result in a constantly expanding outer limit.

The inclusion and addition of the exploitability criterion in 1958 was the result of efforts by the Latin American States whose deliberations and conclusions in the Inter-American Specialized Conference on Conservation of Natural Resources in 1956 proved persuasive with the members of the United Nations International Law Commission.

Only a small number of Latin American States have ratified the Convention on the Continental Shelf or acceded to it.[40] The majority of States remain unfettered by the Convention but in practice do not depart excessively from its provisions concerning the outer limit of the shelf. Indeed, given the virtually unlimited flexibility offered by the exploitability criterion, there is little reason to do so. Only three States have explicitly adopted a more restrictive or more expansive position than the Convention. Ecuador has restricted itself to the limit of the 200-meter isobath, whereas both Costa Rica and Guyana assert unlimited claims over the shelf. For the remainder, the controlling principle appears to be that stated in the Montevideo Declaration, namely "the right to explore, conserve, and exploit the natural resources of their respective continental shelf out to where the depth of the superjacent waters admit of exploitation ... " (Basic Principle 4).

The Santo Domingo Declaration, however, appears to presage an attempt to broaden both the scope and the outer limit of the shelf. The relevant provisions of the Declaration dealing with the shelf provide, firstly, that the shelf "includes the seabed and subsoil of the submarine areas adjacent to the coast" and, secondly, recognize the desirability of defining more precise limits "taking into account the outer limit of the continental rise."[41] The former provision appears to be an attempt to satisfy shelfless or disadvantaged coastal States such as Chile, whereas the latter would have the effect of extending the outer limit of the shelf beyond even the continental slope to the continental rise which is frequently at a depth of between 3500 and 5500 meters. The Santo Domingo Declaration further deals with the problem of the area of the shelf which underlies the patrimonial sea and envisages that this part of the shelf would be regulated by the patrimonial sea regime as distinct from a continental shelf regime to be established for the area beyond.

The recent Latin American declarations are consistent with the overall objectives of Latin American policies which may be summed up as exercising the maximum economic jurisdiction over marine resources. In attempting to push back the outer limit of the shelf as far as possible, the Latin American States are pursuing this objective.

The delimitation of the continental shelf between adjacent Latin American States has not yet been the object of any regional deliberations. The rule contained in Article 6 of the Convention on the Continental Shelf governs the relations of those Latin American States which have ratified the Convention, and there is evidence to suggest that even States which are not parties to this Convention find this provision to be an acceptable basis for bilateral agreements with adjacent States. Geographic or other considerations may of course create special circumstances justifying a departure from the Article 6 rule, as the International Court of Justice recognized in the *North Sea Continental Shelf Cases,*[42] reasoning within the conventional framework of Article 6. Considerations of this nature motivated the Venezuelan reservation to Article 6 of the Convention on the Continental Shelf.[43] Venezuela and Colombia are presently engaged in bilateral negotiations with respect to the delimitation of their adjacent shelves in the Caribbean.

The scope of the rules of international law concerning the continental shelf depends on the definition of the term "natural resources." This was a controversial issue at the Geneva Conference. Article 2, paragraph 4 of the Convention on the Continental Shelf provides that the natural resources referred to shall consist of the mineral and other non-living resources of the seabed and subsoil together with living organisms belonging to the sedentary species only. The Geneva Conference rejected the view of some Latin American States that the natural resources of the continental shelf should include fish and other living resources even of a non-sedentary character and expressly maintained freedom of fishing in the waters above the continental shelf.

The 1958 Convention also maintains the high seas status of the waters superjacent to the shelf. A number of Latin American States, however, have expressly or implicitly claimed sovereignty over the waters of what is sometimes referred to as the epicontinental sea. The Santo Domingo Declaration distinguishes between the shelf of the patrimonial sea and the shelf beyond the patrimonial sea and proposes that the former be governed by the legal regime of the patrimonial sea. This would have the effect of conferring on the coastal State sovereign rights over the waters superjacent to the shelf.

CONCLUSION

One of the most enduring characteristics of the law of the sea throughout the centuries has been its capacity to arouse the passions of writers and governments. The current debate in the United Nations and elsewhere is no exception, and like all emotive issues it tends to create its own rhetoric. Thus, the extensive claims of certain States are depicted as a threat to the fundamental principle of the freedom of the seas — the Grotian legacy regarded as sacred by some but as a symbol of sclerosis by others — and whereas for many coastal States exclusive jurisdiction over a wide marginal sea is an imperative of economic development, for other States economic nationalism in the oceans is undermining the "common heritage of mankind."

This rhetorical dialectic, however, cannot obscure the very real political, economic, or strategic interests and values which are at stake. It is important that these be openly identified and recognized as a first step towards the accommodation of the conflicting interests of the members of the international community which is, after all, the precise objective of contemporary international law.

As far as Latin America is concerned, there can be no doubt that economic interests and values predominate. The economic factor is the Latin American common denominator, the central unifying theme in the Montevideo-Lima-Santo Domingo axis. As is abundantly clear from the United Nations preparatory debates, the States represented at the 1973 conference will divide along economic rather than ideological lines as was the case in Geneva in 1958 and 1960.

The Latin American States will presumably act as a regional group of twenty-one (twenty-two if Cuba is included) and, in addition, will form part of the larger group of less-developed States, sometimes referred to as the Group of 77, which with recent accretions now numbers in excess of eighty members. Assuming that between 120 and 130 States participate in the conference, the less-developed group may muster the two-thirds majority which will be required for the adoption of substantive decisions and important procedural decisions. In order to maintain the homogeneity of this group, however, the coastal States, especially Latin American and African, must accommodate the interests of some twenty land-locked or shelf-locked States.

The Latin American States by their strenuous efforts to reach a regional consensus are also to some extent laying the groundwork for the formulation of a consensus by the larger group. The first public evidence of this demonstration effect came in June 1972 at the Yaoundé seminar of African States.

There are, in summation, a number of factors which suggest that Latin America will play an important, possibly decisive, role in 1973. These include the greater coherence of the Latin American position on all aspects of the law of the sea; the possibility of forming a two-thirds conference majority with Afro-Asian support; the overt support for the 200-mile Latin American claims by the People's Republic of China; and the more independent posture of many Latin American countries in the international system.

Latin America shares with the rest of the world an interest in the successful outcome of the 1973 conference, for no State or group of States can derive satisfaction from an inchoate system of international conventions and unilateral acts which, in the final analysis, contribute to rather than resolve international tensions.

References

1. A selection of the literature devoted to these themes would include W. Friedmann, *The Changing Structure of International Law* (London: Stevens, 1964); P. C. Jessup, *Transnational Law* (New Haven, Conn: Yale University Press, 1956); C. W. Jenks, *A New World of Law? A Study of the Creative Imagination in International Law* (Harlow, England: Longmans, 1969); J. L. Kunz, *The Changing Law of Nations* (Columbus: Ohio State University Press, 1968); O. J. Lissitzyn, *International Law Today and Tomorrow* (Dobbs Ferry, N.Y.: Oceana, 1965); G. Schwarzenberger, *The Frontiers of International Law* (London: Stevens, 1962); R. A. Falk and C. Black (eds.), *The Future of the International Legal Order* (Princeton, N.J.: Princeton University Press, 1969); B. V. A. Röling, *International Law in an Expanded World* (Amsterdam: Djambatan, 1960).
2. M. Bourquin, "Pouvoir scientifique et droit international," *Receuil des Cours,* Vol. 70 (1947), p. 337.
3. Thus, for example, the Peruvian 200-mile claim has been successfully enforced against United States fishing vessels and, more recently, despite an injunctive order of the International Court of Justice and protests by the United Kingdom, Iceland has enforced the extension of its fishing limits. See *The Times,* London, September 13, 1972.
4. C. Chaumont, "Cours général de droit international public," *Recueil des Cours,* Vol. 129 (1970), p. 422.
5. For a recent critical examination of the place of Latin America in the international system from the Argentinian-Brazilian perspective, see C. Lafer and F. Peña, *Argentina y Brasil en el sistema internacional* (Buenos Aires: Editorial Nueva, Visión, 1973).
6. According to one radical critic, the inter-American system is an occult science. See O. M. Carpeaux, "The National Pivot" in *Latin American Radicalism,* I. L. Horowitz, J. de Castro, and J. Gerassi, eds. (New York: Random House, 1969).
7. Brazil's coast, for example, is 4,603 miles in length *(Encyclopaedia Britannica,* Vol. 4 [1967], p. 117). Chile's is about 2,650 miles *(Encyclopaedia Britannica,* Vol. 5 [1967], p. 531). Chile's length is equivalent to the distance from southern Mexico to southern Alaska. Peru's seacoast is 1,400 miles *(Encyclopaedia Britannica,* Vol. 17, [1967], p. 709).
8. As will be seen from the table below, the total value of worldwide production of marine mineral resources was over $7 billion in 1969.

Minerals from the sea in 1969 on a worldwide basis estimated at over $7 billion
(Value in millions of U.S. dollars)

From sea water

Salt	173
Magnesium metal	75
Fresh water	51
Bromine	45
Magnesium compounds	41
Heavy water (D_2O)	27
Others (potassium, calcium salts, sodium sulphate)	1
Total value from sea water	413

From sea floor (surface deposits)

Sand and gravel	100
Shell	30
Tin	24
Heavy mineral sands (ilmenite, rutile, zircon, garnets, etc.)	13
Diamonds	9
Iron sands	4
Total value of surficial deposits	**180**

From sea floor (sub-surface deposits)

Oil and gas	6,100
Sulphur	26
Coal	335
Iron ore	17
Total value of sub-surface deposits	**6,478**
Total	**7,071**

Source: *Marine Science Affairs-Selecting Priority Programmes,* Annual Report of the President to the Congress on Marine Resources and Engineering Development (Washington, D.C.: Government Printing Office, 1970), reprinted in United Nations Doc. E/4973, p. 7.

9. This "insular" psychology is not as far-fetched as it may seem at first sight. Chile, which is 2,650 miles long and averages 110 miles in width, is bordered on one side by the Pacific Ocean and on the other side by the Cordillera of the Andes; Argentina faces the Atlantic Ocean but has its back to the Cordillera; and Peru fronts onto the Pacific Ocean, but its land frontiers meet the Cordillera and the Amazonian jungle.
10. C. J. Colombos, *The International Law of the Sea* (New York: McKay, 1967), pp. 92-93.
11. This is because Article 24 of the Convention establishes a maximum limit of twelve miles for the contiguous zone as measured from the baseline of the territorial sea. See C. J. Colombos, op. cit., note 10 above, pp. 111-113, and M. Sorensen, "Law of the Sea" in *International Conciliation,* No. 520, pp. 240-242.
12. Conferencia sobre Explotación y Conservación de las riquezas marítimas del Pacífico Sur: *Convenios y otros Documentos 1952-1969,* 3rd ed. (Lima, 1970), p. 31.
13. Ibid., p. 44.
14. Declaration of Santiago, preambular paragraphs 1 and 2.
15. Operative paragraph III explicitly states that the maritime zone includes not only the waters but also the seabed and subsoil underlying them.
16. Resolution XIX adopted by the Inter-American Council of Jurists at its Buenos Aires session in 1953 recognized the right of coastal States to protect, conserve, and exploit their maritime resources; the Second Hispano-Luso-American Congress of International Law, which met in Sao Paulo in October 1953, recommended the extension of the territorial sea to twelve miles and the recognition of special fishing rights up to 200 miles in what was termed the "complementary sea"; the Tenth Inter-American Con-

ference held in Caracas in 1954 adopted a Resolution affirming the special rights of coastal States; and the 1956 session of the Inter-American Council of Jurists in Mexico adopted a Resolution which recognized the inadequacy of the classical three-mile rule and postulated the right of every coastal State to determine the breadth of the territorial sea in accordance with its own conditions.

17. With the exception of the South Pacific States and Costa Rica, Nicaragua, and Panama, the majority of Latin American States in 1958 supported a twelve-mile territorial sea or the six-mile territorial sea plus six-mile contiguous zone formula.

18. For example, the seizure in 1954 by the Peruvian authorities of the factory ship *Olympic Challenger* and its fleet of whalers owned by Aristotle Onassis operating about 100 miles off the coast. Ironically, the Onassis ships were flying the Panamanian flag. Despite protests, Onassis reportedly paid $3 million in fines against reimbursement by Lloyds of London. Reported in the *New York Times,* December 13 and 14, 1954.

19. Dominican Republic, Haiti, Mexico, Trinidad and Tobago, and Venezuela.

20. In fact, the Brazilian Decree-Law No. 1.098 provides for derogation from the territorial sea *stricto sensu.* The current Brazilian interpretation of the territorial sea encompasses the following regimes: (1) an inner 100-mile exclusive fishing zone; (2) an outer 100-mile fishing zone for Brazilian and foreign vessels; (3) Brazilian sovereignty over the seabed and subsoil to a distance of 200 miles; and (4) bilateral agreements for special types of fishing which have been concluded, so far, with the United States, Trinidad and Tobago, and the Netherlands. See *International Legal Materials,* Vol. X (1971), p. 1224.

21. See Paragraph 4 of Supreme Decree No. 781, in Conferencia sobre Explotación, op. cit., note 12 above, p. 27; and F. V. García Amador, "Latin America and the Law of the Sea," Law of the Sea Institute, University of Rhode Island, July 1972, Occasional Paper 14, p. 35.

22. This is the position taken by a number of Latin American authors, including R. Ferrero, *Derecho Internacional,* Vol. I (Lima, 1966), pp. 95 and 129-132, and F. V. García Amador, op. cit., note 21 above, p. 2.

23. See F. Pfirter de Armas, Chapter XI.

24. For example, Argentinian law No. 17,094 of December 29, 1966, extends the "sovereignty of the nation" to a distance of 200 miles over the adjacent sea (Article 1) but expressly declares this to be without prejudice to freedom of navigation and overflight (Article 3). See F. V. García Amador, op. cit., note 21 above, p. 8. After several years of considerable uncertainty as to the precise nature and extent of the Argentinian territorial sea, the position was clarified by the Argentina-Chile Joint Declaration of July 22, 1971, in which the two States undertake to maintain the principle of freedom of navigation and overflight in their respective zones of maritime sovereignty and jurisdiction between the twelve-mile and 200-mile limits. Uruguayan Law No. 13,833 of December 29, 1969, establishes a "zone of territorial sea 200 nautical miles wide measured from the baseline" (Article 2). Article 3, however, specifies that the right of innocent passage prevails "through the territorial sea of Uruguay in a zone twelve miles wide" and that beyond the twelve-mile zone the provisions of the law do not affect free navigation and overflight. See F. V. García Amador, op. cit., note 21 above, p. 39.

El Salvador is a classic example of a borderline case of qualification. The formal legislation indicates a 200-mile territorial sea, but the practical implementation of the law leaves considerable doubt whether a territorial sea claim *stricto sensu* can be entertained. This type of situation gives rise to discrepancies in interpretation and induces writers to reach discordant conclusions.

25. Nine States sent delegations to the meeting: Argentina, Brazil, Chile, Ecuador, El Salvador, Nicaragua, Panama, Peru, and Uruguay. Costa Rica, because of a change in administration, notified the Uruguayan Foreign Ministry that it would be unable to participate.

26. In addition to the Montevideo group there were: Barbados, Bolivia, Colombia, Dominican Republic, Guatemala, Honduras, Jamaica, Mexico, Paraguay, and Venezuela.

27. For the text of the Declaration of Montevideo, see *International Legal Materials,* Vol. IX (1970), p. 1031; for the text of the Declaration and Resolutions of the Lima meeting, see *International Legal Materials,* Vol. X (1971), pp. 207-214; the text of the Santo Domingo Declaration appears in United Nations Doc. A/AC.138/80.

28. See, for example, Basic Principle No. 1 of the Montevideo Declaration: "The right of

littoral States to exercise control over the natural resources of the sea adjacent to their coasts and of the seabed and subsoil thereof in order to achieve the maximum development of their economy and to raise the living standards of their peoples." Substantially identical provisions are to be found in Common Principle No. 1 of the Lima Declaration and in the Santo Domingo Declaration, Principle 2, patrimonial sea paragraph (1).

29. Basic Principle No. 2 of the Montevideo Declaration, Common Principle No. 2 of the Lima Declaration, and Principle 2, paragraph (3) of the Santo Domingo Declaration.

30. Basic Principle No. 6 of the Montevideo Declaration, Common Principle No. 3 of the Lima Declaration, and Principle 2, paragraph (2) of the Santo Domingo Declaration.

31. The Preamble of the Montevideo Declaration states that the exhaustion of biological species by irrational or abusive extractive practices ". . . is the foundation of the right claimed by coastal States to prescribe the necessary measures to protect said resources within jurisdictional zones that are broader than the traditional ones. . . ."

32. The United States concluded a number of so-called Liquor Treaties including one with Chile, of May 27, 1930 (League of Nations Treaty Series, Vol. 133, p. 142), based on the Ango-American Liquor Treaty of January 23, 1942 (ibid., Vol. 27, p. 182). A more recent example of a zone of special jurisdiction is contained in the Canadian Arctic Waters Pollution Prevention Act which establishes a 100-mile pollution prevention zone. See *International Legal Materials*, Vol. IX (1970), p. 543.

33. United Nations Doc. A/AC.138/80.

34. Reprinted in Francisco Orrego Vicuña, *Chile y el Derecho del Mar* (Santiago: Editorial Andrés Bello, 1972), pp. 137-150.

35. The expression "epicontinental sea" was first employed by Argentina as early as 1946. Decree No. 14,708 declared the sovereignty of the nation over the Argentinian epicontinental sea and continental shelf. The epicontinental sea is that part of the sea superjacent to the shelf. Article 2 further defined the legal character of the epicontinental sea by expressly stating that freedom of navigation was not affected by the decree.

   The Argentinian decree was based on an erroneous interpretation of the 1945 Truman Declaration which, while extending jurisdiction and control over the resources of the continental shelf, did not modify the legal character of the superjacent waters. Although the epicontinental sea conception was endorsed some years later by a meeting of Central American Foreign Ministers, it has never met with wide adoption.

   The concept of the complementary sea emerged from the Second Hispano-Luso-American Congress of International Law, held in São Paulo in October 1953, the final Act of which contained a provision conferring upon those States which had no continental shelf the right to regulate fishing in zones of the high seas adjacent to the territorial sea to a distance of 200 miles. This zone is referred to as the complementary sea.

36. Treaty for the Prohibition of Nuclear Weapons in Latin America, of February 14, 1967, United Nations Treaty Series, Vol. 634, p. 326.

37. The Yaoundé Declaration calls for the establishment of an economic zone beyond the territorial sea in which the coastal State would exercise exclusive jurisdiction for the purpose of control, regulation, and national exploitation of the resources of the sea without prejudice to the freedom of navigation, overflight, and laying of cables and pipelines. See United Nations Doc. A/AC.138/79.

38. United Nations Doc. A/AC.138/SC.II/L.21.

39. League of Nations Treaty Series, Vol. 205, p. 122. F. Pfirter de Armas, in her chapter on Argentina, points out that one of the first writers to introduce the concept was the Argentinian José León Suárez in a work entitled "El Mar territorial y las industrial marítimas" in *Diplomacia Universitaria Americana* (Buenos Aires, Escoffier, Caraciolo y Compania, 1918). See F. Pfirter de Armas, Chapter IX.

40. Colombia, Dominican Republic, Guatemala, Haiti, Mexico, Trinidad and Tobago, Venezuela.

41. United Nations Doc. A/AC.138/80.

42. Federal Republic of Germany v. Denmark and Federal Republic of Germany v. the

Netherlands, judgment of February 20, 1969, International Court of Justice Reports, 1969, p. 3.

43. For the text of this reservation, see United Nations Treaty Series, Vol. 499, p. 353.

Chapter IV
Mexico and the Law of the Sea

Chapter IV

MEXICO AND THE LAW OF THE SEA

Bernardo Sepúlveda*

INTRODUCTION

Since the 1960 amendment of the constitutional provisions concerning Mexico's maritime territory,[1] there has been no comprehensive organic law on the subject. On the contrary, new provisions have been included in different laws dealing with maritime navigation and commerce, exclusive fishery zones, breadth of the territorial sea and methods for its delimitation, incorporation of a part of the Gulf of California into the regime of internal waters, and fishing rights. Furthermore, the municipal legal order has been enlarged by the accession of Mexico to the four Geneva Conventions on the Law of the Sea. All this legislative activity, however, has failed to provide an organic framework for the legal system of Mexico with regard to the regulation of maritime areas. The trend of Mexican maritime regulations has been one of diversity, as opposed to the adoption of a general law embodying systematic and coherent principles.

Furthermore, Mexico is presently confronted with the basic policy problem of establishing a 200-mile zone of economic interest, contiguous to its coasts, for the exploitation of the natural resources of that area. A decision in this regard must be accompanied by corresponding international negotiations in order to achieve the acceptance of this claim with the least possible friction.

These considerations justify the special interest that Mexico must have in the development of a long-term maritime policy, particularly at this time when the attention of States and of a large number of international organizations is concentrated on the problems of the sea.

LEGAL NATURE OF THE TERRITORIAL SEA

Sovereign Rights

The Mexican Senate approved the Convention on the Territorial Sea and the Contiguous Zone on December 17, 1965 (*Official Gazette,* January 5, 1966), seven years after the Geneva Conference and one year after the Convention came

---

*Parts of this article have also been used in Bernardo Sepúlveda, "Derecho del Mar: Apuntes sobre el Sistema Legal Mexicano," in *La Politica Exterior de Mexico: Realidad y Perspectivas* (Mexico: Centro de Estudios Internacionales, El Colegio de México, 1972), pp. 132-171.

into force. The instrument of accession was deposited with the Secretary General of the United Nations on August 2, 1966.[2]

Article 7 of the Convention defines the legal nature of the territorial sea as follows:

> "The sovereignty of a State extends beyond its land territory and its internal waters, to a belt of sea adjacent to its coast, described as the territorial sea."

Limitations on Sovereignty

The Convention on the Territorial Sea imposes certain limitations upon States, for sovereignty "is exercised subject to the provisions of these articles and to other rules of international law." This means that the parties to the Convention have admitted the possibility of exceptions to their absolute powers over the territorial sea; thus, as a result of treaties or of custom, sovereignty is subject to restrictions. The Convention itself establishes some restrictions, the most important being the right of innocent passage through the territorial sea which ships of all States enjoy.

In accordance with international law, it is possible in particular circumstances for a State to grant rights of utilization over its territorial sea to other States. These rights might be even broader than those established by the Geneva Convention.

A recent example of this is the concession made by Mexico which enables other States to undertake the exploitation of certain areas of the Mexican territorial sea. In accordance with the Law on National Exclusive Fisheries Zone,[3] Mexico established special jurisdiction on fisheries in an area of twelve miles, measured from the baseline. However, the law empowers the Federal Executive to set the conditions and terms whereby nationals of countries which have traditionally exploited living resources of the sea might be authorized to continue such activities, within an area of three miles beyond the territorial sea, which at that time was nine miles. These activities might be undertaken for a period no longer than five years, as from January 1, 1968.

This provision enabled Mexico to enter into agreements on fisheries with the United States (October 27, 1967)[4] and with Japan (March 7, 1968). Fishermen of these two countries were authorized to continue their activities in the exclusive fisheries zone for a period of five years, provided that the number, class, and size of vessels, as well as the catch, would not exceed that employed by that country prior to the agreement.

In December 1969, Article 18 of the *Ley General de Bienes Nacionales* (General Act on National Property)[5] was amended, enlarging the breadth of the Mexican territorial sea from nine to twelve miles. However, Article 3 of the decree containing the amendments expressly provided that such amendments do not affect those agreements already concluded or which might be concluded in

82

the future in accordance with the Law on National Exclusive Fisheries Zone.

For a period of three years (December 1969 to December 1972), Mexico accepted a restriction on the exercise of its sovereign rights over the territorial sea, as provided by the agreements with the United States and Japan permitting the fishing activities of nationals of these countries in a maritime area which is part of the national territory. As will be evidenced below, this concession was a first step in the justification of the enlargement of the Mexican territorial sea to twelve miles.

Sovereignty and Property

In contrast with the concept of State sovereignty over the territorial sea defined by the Geneva Convention, the Constitution and legislation of Mexico maintain the concept of property rights of the nation over its maritime areas. The fifth paragraph of Article 27 of the Constitution[6] declares that "the waters of the territorial seas, within the limits and terms fixed by international law; inland marine waters... " are national property.[7]

Other legislation also refers to the property of the nation, such as, for example, the *Ley General de Bienes Nacionales*[8] which declares that the territorial sea, the seabed, and inland marine waters are the property of the nation and subject to public domain (Article 2, Sections II and IV). The Law of Maritime Navigation and Commerce[9] provides that the territorial sea and internal waters are a part of the maritime domain (Article 9, Section I) and national property, inalienable and imprescriptible (Article 10). A recent Federal Law of Waters[10] also declares that the waters of the territorial sea, within the limits and terms fixed by international law, and inland marine waters are the property of the nation.

In accordance with Article 42 of the Constitution, the national territory includes the waters of the territorial sea, within the limits and terms fixed by international law, and inland marine waters, over which the State exercises sovereign rights. Article 48 further provides that the territorial sea is under the jurisdiction of the Federal Government. The Law on State Secretaries and Departments[11] declares that the Secretary of the Navy is entrusted with "the exercise of national sovereignty over territorial waters, as well as vigilance over the coasts of the territory, navigable waterways, and national islands."

The examination of these provisions reveals a lack of uniformity in Mexican law with regard to the legal nature of the territorial sea — for some of them regard the area as property and others consider it subject to sovereign rights. There is also a certain divergence between Mexican legislation and the rules of international law.

The concept of *jus dominium* is certainly not the most adequate legal approach, for it does not entirely correspond to the nature of the competences which the State exercises over its territorial sea. The idea of property, transplanted from the field of private law to that of public law, is not sufficient to justify the title and authority which the State claims over its maritime areas. On the contrary, the concept of sovereignty, power to command or *jus imperium,* better defines the essential nature of the interests which the State intends to protect, including:

- power to control access to the territorial sea, including the possibility of suspending or denying the right of innocent passage for reasons of security, in order to protect a vital interest, or where the passage will not be innocent;

- power to enforce criminal and civil legislation, determining the degree of jurisdiction which the Mexican State will exercise over persons, ships, or airplanes within the area of the territorial sea;[12]

- power to regulate the uses of the territorial sea, including provisions about routes, navigation procedures, protection of fisheries, communications, sanitary requirements, prevention of maritime pollution, operations of warships, etc.;

- exclusive control over the fishing and mineral resources of the territorial sea, its seabed and subsoil.[13]

With a view to establishing uniform criteria, it is highly desirable, therefore, that Mexican legislation be harmonized with the principles of international law, expressly providing that national sovereignty extends to the territorial sea, the air space above it, its seabed and subsoil, subject to limitations imposed by international law.

BREADTH OF THE TERRITORIAL SEA

The Norm of Customary International Law

Article 27 of the Constitution provides that the waters of the territorial sea, within the limits and terms fixed by international law, are national property. Notwithstanding the international effort to establish a formula which would meet with the general acceptance of States, it has not been possible, however, to codify in a treaty a uniform breadth for the territorial sea. Despite the absence of a universal multilateral agreement on the subject, it is possible to state that there is a norm of customary international law which empowers the State to fix the breadth of its territorial sea at twelve miles.

The origins of this customary rule can be traced to the 1930 Hague Conference for the Codification of International Law. At this meeting it became clear that the "three-mile rule" no longer could be considered a norm of international law, for a certain number of States opposed such a limited breadth. At the same time, the lack of a uniform State practice on the breadth of the territorial waters also became clear.[14]

Neither of the two Geneva Conferences on the Law of the Sea succeeded in the codification of a rule on the breadth of the territorial sea. At both Conferences, however, there was a well-defined tendency to abandon the three-mile rule and to establish a twelve-mile territorial sea. This tendency has been confirmed in the thirteen years which have elapsed since 1960.

The Mexican Territorial Sea

By decree of December 12, 1969, Section II of Article 18 of the *Ley General de Bienes Nacionales* was amended. In accordance with this amendment the territorial sea up to a breadth of twelve miles is national property, in conformity with the provisions of the Constitution, the laws deriving from it, and international law.[15] One of the arguments invoked by the Federal Executive in the Exposition of Motives with which the amendment was proposed is that the tendency in favor of the recognition of a twelve-mile breadth is clear and irreversible. Furthermore, it is a generally accepted norm of customary international law that States may fix a limit of this kind.[16]

The reasons for this amendment may have derived from the international consequences stemming from the Law on National Exclusive Fisheries Zone. By virtue of the agreements concluded with Japan and the United States, both countries recognized the existence of a Mexican jurisdiction over fisheries in a maritime zone of three miles adjacent to the territorial sea, which meant that Mexico had exclusive fishing rights over an area of twelve miles. Notwithstanding the fact that the exclusiveness of this jurisdiction on fisheries did not take effect for five years, during which time special privileges were granted to Japanese and American fishermen, it is nonetheless true that the conclusion of these agreements constituted a precedent in favor of a clear *de facto* recognition (although not *de jure,* for there are reservations about the problem of Mexican sovereignty over a territorial sea of nine miles, which has traditionally been opposed by Japan and the United States) and eased the acquiescence by these two governments of the enlargement of the Mexican territorial sea to twelve miles.

The Mexican claims to a territorial sea beyond the three-mile limit have their origin in a decree of August 29, 1935.[17] It was provided therein that in accordance with the precedents created by treaties concluded by Mexico, the breadth of nine miles had been accepted as determining "the limits of Mexico in the maritime zone." Since the Law of Real Property of the Nation,[18] which established a territorial sea of only three miles, was at variance with the Mexican conventional precedents[19] and did not correspond to the provision of Article 27 of the Constitution, for international law authorizes a larger breadth, the need to amend this law became apparent. Therefore, the law was amended to provide that the territorial waters extend to a distance of nine nautical miles.[20]

The Government of the United States reacted predictably to the enactment of this provision. Seven months after the amendment came into force, the American Ambassador presented a note to the Mexican Ministry of Foreign Affairs, stating that the United States reserved its rights with regard to the effect that the application of a nine-mile territorial sea could have on American commerce.[21]

In his reply to this note,[22] the Mexican Minister of Foreign Affairs indicated that he considered the reservation of rights by the United States Government unjustified. The reasons invoked by the Government of Mexico relied on the provision of the Guadalupe Hidalgo Treaty of 1848,[23] which indicated that the boundary between both countries in the Gulf of Mexico started at three leagues (nine miles, sixteen kilometers) offshore from the mouth of the Rio Bravo. This was, therefore, the limit of the territorial sea for both countries.

The Government of the United States disagreed with this interpretation,[24] pointing out that Article V of the Treaty referred only to the boundary line between both countries and not to the Mexican claim of a nine-mile territorial sea. For the United States to agree that in certain areas the Mexican territorial sea extends three leagues offshore did not mean that Mexico has a right to a similar claim along the whole length of its coasts.

Mexico insisted on the precedent established by the Guadalupe Hidalgo Treaty, which provided for an equitable solution permitting the most rational utilization of the natural resources available to both countries.[25] The United States reiterated its reservations and the nonacceptance of the Mexican interpretation with regard to the application of the nine-mile criteria.[26]

Article 17 of the *Ley General de Bienes Nacionales*[27] provides that the territorial sea, including the adjacent waters up to a distance of nine miles, appertains to the public domain. This provision, which reiterates the breadth of the territorial sea established in the law of 1935, apparently raised no protest on the part of affected countries at the time of its enactment. However, its application resulted in several controversies, particularly with the United States, originating in the capture of American fishing vessels in waters claimed by Mexico as territorial and considered by the United States as belonging to the high seas.[28]

Legal Status of the Epicontinental Waters

Following the Truman Proclamation of 1945, which declared that the natural resources of the subsoil and ocean floor of the continental shelf appertained to the United States, several countries asserted unilateral claims over their continental shelf and, in some cases, over the waters and air space above it. Mexico followed this tendency, which led the Federal Executive to propose to the Mexican Congress an amendment to Articles 27, 42, and 48 of the Constitution; this proposal included the concept that "the waters of the seas above the continental shelf and the continental terrace are the property of the nation." The constitutional amendment was approved by Congress and by the required number of states of the Republic, but never came into force. This situation was clarified by means of the amendment of the same Constitutional provisions in 1960, which do not claim sovereignty over the whole extension of waters and air space above the continental shelf. In the Exposition of Motives of the motion the reasons for this change of attitude are explained:

> "The pretension to exercise sovereignty over all waters above the continental shelf is, in our time, contrary to international law. Such a claim was clearly and definitively repudiated by the United Nations Conference on the Law of the Sea, in which eighty-six States participated — that is, practically all the international community. As an indication of the will of the Community of Nations in this matter, it is sufficient to recall that Article 3 of the Convention, which establishes the regime of the high seas — that is, of a free sea — of the superjacent waters and air space, was approved by the Geneva Conference with no votes against and with only three abstentions. This fact acquires a greater significance when one considers that undoubtedly the Convention on the Continental Shelf is the expression of the law in force on the matter. The situation is so clear and well-defined that the Convention itself prohibits reservations with regard to said Article 3."[29]

Thus, the notion of bringing under national domain a part of the epicontinental sea, which in certain areas extends up to 300 miles from the Mexican coasts, was disregarded. Since international law does not recognize a valid title for the exercise of sovereign rights over the epicontinental waters, any unilateral declaration to that effect would have no legal force.

DELIMITATION OF THE TERRITORIAL SEA

Normal Baselines

In accordance with international law, the normal baseline from which the breadth of the territorial sea is measured seaward is the low-water line along the coast, as marked on large-scale charts officially recognized by the coastal State, with some exceptions which will be mentioned below.[30]

Coincident with international law, Mexican legislation on the matter has provided uniformly that the breadth of the territorial sea is measured from the low-water line along the coasts and of the islands which are part of the national territory.[31]

Straight Baselines

In the new *Ley General de Bienes Nacionales* of 1969, it is provided that in certain circumstances straight baselines may be adopted as the method of measuring the territorial sea. This is a direct influence of the principle contained in Article 4 of the Convention on the Territorial Sea. The method consists of "selecting appropriate points on the low-water mark and drawing straight lines between them."[32] It may be applied not only in the case of well-defined bays but also in smaller indentures of the coast. The basic difference between the normal baselines and straight baselines is that the former are drawn along the coast, following its sinuosities, while the latter are drawn through the sea joining coastal points.

When Mexico became a party to the Convention on the Territorial Sea, its provisions including the baseline rule were incorporated into municipal law by means of the amendment of Article 17 of the *Ley General de Bienes Nacionales*, introduced by Congressional Decree of December 29, 1967. The *Ley General de Bienes Nacionales* of 1969 also included this rule.[33]

Application of the Straight Baseline Method
in the Interior of the Gulf of California

Thus far, Mexico has applied the straight baseline method for the delimitation of its territorial sea on only one occasion. This was the case of the delimitation of the Mexican territorial sea in the interior of the Gulf of California.[34] The pertinent decree originated in the recommendations of an Intersecretarial Commission, which supported the drawing of baselines from which the breadth of territorial waters would be measured within the Sea of Cortes. As a result, the waters on the landward side of the baselines would be subject to the regime of internal waters.

In this case the straight baseline method was applied because there was a fringe of islands along both coasts in the interior of the Gulf of California, located in its immediate vicinity and which did not depart to any appreciable extent from the general direction of the coasts. The islands were joined with the most seaward points of the coast by means of two systems of straight baselines drawn along each one of the interior coasts of the Gulf, following approximately a southeast direction. The drawing, which runs along the Peninsula of Baja California, begins at a point known as Punta Arenas in the territory of Baja California and ends, after linking several islands and points of the coast, in the southwest extremity of the Island of San Esteban. The second drawing begins in the northwest extremity of the Island of San Esteban and runs down, touching several points of the coast of Sonora, along the western coast of the Gulf of California up to a point known as Punta San Miguel in the State of Sinaloa. The Island of San Esteban, located in the middle of the breadth of the Gulf, was chosen as the starting point of both systems of straight baselines, mainly because of its geographical position. Thus, the waters to the north of the Island of San Esteban were enclosed as internal waters, as well as those on the landward side of the straight baselines drawings.

An unfavorable geographical condition did not make possible the application of Article 7 of the Convention on the Territorial Sea. Section 4 of this Article provides that "if the distance between the low-water marks of the natural entrance points of a bay does not exceed twenty-four miles, a closing line may be drawn between these two low-water marks, and the waters enclosed thereby shall be considered as internal waters." The Government of Mexico sent a special expedition, provided with the most modern equipment for the measurement of distances, to the Gulf of California. The expedition concluded that Article 7 was not applicable, for at no point, not even in the area of the fringe of islands located in the middle of the Gulf, did the distance exceed twenty-four miles.

In spite of certain opinions that the drawing of baselines in the Gulf of California is not in accordance with the provisions of the Geneva Convention, and that therefore the waters to the north of parallel 29 cannot be considered internal waters of Mexico, it is evident that there is a legitimate basis for extending Mexican sovereignty to this area of the sea.

The delimitation of the Gulf of California corresponds to the criteria advanced by the International Court of Justice in the *Anglo-Norwegian Fisheries Case,* which were considered by the International Law Commission as the expression of the law in force and incorporated into Article 4 of the Convention on the Territorial Sea.

The coastal State is the only one which can determine, within the limits of reasonableness, the local conditions which will justify the adoption of the straight baselines method for the delimitation of its territorial sea. To that end it must take into account the ensemble of elements required by public international law for the application of the method.

In the case of Mexico, it is considered that the delimitation of the territorial sea in the interior of the Gulf of California has been done in strict compliance with the conditions fixed by international law. The waters located to the north of the area of San Esteban Island, that is, to the north of parallel 29, have been enclosed by straight baselines, thus acquiring the character of internal waters. This is justified because the Island of San Esteban, located in the middle of the breadth of the Gulf, is sufficiently close to the Island of San Lorenzo, to the west, and to the Island of Tiburon, to the east, as to be used as the starting point of the straight baselines. The fringe of islands along the area of parallel 29 determine that the maximum length of the baselines is quite moderate and considerably shorter than those drawn in other coasts, such as those of Norway, Iceland, and Canada.

The baselines do not depart to any appreciable extent from the coast. The fringe of islands along the coast, and located in its immediate vicinity, makes possible the joining of the pertinent points without departing from the coast. It is true that in the middle of the breadth of the Gulf of California, the baselines do not follow the general direction of the coast, which could be invoked as an argument against the validity of such delimitation. Nevertheless, such argument has no justification. The existence of islands close to each other, and near the coast, naturally compels the drawing of straight baselines through those points of the coast and of the islands where geography will make it necessary and logical. Furthermore, due to the geographical peculiarities of the Gulf, the requirements that the sea areas lying on the landward side of the baselines be so closely linked with land domain as to be subject to the regime of internal waters is also met.

It is also evident that the economic interests peculiar to the region justify that this sea area be considered Mexican territory.

The decree of August 30, 1968, determined that the sea areas to the north of the Island of San Esteban be transformed into internal waters. In spite of the diplomatic protests presented by affected governments, it is a fact that there is a valid legal basis for incorporating this area into Mexican territory.

The Gulf of California as an Exclusive
Fisheries Zone and a National Bay

The southern maritime area of the Gulf of California — that is, the area lying between the entrance of the Gulf and the lower part of the Island of San Esteban — still enjoys the status of high seas. However, distinguished Mexican writers, particularly César Sepúlveda,[35] have advanced several arguments that would transform the whole of the Gulf of California into a Mexican sea. There has also been legislative attempts to proclaim Mexican sovereignty over the entire area. In November 1965 the parliamentary representatives of the National Action Party, introduced in the House of Representatives a motion to amend Articles 27, 42, and 48 of the Constitution, expressly including the Gulf of California in the territory of Mexico.[36] From the point of view of international law, the technical arguments invoked in the Exposition of Motives of the motion are rather confused.

Apart from citing writers who advocate that the Gulf of California should be considered an "historic bay," the motion attempts to justify the incorporation of the Gulf into Mexican territory on the basis that the regime of bays would be applicable. It seems difficult to accept the legal possibility that the Gulf of California could be subsumed under the concept of a bay, for although it meets some of the requirements of the Convention on the Territorial Sea, it also lacks at least one of them — namely, that the entrance of the bay does not exceed twenty-four miles. The distance between any point of the coast of the Peninsula of Baja California and the corresponding point in the coast of Sinaloa or Sonora exceeds by far the maximum of twenty-four miles. Without deriding the importance of the motion, it could have had more positive results had it been prepared with a stricter technical approach.

Due to the geographical characteristics of the Gulf of California and the close relationship between the Sea of Cortes and Mexican interests, in the immediate future this sea area will have to be claimed by Mexico as internal waters, thus extending the exercise of sovereign rights over the entire maritime area. At the present time, however, what is important is the determination of the legal basis for such a claim and the evaluation of its legal feasibility in terms of international law. Mexico has accepted the rules of the law of the sea provided by the four Geneva Conventions. Although this *corpus juris* is not immutable and does not contain the totality of the rules of the law of the sea, it is evident that it would not be legally valid to violate the provisions of these treaties. It is necessary, therefore, to examine whether the legal justification of such a claim can be found in conventional law, customary principles or, in their absence, in circumstances which would allow the development of a new rule applicable to this particular case. The effectiveness of the new rule will depend on the evolution of international law, which is not a static order but responds to the continuous incorporation of rules which reflect the interests of the subjects of such rules.

It is important, however, to emphasize that the legal validity of any claim to a sea area requires a basis in international law. In the words of the Court:

> "The delimitation of sea areas always has an international aspect; it cannot be dependent merely upon the will of the coastal State as expressed in its municipal law. Although it is true that the act of delimitation is necessarily a unilateral act, because only the coastal State is competent to undertake it, the validity of the delimitation with regard to other States depends upon international law."[37]

From a geographical point of view the Gulf of California is properly speaking a bay. However, as was explained above, it does not meet one of the formal requirements of the Convention on the Territorial Sea. Thus, Article 7 of the Geneva Convention is not applicable, and therefore Mexico cannot claim sovereignty over the area which is characterized as high seas.

Apart from that formal requirement, and notwithstanding other legal considerations, it has been argued that it is not equitable to identify the Gulf of California with the concept of a bay as defined by the Geneva Convention and thereby making automatically applicable the twenty-four mile rule. In fact, the geographical nature of the Gulf of California is so unique that it justifies the creation of an exceptional status. The length of the sea area which penetrates landward between the two coasts of the Gulf is four times larger than the line which closes the entrance. It is only just to apply in such cases a criteria which will take into account the proportion between the maritime area concerned and the dimensions of the mouth of the bay. The special legal status of the Gulf of California should be proposed by Mexico in the next Conference on the Law of the Sea.

On the other hand, although the legal regime of "historic bays" is not included in the Geneva Conventions, general international law admits the validity of claims over certain waters which have the characteristics of a bay, but the entrance of which is larger than the one permitted for bays in general. The effect will be that the coastal State will exercise its sovereignty over areas which normally would be subject to the regime of the high seas. In consenting to this exception, international law imposes certain rights by Mexico over the Sea of Cortes. However, it could be considered that recent developments in the law of the sea recognize the existence, although only in an embryonic stage, of a rule of international law conceding certain powers to the coastal State for the exclusive exploitation of the natural resources of the maritime areas adjacent to its coasts. This tendency is confirmed by the practice of an increasing number of States.

For the first time Mexico has supported principles involving jurisdiction over extraterritorial waters. Although it has not yet enacted national legislation to this effect, the Government of Mexico has stated that "Mexico shall fight at the Conference on the Law of the Sea in 1973, in order that legally and by means of an international convention a patrimonial sea of up to 200 miles be recognized and respected, conferring upon the coastal State the power to exercise without controversy exclusive or preferential fishing rights and, in general, rights over all its economic resources."[38] This signals an important change in Mexican policy on the law of the sea. It is necessary that this change be supplemented by measures which will make possible the exploitation, exploration, and administration of the 200-mile zone to the benefit and advantage of the nation. Many other States have enacted provisions which depart from the conventional or customary rules of international law with the intention of enlarging State jurisdiction over areas of the sea, including the Soviet Union, Canada, Iceland, Ceylon, Ghana, India, and Pakistan.

The unilateral acts of several countries claiming historic, economic, strategic, fishing, or conservation rights over areas which traditional international law considers high seas signals the existence of a clear tendency in favor of the creation of new rules of world public order which will consecrate the preferential rights of coastal States to explore, exploit, and conserve the living and mineral resources found in areas adjacent to their coasts. Within this context Mexico has the option of following the new tendencies on the law of the sea to proclaim an exclusive zone in the Gulf of California, as well as in other areas rich in natural resources, establishing a special jurisdiction with the exclusive purpose of exercising the rights which are inherent to the conservation and administration of the living resources of the sea, to their exclusive exploitation by Mexican nationals, and to the adoption of measures to prevent the pollution of the marine environment and the coasts. To this end it will be necessary to enact the pertinent legislative provisions, as Congress is empowered to do by Article 73, Section XIII, of the Constitution.

By means of such a law, Mexico could proclaim its exclusive jurisdiction over fisheries and for the exercise of other special powers in those areas of the Gulf of · California which are not at the present time Mexican internal waters. The drawing of a straight line between Punta Arena in the Peninsula of Baja California and Altata, or perhaps Mazatlan, in the coasts of Sinaloa, would enclose the sea area extending to the north, to the point where it meets the outer limit of the Mexican territorial sea in the interior of the Gulf of California. It is probable that a measure of this kind would have to include provisions for the gradual withdrawal of foreign fishermen traditionally active in the area. The political advantage, in the light of international conditions, of claiming a special zone in the Gulf of California at the United Nations Conference on the Law of the Sea, must also be taken into consideration.

The proclamation by Mexico of a special jurisdiction in the Gulf of California would only be a first step to ensuring the existence of a national bay in the entire area, perhaps on solid legal grounds. With the evolution of international law, Mexican authority over the Gulf of California will come to be accepted, thereby confirming the reasons stated by César Sepúlveda:

> "The physical disposition of that marine area is entirely favorable, for it is closed by most of its entrances and offers in addition a uniform functional characteristic with regard to the national territory. There are economic and political links with the mainland. . . . The existence of a vital interest is evident for the fishing resources are indispensable to us . . . there is no valid pretension by others which might be opposed to the reasonable interest of the coastal State . . . the international interest in navigation is not at stake."[39]

These ideas, based on the higher interest of Mexico and vigorously stated for some time, must sooner or later find their place in the Mexican legal order.

JURISDICTION IN THE TERRITORIAL SEA

The Right of Innocent Passage

Since 1940 the Law on General Ways of Communication[40] has established the rules which shall be observed by ships entering the Mexican territorial sea. With regard to innocent passage it provides that there is freedom of navigation through the territorial sea of the Republic *in accordance with international law and treaties*. However, national legislation is to be observed by foreign ships navigating through Mexican waters. Seaports of the Republic are open to commerce of all nations.[41]

Jurisdiction over Foreign Vessels

The sovereign power of Mexico over its territorial sea has not been implemented by virtue of legislation indicating how it is to be exercised. There are only a few provisions establishing the principles that must be observed by foreign vessels navigating in Mexican territorial sea. The following should be mentioned:

Criminal Jurisdiction. Crimes committed on board foreign ships anchored in national ports or in Mexican territorial waters are considered as having been committed in the national territory if they disturb the peace or when the offender or offended do not belong to the crew.[42] This provision of the Penal Code is supplemented by the Law of Maritime Navigation and Commerce,[43] which provides that Mexican authorities will intervene and apply Mexican law when the crimes or offenses committed on board foreign ships in national waters disturb public order, or when such assistance is requested by the captain or the Consul of the country whose flag the ship flies. These provisions are similar, though not identical, to those of Article 29 of the Convention on the Territorial Sea.

Fiscal Measures. Mexican law is silent on the exercise of fiscal jurisdiction in territorial waters. The Customs Code establishes the conditions which are required for a ship, entering or departing from a national port, to observe fiscal obligations.[44] But fiscal control in the territorial sea is not regulated.

Sanitary Measures. The Sanitary Code regulates the administration of sanitary services in national ports, the visit and inspection of foreign ships, the measures for the prevention of communicable diseases, and the sanitary rules which shall be observed by ships which are presumed to be or actually are infected by any disease subject to quarantine.[45] However, there are no rules on sanitary supervision in Mexican territorial waters.

There is no doubt that the Mexican State is entitled to sovereign rights over the territorial sea, but such rights cannot be exercised abstractly. There is, therefore, a need for Mexican legislation to provide the authorities with specific powers in civil, fiscal, custom, defense, and other matters, so that there be a precise legal framework for the exercise of different actions in the area of Mexican maritime jurisdiction.

Fishing Rights

In May 1972, the Federal Law on Promotion of Fishing was enacted[46] to serve as an instrument of promotion in the area of fishing resources, which is one of the most important items of the national economy and which had not been properly regulated as far as exploitation is concerned.

It is interesting to examine those aspects of the law which may have international consequences. The law purports to regulate and promote fishing in Mexican internal waters, in the territorial sea, in international waters with regard to Mexican vessels, in preferential or exclusive fishing zones proclaimed by the Republic, in the continental shelf and its superjacent waters, and in the high seas.[47] The last two points are an unnecessary repetition, for the waters above the continental shelf and beyond twelve miles are a part of the high seas.

Regulation and promotion are concepts which involve the exercise of jurisdiction; from this point of view the law purports to extend its jurisdiction to the high seas. However, it does not provide any criteria on the nature or characteristics of such powers. The interpretation of the law could lead to absurd conclusions, for Mexican jurisdiction could be exercised in any part of the high seas, whether it be the Indian Ocean or the Caspian Sea. This, of course, would conflict with international law and the conventional obligations entered into by Mexico which is a party to the Convention on the High Seas, which provides that no state is entitled to subject any part of the high seas to its sovereignty.[48] The Law on the Development of Fisheries is cast in such broad terms that it appears to be incompatible with international law.

It should have been possible, by use of a better legal technique, to include criteria for the definition of the extent of the regulation and promotion in extraterritorial waters. A basic element would be proximity. Thus, the idea of establishing a special jurisdiction over maritime areas contiguous to the Mexican territorial sea should be given some consideration. Also, for example, to have included the conservation measures accepted by the Convention on Fishing and Conservation of the Living Resources of the High Seas would have enriched the text of the law, clearly and precisely determining the characteristics of such measures.

It is evident that this was the proper occasion to define the extension of certain special jurisdictions of the Mexican State over the extraterritorial maritime areas, thus incorporating the most recent developments of international law. The law accomplishes this purpose to a certain extent, but does not properly regulate the matter. It is of interest to note that for the first time a provision empowering the Federation to establish exclusive or preferential fishing zones has been included. Thus, the legislation has incorporated a power of profound international significance, but has not established its meaning or content. In spite of the economy of this provision, it is desirable that it should be made effective, to mention only the case of the Gulf of California.

In principle, Article 37 of the law prohibits commercial fishing by foreign vessels in territorial waters, which are erroneously referred to by the law as national waters. However, the Secretary of Industry and Commerce might grant permits to foreign vessels, but only exceptionally and for each trip and provided that certain requirements be observed, especially the following:

(1) that they leave the territorial sea at the agreed time;
(2) that they do not unload their catch in national territory;
(3) that at least 50 percent of the crew be of Mexican nationality;
(4) that the national crew be engaged in Mexican territory;
(5) that no commercial fishing of sardines, anchovies, or species reserved to cooperatives be undertaken in reserved zones;

(6) that the observance of these obligations be guaranteed with a cash deposit, which shall not exceed one hundred thousand pesos.

Fishing in territorial waters or in exclusive zones by foreign vessels without permit is penalized with a fine of $ 6,000 to $ 24,000, the confiscation of the fishing gear and the catch.[49]

In addition to these provisions of municipal law, mention must be made of the Convention on Fishing and Conservation of the Living Resources of the High Seas,[50] to which Mexico is a party.

This Convention provides that nationals of all States have the right to engage in fishing on the high seas and the duty to adopt such measures as may be necessary for the conservation of the living resources of the high seas. The latter expression means "the aggregate of the measures rendering possible the optimum sustainable yield from those resources so as to secure a maximum supply of food and other marine products."[51] It is admitted that the coastal State has a special interest in the maintenance of the productivity of the living resources in any area of the high seas adjacent to its territorial sea, for which purpose and under certain conditions it may adopt unilateral measures of conservation appropriate to any stock of fish or other marine resources.[52] A special commission is created for the settlement of any dispute which may arise in the application of these provisions; its decisions are binding on the parties.[53]

It is interesting to note that neither Mexico nor any other State party to the Convention has enforced the measures of conservation provided therein, and that the mechanism has remained inoperative in practice.[54]

Legal Regime of Ships

The Convention on the High Seas contains provisions regarding the nationality of ships and on the legal regime applicable to them. It provides that each State shall fix the conditions for the granting of its nationality to ships, for the registration of ships in its territory, and for the right to fly its flag. Ships have the nationality of the State whose flag they are entitled to fly, but there must exist a genuine link between the State and the ship. Ships shall sail under the flag of one State only and, except in exceptional cases, shall be subject to its exclusive jurisdiction on the high seas. A ship may not change its flag during a voyage or while in a port of call, except in the case of a real transfer of ownership or change of registry.[55]

The Convention grants a complete immunity from jurisdiction of any State other than the flag State to those ships which are government owned or operated but used only on government noncommercial service, when on the high seas.[56] This Article was subject to an express reservation on the part of Mexico when it deposited its instrument of accession to the Convention with the Secretary General of the United Nations, for it considered that "ships which are the property of the State enjoy immunity independently from their use," and therefore would not accept the limitations imposed by the Convention.[57] Mexico's reservation is a legitimate one. A nation that has a decentralized system of organs and enterprises with state participation, some of which operate commercial ships, in the public interest, has the right to exclude any interference by third States. Ships of a public enterprise, such as Petróleos Mexicanos, which are the property of the nation, must be protected by a regime that guarantees their immunity. As was pointed out by the International Law Commission in its comments to draft Article 33: "as regards navigation on the high seas, there were no sufficient grounds for not granting to State ships used on commercial government service the same immunity as other State ships."[58] At the Geneva Conference, however, this approach did not prevail and commercial ships of the State were excluded from immunity of jurisdiction.

The legal regime of ships is regulated in Mexican municipal law by the Law on General Ways of Communication and the Law of Maritime Navigation and Commerce. Mexican ships on the high seas are considered by the law as Mexican territory. When in foreign waters, legal acts related to the ships shall be subject to Mexican law to the extent compatible with the application of the legislation which the foreign State might require. Mexican law is also applicable to crimes and offenses committed on board national ships, unless they were committed in foreign waters, and those responsible are subject to the jurisdiction of another country.[59]

Mexican ships must be registered with the port authorities before being entitled to fly the flag. The nationality of the ship is proved by means of the patent of navigation or the certificate of registration. The registration must be filed with the National Maritime Public Registry.[60]

Mexican ships are those registered and flying the Mexican flag, those abandoned in waters under national jurisdiction, those attached or expropriated by Mexican authorities, those captured as a prize from the enemy, and those which are the property of the State.[61] For a corporation to have ships registered and flying the Mexican flag, it must provide evidence of the Mexican character of its capital and of its governing board.[62]

Ships acquired abroad must be provisionally registered with Mexican consular authorities in the port of departure. From the moment in which it becomes definitively registered, its crew shall be composed entirely of Mexican nationals by birth.[63]

The registration and right to fly the flag is terminated by the transfer of the ship to foreign ownership, by its capture in case of war, by its loss, shipwreck, or fire, or by demission of the flag, which has to be authorized by the Federal Executive.[64]

With regard to foreign ships in internal or territorial waters, the law provides that they are subject to the law of the foreign State, to the extent compatible with the application of Mexican laws.

THE CONTINENTAL SHELF

The idea that the coastal State might exercise authority and jurisdiction over the continental shelf is quite recent. In September 1945, the President of the United States issued a proclamation declaring that the natural resources of the subsoil and seabed of the continental shelf adjacent to the coasts appertained to the United States and were subject to its jurisdiction and control. Mexico did not escape the chain reaction which followed, and on October 29, 1945, the President of Mexico claimed for the nation the whole of the continental shelf adjacent to its coasts, and all of the natural resources, known or unknown, which are found in it, leading to the supervision, use, and control of the zones of protection of fisheries necessary for the conservation of this source of prosperity. The application of these measures is without prejudice to the legitimate rights of third States and the freedom of navigation. On December 6, 1945, the President of Mexico introduced a motion to amend Articles 27, 42, and 48 of the Constitution, in order to incorporate the continental shelf to the national territory. This proposal purported to establish the principle that "the waters of the sea above the continental shelf and the submarine terrace are the property of the nation."

As mentioned above, the proposal was approved by Congress and state legislatures. However, the amendments were never enacted by the Executive. The pretension of sovereignty over the epicontinental waters had no justification.

In February 1949 an area of the continental shelf of the States of Campeche, Tabasco, and Veracruz was declared the property of Petróleos Mexicanos for the exploitation of oil resources of the subsoil.[65] In 1958 a further step was taken in declaring that the nation has the direct, inalienable, and imprescriptible right over all deposits of oil which are found in the national territory, including the continental shelf.[66]

In 1959, as a consequence of the Geneva agreements, Mexico considered it necessary to adapt its national legislation to the new international situation. For this purpose, the Executive introduced a motion to amend Articles 27, 42, and 48 of the Constitution,[67] so that the country could have "more effective legal instruments for the defense of its rights and the protection of its resources." It is accepted as a constitutional principle that the nation has a direct right over all the natural resources of the continental shelf and submarine terrace. The submerged region is considered as a part of the national territory, under the authority of the Federal Government.[68] Mexico deposited its instrument of accession to the Convention on the Continental Shelf on August 2, 1966.

CONCLUSIONS

The law of the sea is composed of an aggregate of norms in constant evolution. Among the many branches of international law, this particular one has proven since the days of Grotius to be the most dynamic, modifying the content of its norms and always incorporating new principles. The breadth of the territorial sea, the sacred freedom of the high seas, the regime of the continental shelf and of the seabed and ocean floor, freedom of fishing and the right to establish exclusive or preferential fishing zones are concepts, among others, which have had a great flexibility and which are subject to important legal transformations. The interests and practice of States determines that the legal order of the sea never remains stationary.

Notwithstanding its long tradition, the law of the sea has no immutable principles or, with the exception of the repression of piracy, rules of *jus cogens,* that is, peremptory norms of international law from which no derogation is permitted. The regime of the sea is in a constant state of transition, and when it has been codified it is subject to a condition of suspension, until new developments will require additional modifications. Technological developments and economic necessities of States lead to a permanent revision of the law of the sea.

In spite of the importance of the subject, Mexico has lacked until now an organized policy towards the law of the sea. The absence of a coherent and systematic strategy, based on uniform criteria, for planning, designing, and implementing measures related to the marine environment, is very obvious. As a result there is no legislative policy which can translate into legal provisions the objectives of the strategy.

The matter is far too important to be left to chance decisions or for Mexico to follow only the ideas or the initiatives advanced by other States. Due to its geographic conditions, the extension of its coasts, and the wealth of its fishing and mineral resources in areas near to the coasts, the Government of Mexico has a special responsibility in the process of creation of a law of the sea, for the purpose of which it must actively participate in its formulation.

The forthcoming United Nations Conference, which will reconsider the basic problems of the law of the sea, suggests the need for a change of attitudes. It is necessary to define the position that Mexico will take at this meeting and to initiate the planning of a long-term maritime policy. The possibility of creating a technical organ exclusively dedicated to the matter must be considered. This organ, composed of high level personnel and directly responsible to the Chief Executive, would ensure the participation of experts in the different areas involved: lawyers, biologists, economists, oceanographers, geographers, mining and oil engineers, geologists, and experts in fishing, problems of defense and naval strategy and marine pollution. It would be desirable to ensure the participation and direction of a well-known international lawyer, with a solid tradition in United Nations activities on the law of the sea and experience in the bilateral and regional negotiations undertaken by Mexico in maritime problems.

The functions of this body would be to collect all the pertinent information on the marine area. It would also be entrusted with the responsibility of formulating a national and international maritime policy in accordance with the national interest. This organ should be a permanent body, for once its policy recommendations are approved it should implement them in close coordination with the different organs dealing with maritime matters.

The functions of this body would be to collect all the pertinent information on the marine area. It would also be entrusted with the responsibility of formulating a national and international maritime policy in accordance with the national interest. This organ should be a permanent body, for once its policy recommendations are approved it should implement them in close coordination with the different organs dealing with maritime matters.

Should such a technical organ be provided with the economic and human resources needed for effective work, then the sea could be truly transformed into a patrimony of benefit to the nation.

References

1. J. Castañeda. "Las reformas a los Artículos 27, 42 y 48 Constitucionales, relatives al dominio Marítimo de la Nación y al Derecho Internacional," in *El Pensamiento Jurídico de México en el Derecho Internacional* (Mexico: Porrúa, 1960), p. 50.
2. It is interesting to note that for Mexico the Convention came into force thirty days after the deposit of the instrument of accession (Article 29 [2] of the Convention), that is, on September 1, 1966. However, in the municipal order the situation was different. The Convention was enacted by the Executive on August 17, 1966, although it was not published in the *Official Gazette* until October 5, 1966 – that is, thirty-five days after it was in force in terms of international law. In accordance with Article 3 of the Civil Code for the Federal District and Territories, "Laws, regulations, instructions, or any other provision of general observance, are binding and effective three days after their publication in the *Official Gazette.*" Therefore, for thirty-eight days there was a legal disparity between the internal and the international obligations of Mexico. This form of *vacatio legis* could have been a source of controversy. With regard to the three other Geneva Conventions there was a similar situation, only longer in time. For an examination of the effect of treaties in municipal law, see C. Sepúlveda, "La situación de los Tratados en el orden Legal Mexicano," in *Comunicaciones Mexicanas al VI Congreso Internacional de Derecho Comparado* (Hamburg, 1962) (Mexico: Instituto de Derecho Comparado, UNAM, 1962), pp. 203-207. This study concludes that treaties are not enforceable in municipal law if they have not been enacted and published, for the addressees of the norm are entitled to know the rights and obligations imposed.
3. *Official Gazette,* January 20, 1967.
4. *International Legal Materials,* Vol. VII (March 1968), No. 2, pp. 312-319. See also D. W. Windley, "International Practice Regarding Traditional Fishing Privileges of Foreign

Fishermen in Zones of Extended Maritime Jurisdiction" in *American Journal of International Law,* Vol. 63 (July 1969), pp. 490-503.

5. *Official Gazette,* December 26, 1969.

6. Amended by decree of January 6, 1960, published in the *Official Gazette* of January 20 and in force from that date. This amendment added to paragraph 5 the expression "inland marine waters," that is, those to landward side of the baseline of the territorial sea.

7. It is interesting, however, to mention the comments included in the Exposition of Motives of the motion to amend paragraphs 4 and 5 of Article 27 and Articles 42 and 48 of the Constitution, introduced by the Federal Executive in the Senate on October 1, 1959. This document states that the proposal "refers to Article 42 of the Constitution so that the national territory will include the territorial seas, internal waters, and national air space. As was indicated, Article 27 of the Constitution provides that the waters of the territorial seas are the property of the nation. However, the sole reference to the legal concept of property is not sufficient. In the opinion of the Federal Executive, it is desirable that the exercise of the sovereign rights by the Mexican State over the territorial sea be derived more directly from the Constitution. Though when the latter was enacted there could have been doubts about the legal nature of the rights of the coastal State over the territorial sea, nowadays the situation is clear. In accordance with contemporary international law, the territorial sea is a part of the territory of the State; the sovereignty which the State exercises over the territorial sea has the same nature as the one exercised over its territorial domain. Therefore the Constitutional amendment consists of including the territorial seas among the composing elements of the national territory." Text in *Derechos del Pueblo Mexicano: México a través de sus constituciones,* XLVI Legislatura de la Cámara de Diputados, México, Vol. IV, p. 823. It may be concluded, therefore, that there is a dual regime for the Mexican territorial sea: property and sovereignty. On the other hand, the first paragraph of Article 27 of the Constitution provides that "ownership of the lands and waters within the boundaries of the national territory is vested originally in the Nation. . . ." The territorial sea being a part of the national territory, it follows that the ownership of these waters is also vested in the nation. Can it be assumed that property over the three-mile belt which was a part of the high seas until incorporated into the Mexican territorial sea when enlarged to twelve miles in 1969 is also vested in the nation?

8. *Official Gazette,* January 30, 1969.

9. Ibid., November 21, 1963.

10. Ibid., January 11, 1972, Article 5, Sections I and II.

11. Ibid., December 24, 1958, Article 5, Section IV.

12. See Article 5 of the Law of Maritime Navigation and Commerce; Article 5, Sections III and IV of the Penal Code for the Federal District and Territories; and Articles 19 and 20 of the Convention on the Territorial Sea.

13. M. S. McDougal and W. T. Burke, *The Public Order of the Oceans: A Contemporary International Law of the Sea* (New Haven, Conn.: Yale University Press, 1962), pp. 174-302; D. W. Bowett, *The Law of the Sea* (Manchester, England: Manchester University Press, 1967), pp. 5-6.

14. See Alfonso García Robles, *La Conferencia de Ginebra y la Anchura del Mar Territorial* (Mexico: Fondo de Cultura Economica, 1959), pp. 51-65. For historical background, see J. K. Oudendijk, *Status and Extent of Adjacent Waters* (Leyden: Sijthoff, 1970).

15. *Official Gazette,* December 26, 1969; in force the day following its publication.

16. In accordance with Article 24, Section II, of the Convention on the Territorial Sea, the contiguous zone may not extend beyond twelve miles from the baseline from which the breadth of the territorial sea is measured. These provisions are no longer relevant in the case of Mexico, for the breadth of the territorial sea and the contiguous zone are identical.

17. *Official Gazette,* August 31, 1935.

18. December 18, 1902.

19. For the text of bilateral treaties incorporating a three marine leagues territorial sea, see

García Robles, op. cit., note 14 above, Appendices V and VI.

20. See Article 4, Section I, of the Law on Real Property, of 1902, as amended in 1935.
21. For the exchange of diplomatic notes between the Governments of Mexico and the United States, see M. Whiteman, *Digest of International Law* (Washington, D.C.: Government Printing Office, 1965), Vol. 4, pp. 1210-1229.
22. Note of May 6, 1936. See M. Whiteman, op. cit., note 21 above, pp. 1210-1213.
23. Article V of the Treaty of Peace, Friendship, and Limits Between the United States and Mexico, February 2, 1848.
24. Note of June 3, 1936. See M. Whiteman, op. cit., note 21 above, pp. 1213-1214.
25. Note of July 8, 1936. See M. Whiteman, op. cit., note 21 above, pp. 1214-1218.
26. Note of August 25, 1936. See M. Whiteman, op. cit., note 21 above, pp. 1218-1219. The interpretation of the Mexican Ministry of Foreign Affairs was confirmed years later by the Supreme Court of the United States. When the Submerged Lands Act of 1953 was enacted, a conflict of interpretation arose between the United States Government and some states of the Union with regard to the extension of the rights of the latter over the submerged areas, particularly in relation to the exploitation of oil and natural resources of such areas. In *U.S. v. Louisiana, Texas, Mississippi, Alabama, and Florida* (1960), the Supreme Court admitted that the State of Texas had the right to the natural resources of the Gulf of Mexico up to a distance of three leagues from its coast. The Court based its decision on Article V of the Guadalupe Hidalgo Treaty. See M. Whiteman, op. cit., note 21 above, p. 67.
27. This law has been published twice: *Official Gazette* of July 3, 1942, and of August 26, 1944. The latter publication was made necessary by the omission of the signatures of five Ministers.
28. Between 1956 and 1963 only forty-two American fishing vessels were captured by Mexican authorities for carrying out activities in waters under national jurisdiction. The fines applied ranged between $1,200 and $3,200. These cases are only those in which the Government of the United States undertook to pay the fine. Cases in which the Government of the United States did not assume responsibility for the payment are not registered. See M. Whiteman, op. cit., note 21 above, pp. 1232-1238.
29. *Derechos del Pueblo Mexicano*, cit., note 7 above, pp. 821-822.
30. Convention on the Territorial Sea, Article 3.
31. *Ley General de Bienes Nacionales*, Article 18 (II), *Official Gazette*, January 30, 1969; Ibid., Article 17, *Official Gazette*, July 3, 1942; Law on Real Property of the Federation, Article 4, December 18, 1902.
32. *Anglo-Norwegian Fisheries Case*, International Court of Justice Reports, 1951, pp. 129-130.
33. "In localities where the coastline of the national territory is deeply indented and cut into or where there is a fringe of islands along the coast in its immediate vicinity, the method of straight baselines joining the outermost points may be employed in drawing the baseline from which the breadth of the territorial sea is measured. The drawing of such baselines shall not depart to any appreciable extent from the general direction of the coast, and sea areas lying within the lines must be linked closely to the land domain to be subject to the regime of internal waters. These baselines may be drawn to and from low-tide elevations when lighthouses or similar installations which are permanently above sea level have been built on them, or when such elevations are totally or in part at a distance from the coast of the mainland or of an island which does not exceed the breadth of the territorial sea. For the purpose of delimiting the territorial sea, the outermost permanent harbor works which form an integral part of the harbor system shall be regarded as forming part of the coast." *Ley General de Bienes Nacionales*, Article 18, Section II, as amended by decree of December 12, 1969, *Official Gazette*, December 26, 1969.
34. *Official Gazette*, August 30, 1968.
35. C. Sepúlveda, *Curso de Derecho Internacional Público*, 4th ed. (Mexico: Porrúa, 1971), pp. 167-169.
36. Congress of the United States of Mexico, House of Representatives: *Iniciativa para*

reformar los artículos 27, 42 y 48 de la Constitución Política de los Estados Unidos Mexicanos para incluir expresamente el Golfo de California dentro del territorio nacional, bajo el dominio de la Federación, suscrita por los C. C. Diputados a la XLVI Legislatura, miembros del Partido Acción Nacional. Mexico, November 19, 1965.

37. *Anglo-Norwegian Fisheries Case,* International Court of Justice Reports, p. 132.

38. Address by the President, Luis Echeverría Alvarez, before the Third UNCTAD Conference, Santiago, Chile, April 19, 1972. *El Trimestre Económico,* Vol. XXXIX, No. 155, 1972, pp. 665-673.

39. *Curso de Derecho Internacional Público,* loc. cit., note 35 above, pp. 168-169.

40. *Official Gazette,* February 19, 1940.

41. Law on General Ways of Communication, Articles 189 and 190.

42. Penal Code for the Federal District and Territories, Article 5 (III). See also General Regulations of Port Police, Articles 66-75. *Official Gazette,* October 9, 1941.

43. Law of Maritime Navigation and Commerce, Article 5.

44. Customs Code of the United States of Mexico, Articles 47-114. *Official Gazette,* December 31, 1951.

45. Sanitary Code of the United States of Mexico, Articles 26 (III), 32-47. *Official Gazette,* March 1, 1955.

46. *Official Gazette,* May 25, 1972.

47. Law on the Development of Fisheries, Article 5.

48. Mexico deposited its instrument of accession on August 2, 1966. The Convention entered into force for Mexico on September 1, 1966, although it was published in the *Official Gazette* of October 19, 1966. The Convention came into force in terms of international law on September 30, 1962. By 1971, forty-eight States were parties to the Convention. See in general, A. Sobarzo, *Régimen Jurídico del Alta Mar* (Mexico: Perrúa, 1970).

49. Law on the Development of Fisheries, Article 93.

50. *Official Gazette,* October 22, 1966. The Convention entered into force on March 20, 1966; thirty-two States are party to the Convention.

51. Article 2 of the Convention.

52. Articles 6 (1) and 7 of the Convention.

53. Articles 9-11 of the Convention.

54. To this effect see *The Law of the Sea: Offshore Boundaries and Zones,* Lewis M. Alexander, ed. (Columbus, Ohio: Ohio State University Press, 1967); D. M. Johnston, *The International Law of Fisheries* (New Haven, Conn.: Yale University Press, 1965). See also Lewis M. Alexander, ed., *The Law of the Sea: The Future of the Sea's Resources.* Proceedings of the Second Annual Conference of the Law of the Sea Institute, the University of Rhode Island, June 1967; and *International Rules and Organizations for the Sea,* Proceedings of the Third Annual Conference of the Law of the Sea Institute, the University of Rhode Island, June 1968.

55. Articles 5 and 6 of the Convention on the High Seas.

56. Article 9 of the Convention on the High Seas.

57. A similar reservation was made by Mexico when it acceded to the Convention on the Territorial Sea, with regard to Article 21 and its application to Article 19, Sections 1-3, and Article 2, Sections 2 and 3. *Official Gazette,* October 5 and 19, 1966. The Government of the United States objected to these reservations in a note to the Secretary General of the United Nations in September 1966.

58. Report of the International Law Commission, *Yearbook of the International Law Commission,* 1956, Vol. II, p. 280.

59. Law of Maritime Navigation and Commerce, Articles 2, 3, and 4.

60. Ibid., Articles 88, 89, and 91.

61. Ibid., Article 90; Law on General Ways of Communication, Article 275.

62. Law of Maritime Navigation and Commerce, Article 92.

63. Political Constitution of the United States of Mexico, Article 32; Law of Maritime Navigation and Commerce, Article 94; Law on General Ways of Communication, Article 278.

103

64. Law of Maritime Navigation and Commerce, Article 95; Law on General Ways of Communication, Articles 281, 282, 283, and 284.
65. Decree incorporating into the property of Petróleos Mexicanos the subsoil of the area below the territorial waters of the Gulf of Mexico. *Official Gazette,* March 11, 1949.
66. Law regulating Article 27 of the Constitution with regard to oil. *Official Gazette,* November 29, 1958.
67. For the text of the motion and the debate in the Senate and House, see *Derechos del Pueblo Mexicano,* cit., note 7 above, pp. 819-875.
68. *Official Gazette,* January 20, 1960.

Chapter V
Central America and the Caribbean

Chapter V

CENTRAL AMERICA AND THE CARIBBEAN

Francisco Villagrán Kramer

INTRODUCTION

Central America and the Caribbean represent a microcosm of the several distinct approaches to the problem of maritime sovereignty. The similarities and differences which are produced in a global framework are here reproduced on a smaller scale.[1]

The fact that the Caribbean Sea is a sensitive and strategic area from the point of view of the United States cannot be disregarded in any global or regional approach. On the other hand, both the Central American countries and the independent Caribbean Islands claim the lawful right to use their maritime areas for economic purposes in order to promote their exports and imports and improve commercial intercourse and the balance of payments. The resources of the sea have a strong economic impact in these countries. Large-scale fishing and the exploitation of oil are important sources of fiscal revenue through the payment of royalties and concession rights as well as sources of foreign exchange.

The fact that the industrialized countries have greater financial and technological possibilities for the exploitation of natural resources has induced some of the countries of the area to enlarge the territorial scope of their legal systems through the exercise of sovereignty or special jurisdiction over new geographical areas. In particular, it has been the policy of those countries which have moved toward the expansion of their maritime domain, whether by enlarging the breadth of their territorial sea or by establishing exclusive fishery zones, to defend the existing resources in order to prevent their diminution or deterioration.

Taking into account the strategic character which the Caribbean Sea has for the United States, and giving due consideration to the rules of international law, all the countries of the region which have enlarged their sovereignty or jurisdiction have safeguarded to the greatest possible extent the right of innocent passage and overflight in the territorial sea and adjacent zones subject to the jurisdiction of the coastal State, thereby avoiding legal controversies.

In general, these political, economic, and strategic factors explain the cautious attitude which the countries of the region have taken in this matter, in addition to the Anglo-Saxon tradition followed in maritime affairs by the Caribbean Islands. Although Cuba and the Dominican Republic have a different tradition, their interests are very much linked to fishing, both with regard to internal consumption and to foreign trade, the main fishing activities of Cuba being carried on outside its territorial sea.

It must be mentioned also that the rights of the coastal State are exercised not only with regard to fishing and the exploitation of oil, but also in matters such as customs, health, and national security. Therefore, the extent of national jurisdiction varies in accordance with the different purposes pursued, such as in the case of Colombia, Cuba, or Venezuela; however, some other countries have included all forms of jurisdiction in the principal category of the territorial sea, thereby having in each individual case a uniform breadth whatever the purpose pursued.

CENTRAL AMERICA

The fact that five of the nine American countries having coasts both on the Atlantic and Pacific oceans are located in the Central American Isthmus is an important fact. Only El Salvador borders the Pacific and not the Atlantic; but because of its geographical location, it is also considered as a part of the Caribbean region.

The great abundance and variety of the fisheries resources of the Pacific Ocean has made it attractive to the fishing interests of the United States, Mexico, and Japan. This situation has influenced the fishing policy of two countries, El Salvador and Panama, and is directly related to their 200-mile territorial sea claims. It also explains why Costa Rica, Honduras, and Nicaragua have had, in different periods, 200-mile fisheries jurisdictions. Only Guatemala has had, since 1934, a twelve-mile breadth for its territorial sea and national fishing zone.

The continental shelf in the Pacific or Atlantic oceans is not very significant from a geological point of view, and therefore fishing is the priority interest in the law of the sea, particularly in the Pacific area.[2] The largest extension of the continental shelf in the Caribbean is not more than 125 miles, off Honduras and Nicaragua.

THE EPICONTINENTAL SEA

In spite of the close economic and political relations within the area, and the existence of a regional machinery of cooperation and economic integration, the countries of the region have not developed a uniform policy on the law of the sea, nor have they established a basis for the joint exploitation of the resources

108

of the sea. The only precedent in this regard is the Declaration of Antigua Guatemala, approved in August 1955, by the First Meeting of Ministers of Foreign Affairs of Central America. This declaration, which is closely linked to the plans for creating a customs union, states:

> "The First Meeting of Ministers of Foreign Affairs of Central America, DECLARE: ... their purpose to defend the territorial, economical, and cultural patrimony of the Central American States, including the continental shelf and the territorial and epicontinental sea, in order that their exploitation might benefit the people of all the countries."

The declaration revives the concept of the "epicontinental sea," which was first used in the legislation of Argentina[3] to mean the waters above the continental shelf. If this concept had been implemented at the regional level by means of a convention, it would have provided the basis for a clear definition leading to the establishment of a common position of the Central American countries, particularly since the breadth of the epicontinental sea would be determined by the size of the continental shelf itself.

At the time of its approval, the declaration was in accordance with the legislation and regulations of most of the Central American States. Costa Rica, by means of Legislative Decree 116 of July 27, 1948,[4] had proclaimed "national sovereignty over the seas adjacent to the continental and insular coasts of the national territory, whatever their depth, and to the extent necessary to protect, conserve, and utilize the natural resources and wealth" (Article 2). This decree also declared "the protection and control of the State ... over all the sea included within the perimeter formed by the coasts and by a mathematical parallel, projected out to sea at a distance of 200 marine miles" (Article 4). Although this decree was revised by Legislative Decree 803 of November 1949, changing the expression "national sovereignty" applicable to the adjacent seas to the expression "rights and interests of Costa Rica," and exchanging the words "control applicable to the 200-mile zone" to "protection of the State over that maritime zone," the law provided sufficient ground for the exercise of certain kinds of jurisdiction over the epicontinental sea. In addition, upon approval of the Declaration of Antigua Guatemala, Costa Rica acceded by Protocol to the Declaration of Santiago signed by Chile, Ecuador, and Peru in 1952; this Protocol, however, was never ratified.

In 1950, El Salvador established by its Constitution a 200-mile territorial sea. Honduras, by means of Legislative Decree 25 of January 17, 1951, and Decree 96 of January 28, 1951, declared that "... the sovereignty of Honduras extends to the continental shelf of the national territory, both of the mainland and of the islands, and to the waters covering it, at whatever depth and to whatever extent, and that the nation has full, inalienable, and imprescriptible domain over all wealth which exists or may exist in it, in its lower strata or in the area of water bounded by the vertical plane passing through its borders." Furthermore, the same decree also declared "the protection and control of the State in the Atlantic Ocean" over a 200-mile zone. Therefore, this law distinguishes between the superjacent waters of the continental shelf, over which Honduras exercises sovereignty, and the waters of the 200-mile zone over which it exercises "protection and control."

The Constitution of Panama of 1946 included in the category of State property and public use the territorial sea and the continental shelf. Decree 449 of December 17, 1946,[5] established that "For the purposes of fisheries in general, national jurisdiction over the territorial waters of the Republic extends to all the space above the seabed of the submarine continental shelf. For this reason the product of any fishing within the limits indicated is considered a national product, and is therefore subject to the provisions of the present decree" (Article 3).

At the time of the Declaration of Antigua Guatemala, which was not signed by Panama, four countries of the region had national legislation claiming rights over the epicontinental sea. Only Guatemala and Nicaragua had not claimed rights over the superjacent waters of the continental shelf. Some years later this situation changed — the claims of Honduras were modified while those of Panama were reaffirmed.

The Central American countries attended the Third Meeting of the Inter-American Council of Jurists, held in Mexico in 1956, and supported the Declaration of Principles on the territorial sea. After this expression of solidarity with the other American countries which also approved the declaration, the construction of a common policy and a uniform regulation of the territorial sea was again deferred for many years, each State remaining free to exercise its sovereign rights and to fix unilaterally the breadth of its territorial sea.

It was not until 1972 that a new regional meeting would take place, this time with the participation of the other countries of the Caribbean area, from which a regional consensus would emerge on the concept of the patrimonial sea, with a view to harmonizing the legislative differences and permitting a more flexible position for the coming conference on the law of the sea.

With regard to the central American participation in the Geneva Conventions, it must be mentioned that El Salvador, Honduras, and Nicaragua did not sign or accede to any one of them; Guatemala signed all the 1958 Conventions except for the one on Fishing and Conservation of the Living Resources of the Sea, but ratified only the Conventions on the High Seas and the Continental Shelf; and Costa Rica and Panama signed all four Conventions but with no subsequent ratification.

The Montevideo meeting on the law of the sea, held in May 1970, was attended only by El Salvador, Nicaragua, and Panama, all of which signed the

Declaration of Montevideo. The Lima meeting in August 1970 was attended by El Salvador, Guatemala, Honduras, Nicaragua, and Panama. Costa Rica was represented by an observer. This larger participation in the Lima meeting emphasizes the active developments which were taking place in the law of the sea.

THE TERRITORIAL SEA

In spite of these developments and the close links existing in the field of economic cooperation and integration, the legislation of the Central American countries on the law of the sea is still heterogeneous. In 1973 the situation was as follows.

● *Nicaragua* has no legislative provision fixing the breadth of its territorial sea, which means that it follows whatever is the rule of international law in this matter. The Constitution, however, proclaims sovereignty over the territorial sea; and special legislation has established a 200-mile zone with regard to fishing and conservation of resources.

Article 5 of the Constitution of 1950, which is similar to the corresponding provision of the Constitution of 1948, provides that:

> "The national territory extends between the Atlantic and the Pacific oceans and the Republics of Honduras and Costa Rica. It also comprises the adjacent islands, the subsoil, the territorial waters, the continental shelf, the submerged foundations, the air space, and the stratosphere. Such frontiers as may not yet be determined shall be fixed by treaties and by law."

The territorial sea, which is considered a part of the national territory, is certainly different from the national fishing zone of 200 miles established by Executive Decree I-L of 1965, as amended by Executive Decree 13-L of April 7, 1970; the latter has not modified the breadth of this fishing zone.

● *Costa Rica.* Article 6 of the Constitution of Costa Rica declares that "the State exercises complete and exclusive sovereignty over the air space above its territory and over its territorial waters and continental shelf, in accordance with the principles of international law and the treaties in force."

No legislative provision has yet defined the breadth of the territorial sea. Therefore, the decision given in 1950 by the Costa Rican Supreme Court, interpreting the principles of international law in favor of the three-mile rule, still regulates this breadth inasmuch as it has not been contradicted by any other decision. However, Costa Rica, as well as Nicaragua, has constantly made a distinction between the territorial sea and other areas over which jurisdiction is exercised with regard to marine fishing and hunting, with a view to the protection, conservation, and exploitation of natural resources. At the present time, this maritime area is considered to be a "patrimonial sea" with an extension of 200 miles measured from the low-water line.

The distinction between the territorial sea and the zone adjacent to it has been established by means of two instruments. On the one hand, Decree 2204 of the Ministry of Foreign Affairs, of February 10, 1972, fixed a twelve-mile territorial sea to "ensure to nationals an exclusive fishing zone and the exploitation of the resources of the sea." On the other hand, a decree also enacted on February 10, 1972, declared that Costa Rica will exercise a special jurisdiction over the seas adjacent to its territory to the extent necessary to protect, conserve, and exploit the natural wealth and resources existing in the zones corresponding to the "patrimonial sea." The breadth of the patrimonial sea is fixed at 200 miles measured from the low-water line.

• *Guatemala and Honduras* have also fixed the breadth of their territorial sea at twelve miles — Guatemala by means of the law regulating the administration and policing of ports, of June 10, 1934, except the bay of Amatique in the Caribbean which is considered a historic bay; Honduras by means of its Constitutional Amendment of 1965, Article 5 of which provides that:

> "The subsoil, the air space, the territorial sea to a distance of twelve nautical miles, the bed and subsoil of the submarine platform, continental and insular shelf, and other underwater areas adjacent to its territory outside the zone of territorial waters and to a depth of 200 meters or to the point where the depth of the superjacent waters, beyond this limit, permits the exploitation of the natural resources of the bed and subsoil, also belong to the State of Honduras and are subject to its jurisdiction and control."

The position of Guatemala in favor of twelve miles has remained unchanged since 1934, a breadth which was considerably larger than the one prevailing at the time. On the other hand, in 1965 Honduras changed its 1951 claims in favor of the epicontinental sea and its sovereignty over the continental shelf and superjacent waters, as well as a 200-mile zone of protection and control, to a twelve-mile territorial sea. However, Honduras has reserved the right to establish the limits of zones of control and protection over the natural resources under its jurisdiction, as well as to modify such limits in accordance with circumstances, discoveries, studies, and other reasons.

The violation of the Guatemalan territorial sea by foreign fishermen[6] gave rise to the enactment of the proper penalties in Decree 1412 of the National Congress of December 6, 1960, as well as to a more adequate regulation of fishing in the territorial sea by Decree 1470 of June 23, 1961. These decrees introduced no modifications in the twelve-mile rule in force since 1934, but defined more precisely the geographical area, thus imposing upon the captains of

Guatemalan ships the obligation to observe the territorial sea limits of other nations established by their legislation. This means that Guatemala has recognized at the legislative level the legal validity of the breadth of the territorial sea as fixed by third countries.

• Only *El Salvador and Panama* have clearly established in their legislation a 200-mile territorial sea. The 1962 Constitution of El Salvador, which retains the same provision as the 1950 Constitution, declares:

> "The Territory of the Republic within its present boundaries is irreducible. It includes the adjacent seas to a distance of 200 sea miles from the low-water line and the corresponding air space, subsoil, and continental shelf.

> "The provisions of the foregoing paragraph shall not affect freedom of navigation in accordance with the principles recognized under international law.

> "The Gulf of Fonseca is a historic bay subject to a 'special regime.' "

This constitutional provision has also been implemented with regard to fishing and marine hunting by means of Law No. 1961 of October 25, 1955, and of the law on distant-water and middle-distance fishing, established by Decree 97 of September 22, 1970. The first instrument provides that coastal fishing is that fishing carried out up to twelve miles from the coast, middle-distance fishing between twelve and 200 miles and distant-water fishing beyond 200 miles. The second instrument modified the area of middle-distance fishing to include the area between sixty and 200 nautical miles in the territorial sea.

With respect to the law of the sea, Panama has evolved differently than other Central American countries. The Constitution of 1946 included within the property of the State both the territorial sea and the continental shelf. Thereafter, Decree 449 of December 17, 1946, proclaimed "national jurisdiction for the purpose of fishing in general over the territorial waters of the Republic" and the whole area overlying the seabed of the continental shelf; all fishing within these limits was subjected to the provisions of national legislation. Law No. 58 of December 18, 1958, fixed the breadth of the territorial sea at twelve miles. Finally, Law No. 31 of February 2, 1967, extended the territorial sea to 200 miles:

> "The sovereignty of the Republic of Panama extends beyond its continental and insular territory and its inland waters to a zone of territorial sea 200 nautical miles wide, to the seabed and the subsoil of that zone, and to the air space above it."

The claims of El Salvador and Panama over the territorial sea are very clear with regard to its breadth and the exercise of sovereign rights by the State, although in the case of El Salvador the latter are not absolute.

Bearing in mind that Colombia, Guatemala, Jamaica, Honduras, Mexico, Trinidad and Tobago, and Venezuela have fixed the breadth of their territorial sea at twelve miles, that Costa Rica defers to international law, and that Nicaragua has remained silent, it may be asserted that this is the prevailing rule of international law in the region. As the Mexican jurist and diplomat Jorge Castaneda has observed, to the extent that legislation and statements before United Nations organs can be considered as evidence of *opinio juris,* there is a rule of customary international law enabling States to claim a twelve-mile territorial sea.[7] The Mexican authorities have undoubtedly taken this into consideration as well as the 200-mile claims in accepting the idea of a patrimonial sea — that is, the exercise of a specialized jurisdiction over a 200-mile area.

LIMITATIONS IN FORCE IN THE TERRITORIAL SEA

The breadth of the territorial sea does not indicate the whole of the jurisdiction which the Central American countries exercise over their maritime domains, but only the area over which sovereignty is exercised with the limitations imposed by international law with regard to innocent passage.[8] Beyond the territorial sea, the coastal State exercises certain powers or special jurisdiction, such as those relating to fishing, conservation, rational exploitation of the resources of the sea or sanitary, fiscal, customs, and national security matters.[9]

It is important, therefore, to examine the different limitations which the States of the region have accepted with regard to their territorial seas.

Guatemala recognizes the freedom of overflight, in accordance with the provisions of the law, treaties, or international agreements. El Salvador and Honduras have not indicated the kind of navigation which is permitted, stating only that the constitutional provisions do not affect freedom of navigation in accordance with the accepted principles of international law. However, in accepting the Declaration of Montevideo of 1970, El Salvador declared that freedom of overflight was also granted. Nicaragua exercises sovereignty over the air space above its territory and its territorial sea, declaring at the time of voting in favor of the Declaration of Montevideo that the right of overflying the territorial sea was subject to its national legislation. Panama declared in Montevideo that national sovereignty over the 200-mile territorial sea "does not affect the principles established by international law." Costa Rica has not provided for any special regime in this matter.

THE CONTINENTAL SHELF AND THE
RESOURCES OF THE SEABED AND SUBSOIL

Every Central American country has laid claims to rights over the continental shelf and the resources of the seabed and subsoil thereof, although the extent of these claims has been different. Honduras claims rights "to a depth of 200 meters, or, beyond that limit, up to where superjacent waters permit the exploitation of the natural resources of the seabed and subsoil." El Salvador and Panama claim a 200-mile territorial sea which includes the continental shelf and the seabed. Costa Rica, Guatemala, and Nicaragua claim rights over their respective continental shelves, but without any specific reference to distance or depth.

SPECIAL JURISDICTION

Some countries of the region also exercise special kinds of jurisdiction beyond their territorial sea. This is not the case, of course, of El Salvador and Panama whose 200-mile territorial sea embraces a special jurisdiction with regard to fishing and maritime hunting. Special jurisdictions exclude the rights over the continental shelf and its resources, for these are sovereign rights.

Thus the problem is reduced to the exercise of special kinds of jurisdiction, particularly of an economic nature, by those countries – Costa Rica, Guatemala, Honduras, and Nicaragua – which have a territorial sea of twelve miles or less. Guatemala is the only country which has not proclaimed any special jurisdiction beyond its territorial sea. The situation of the other countries is examined in detail below.

● *Honduras.* Article 5 of the Constitution of 1965 regulates, on the one hand, those areas over which the State exercises sovereignty and, on the other hand, those areas over which it exercises jurisdiction and control. The right to establish the limits of the latter zone has also been reserved. Sections 3 and 4 of the Constitutional provision, clearly state the position of Honduras:

> "3. The subsoil, the air space, the territorial sea to a distance of twelve nautical miles, the bed and subsoil of the submarine platform, continental, and insular shelf, and other underwater areas adjacent to its territory outside the zone of territorial waters and to a depth of 200 meters or to the point where the depth of the superjacent waters, beyond this limit, permits the exploitation of the natural resources of the bed and subsoil, also belong to the State of Honduras and are subject to its jurisdiction and control.
>
> "In the cases referred to in the . . . preceding paragraphs, the domain of the nation is inalienable and imprescriptible, and concessions may be granted only by the Republic to individuals or civil or commercial companies organized or incorporated under Honduran laws, subject to the condition that regular undertakings be established for exploitation of the elements mentioned and that requirements prescribed by law are met. In

115

the case of petroleum and other hydrocarbons, a special law shall determine the manner in which exploitation of these and similar products is to be undertaken.

"4. As a consequence of the foregoing declarations, the State reserves the right to establish the boundaries of zones for the control and protection of natural resources in the continental and insular seas that are under the control of the Government of Honduras and to change such boundaries according to circumstances that may arise by reason of new discoveries, studies, and national interests that may occur in the future.

"5. The present declaration of sovereignty does not ignore similar legitimate rights of other States on a basis of reciprocity, nor does it affect the rights of free navigation by all nations, in accordance with international law."

• *Nicaragua*, by means of Executive Decree I-L of 1965, claimed a 200-mile area establishing a "national fishing zone":

"Article 1. In conformity with Article 5 of the Constitution, in order to promote the better conservation and rational exploitation of Nicaragua's fishing and other resources, the waters lying between the coast and a line drawn parallel to it at a distance of 200 nautical miles seaward, both in the Atlantic and in the Pacific oceans, shall be designated a 'national fishing zone.'

"Article 2. Any fishing activity carried on within the 'national fishing zone' shall be subject to the provisions of the General Act on the Exploitation of the Natural Wealth, the legislation supplementing it, and legislation which may be adopted in the future."

The General Act referred to by this provision is Legislative Decree 316 of March 12, 1958, published in the *Official Gazette* of April 17, 1958, which established "the basic conditions for the exploration and exploitation of the natural resources which are the property of the State." Fishing activities were regulated by the Special Law of January 20, 1961.

The wording of the laws mentioned creates the impression that Nicaragua extended national sovereignty over a 200-mile area. However, the Constitution — which is invoked by the law of 1965 establishing the national fishing zone — only considers as a part of the national territory the territorial sea, the continental shelf, and the continental terrace, providing furthermore that those limits still undetermined shall be fixed by treaties or by the law. The general law on the exploitation of natural resources enacted in 1958, again mentioned in the law of 1965, did not fix the limits of the territorial sea *stricto juris* but only regulated such exploitation and the fishing activities in the "national fishing zone," and should be characterized accordingly as the exercise of a special jurisdiction.

This situation is further confirmed by the fact that Nicaragua voted in favor of the Declaration of Santo Domingo in 1972 which embraced the concept of a patrimonial sea and clearly provided that the State can exercise sovereign rights over a territorial sea of twelve miles. Nicaragua did not abstain as did El Salvador and Panama which claim a territorial sea of 200 miles.

• *Costa Rica.* By means of Decree 2204 of the Ministry of Foreign Affairs of February 1972, Costa Rica enlarged its territorial sea to twelve miles, to safeguard for its nationals an exclusive fishing zone and the exploitation of the resources of the sea. A further decree of the same date established a special jurisdiction over the seas adjacent to the territory, to "protect, conserve, and exploit" the resources; this area is called the patrimonial sea and its breadth was fixed at 200 miles. The situation is somewhat similar to the one of Nicaragua, although the legislation of Costa Rica clearly refers to a special jurisdiction.

In accordance with this legislation, foreign fishermen will be admitted to the area of the patrimonial sea under the conditions which will be established by special legislation. The jurisdiction of Costa Rica does not affect in any other way the regime of the high seas in the area, nor does it affect the rights which other nations may have in accordance with treaties on conservation and exploitation of species.

THE ISLANDS OF THE CARIBBEAN

In addition to the independent States of the Caribbean — Barbados, Cuba, Dominican Republic, Jamaica, Haiti, Trinidad and Tobago — three European nations — France, the Netherlands, and the United Kingdom — still exercise sovereignty over portions of this area. Furthermore, the United States, Colombia, Venezuela, and Guyana are also present in the region. For the purpose of this study, the concept of the Caribbean subregion must be limited to those islands which are independent States but without necessarily ignoring the countries mentioned above. In contrast to the Central American region, the policy of the Caribbean States with regard to the law of the sea is more homogeneous: the breadth of the territorial sea varies only between three and a maximum of twelve miles and special kinds of jurisdiction do not extend beyond fifteen miles. The policy of the continental countries of the area is also compatible with that of the island States. Colombia and Venezuela have a twelve-mile territorial sea, while Guyana and the United States have traditionally followed the three-mile rule, although the United States has recently moved in the direction of preparing legislative action in favor of twelve miles.[10] Therefore, a homogeneous policy in this area is more feasible.

THE TERRITORIAL SEA

Only Cuba and Barbados follow the three-mile rule. Cuba enacted this breadth by means of Decree-Law 704 of March 28, 1936, which also provided for exclusive fishing rights in this area. However, special kinds of jurisdiction have also been proclaimed over larger distances: ten miles for fisheries conservation, twelve miles for customs, five miles for sanitary matters and pollution. In the case of Barbados the rule has been inherited from the United Kingdom.

Haiti and the Dominican Republic have proclaimed a breadth of six miles. Haiti bases its position on that adopted by the *Institut de Droit International* in 1894 and by the International Law Association, which it confirmed upon signing and approving the Geneva Convention on the Territorial Sea. The Dominican Republic, by Law 3342 of July 1952, had originally fixed a three-mile territorial sea; however, Law 186 of September 13, 1967, enlarged this breadth to six miles.

The Dominican Republic, as is the case of the Central American countries, incorporated into its 1966 Constitution the claims of sovereignty over certain maritime areas, in the following manner:

"The corresponding territorial sea and the submarine surface and subsoil, as well as the air space above them, are also parts of the national territory. The extent of the territorial sea, of the air space, and of the contiguous zone and its defense, as well as of the submarine surface and subsoil, and the utilization thereof... shall be fixed and regulated by law."

In addition to the territorial sea, the 1967 legislation established a *supplementary zone contiguous to the territorial sea* of six miles, over which the State exercises the powers of jurisdiction and control necessary to prevent the infringement of its sanitary, fiscal, and customs laws, as well as to protect and conserve fishing and other natural resources. This jurisdiction will be examined further below.

Trinidad and Tobago and Jamaica have a twelve-mile territorial sea — the former by Act No. 38 of 1969 and the latter by the Territorial Sea Act No. 14 of July 19, 1971. Earlier both countries had followed the three-mile rule; both are parties to the Geneva Convention on the Territorial Sea. Exclusive fishing rights are also exercised within the twelve-mile area.

THE CONTINENTAL SHELF

Every country of the region has claimed sovereignty over the continental shelf, either by being a party to the Geneva Convention of 1958 or by unilateral legislation. Barbados is a party to the Convention, the United Kingdom's ratification having been applied to Barbados and considered to be still in force; in 1968 it enacted the Petroleum Act No. 1950. Cuba claimed sovereignty over the shelf by Presidential Decree 952 of April 30, 1954. The Dominican Republic is also a party to the Convention since August 11, 1964, and has special legislation regulating the rights over the area: the Mining Code approved by Law 4550 of October 13, 1956 and Law 186 of September 13, 1967.

The rights of Jamaica over the continental shelf were proclaimed by Order in Council No. 2575 of November 26, 1948 — Alteration of Boundaries. This order did not define the area subject to sovereignty; however, Jamaica acceded to the Geneva Convention on October 8, 1965, and is, therefore, now bound by the definition of Article 1.

Trinidad and Tobago also became a party to the Convention on July 11, 1968. However, its national legislation has not followed the depth criteria but proclaims rights to a distance of 200 miles. The boundary of the submarine areas between Trinidad and Venezuela in the Gulf of Paria were established by the Treaty of February 26, 1942.

SPECIAL JURISDICTION

In general, the countries of the region have not proclaimed special jurisdiction over distances different from the breadth of the territorial sea except for the rights over the continental shelf. Only Cuba and the Dominican Republic have proclaimed such special zones.

The Cuban Decree-Law 1948 of January 25, 1955, mentions in its preamble the right of the coastal State to extend its maritime jurisdiction over areas of the high seas, to the extent required for "the protection and conservation of the resources of the sea." Article 2 of the decree provides:

"The Cuban State may take the legal, administrative, or technical measures for the protection and conservation of the marine resources of the areas of the high sea contiguous to the Cuban territorial sea."

As previously mentioned, Cuba has also proclaimed, since 1942, special jurisdiction for customs over twelve miles and, since 1936, for sanitation and pollution over five miles.

The Dominican Republic, by Law 3342 of July 13, 1952, and particularly by Law 186 of September 13, 1967, established a supplementary zone contiguous to the territorial sea of six miles, over which "the Dominican State shall exercise the powers of jurisdiction and control necessary for preventing contraventions of Dominican legislation governing public health, public revenue, customs, and the protection and conservation of fisheries and other natural resources of the sea" (Article 3) and further declared to be of national interest the conservation and sustained yield of the resources of the sea in the Silver and Navidad Banks. To

119

this end the special jurisdiction for exclusive fishing is extended six miles beyond the territorial sea, bringing the exclusive fishing rights to a total of twelve miles.

THE PATRIMONIAL SEA: A REGIONAL CONSENSUS

The previous examination reveals that considering the area as a whole, there is some basis for a regional consensus. Except for El Salvador and Panama, which proclaim a 200-mile territorial sea, all the other countries have established a maximum breadth of twelve miles.

The countries having a territorial sea of not more than twelve miles also have in common the policy of exercising some special kinds of jurisdiction beyond the territorial sea; in the case of Central America this jurisdiction generally extends to 200 miles, while other countries, such as Colombia, Guatemala, Jamaica, Trinidad and Tobago, and Venezuela, have fixed shorter distances.

This distinction between the territorial sea and the zone adjacent to it, over which the coastal State exercises a special jurisdiction, particularly of an economic content, has given place to the appearance of the new concept of the patrimonial sea.[11]

The Delegation of Venezuela in the Committee on the Peaceful Uses of the Seabed and Ocean Floor Beyond the Limits of National Jurisdiction explained this concept in the Geneva Session of August 12, 1971, stating that a possible consensus for the 1973 Conference on the Law of the Sea could be based upon the following considerations:

(1) A territorial sea under the coastal State's exclusive sovereignty and jurisdiction, with a reasonable breadth of, say, twelve miles;

(2) An economic zone, called the patrimonial sea, not more than 200 miles in breadth from the baseline of the territorial sea. In that zone, there would be freedom of navigation and overflight but the coastal State would have an exclusive right to all resources.

The concept had already been subject to consideration and study by other countries, although mainly at the academic level. Since 1971 the idea has developed at the official level and has been the subject of diplomatic and academic discussions in a Caribbean regional framework.[12] As previously mentioned, Costa Rica is the first country to have introduced the concept at the legislative level. The countries of the region have also supported the concept in the Conference of Santo Domingo of June 1972, where the Declaration of Santo Domingo was adopted with the abstentions of El Salvador and Panama. It may be said, therefore, that a regional consensus is emerging.

References

1. See Manuel Noriega Morales, "El área del Caribe como un Nuevo Concepto de Integracion" (mimeo paper), Second Seminar on the Integration of Caribbean Countries,

Antigua, Guatemala, June 1971; Robert Hodgson, "The American Mediterranean, One Sea, One Ocean?" (mimeo paper), University of Rhode Island, Law of the Sea Institute, Gulf and Caribbean Workshop, Caracas, February 1972; Andres M. Aguilar, Address in the Opening Session of the Preparatory Committee of the Conference of the Caribbean Countries on the Problems of the Sea, Bogotá, February 1972.

2. G. L. Kesteves, "A Sketch for a Survey of Gulf and Caribbean Fisheries" (mimeo paper), University of Rhode Island, Law of the Sea Institute, Gulf and Caribbean Workshop, Caracas, February 1972. It must also be noted that the United States, Mexico, and Costa Rica have concluded agreements on fishing the Pacific Ocean; in the case of Central American States their principal fishing grounds are also located in the Pacific.

3. Decree No. 1386, January 24, 1944. See also F. V. García Amador, "La Jurisdicción Especial sobre las Pesquerías, Legislaciones Nacionales y Propuestas de los Gobiernos" (mimeo paper), Provisional Edition (Washington, D.C.: Pan American Union, 1972); and by the same author, "América Latina y el Derecho del Mar" (mimeo paper) (Washington, D.C., 1972).

4. *La Gaceta, Official Gazette* of July 29, 1948. See also, *Limits and Status of the Territorial Sea, Exclusive Fishing Zones, Fishery Conservation Zones and the Continental Shelf* (United Nations Doc. A/AC.138/50 [August 1971] with regard to the statement of the Ministry of Foreign Affairs concerning the extent of the claims.

5. *Official Gazette,* December 24, 1946.

6. On the fishing incidents which culminated in the severance of diplomatic relations between Mexico and Guatemala, see Francisco Villagrán Kramer, *Casos y Documentos de Derecho Internacional* (Guatemala: Editorial Pineda Ibarra), 1960.

7. "Alternatives to Fisheries Management," Working Paper (mimeo), University of Rhode Island, Law of the Sea Institute, Gulf and Caribbean Workshop, Caracas, February 1972, p. 1.

8. Robert D. Hayton, "Jurisdiction of the Littoral State in the Air Frontier," in *Philippine International Law Journal* (1964), pp. 369-398. The declarations of the countries attending the Montevideo and Lima meetings also provide additional background on this matter.

9. The United States, for example, has provided for the exercise of sanitary jurisdiction over three miles, but with regard to customs (Anti-Smuggling Act, United States Code, Vol. 19, pp. 1701-1711) the jurisdiction covers 100 nautical miles. The security zone established by the Declaration of Panama of 1939 was 300 miles, and the neutrality zone was 200 miles. Colombia has customs and sanitary jurisdiction over twenty kilometers (twelve miles). Customs, security, and sanitary jurisdiction of Venezuela is exercised over fifteen miles, although the territorial sea is only twelve miles. See Department of State, Bureau of Intelligence and Research, International Boundary Study, Series A, *Limits in the Seas: National Claims to Maritime Jurisdictions,* No. 36, (January 3, 1972).

10. In October 1972 the Department of State recommended to Congress the possibility of enlarging the breadth of the territorial sea from three to twelve miles, suggesting a study on the problems of fishing. Earlier, the United States and the Soviet Union prepared a common draft establishing a twelve-mile territorial sea to be submitted to the United Nations Conference on the Law of the Sea.

11. The Inter-American Juridical Committee examined the problem during its 1971 session. See also Reynaldo Galindo Pohl, "Consecuencias eventuales del nuevo regimen del mar en la zona del Caribe" (mimeo paper), University of Rhode Island, Law of the Sea Institute, Gulf and Caribbean Workshop, Caracas, February 1972. In this study Galindo Pohl considers the concept as a valuable element of the regional consensus and an eventual way of solving the difficult problems encountered by the countries which have established a 200-mile territorial sea.

12. Informal Consultative Meeting of the Ministers of Foreign Affairs of the Countries of the Caribbean Sea, Caracas, November 1971; and the subsequent meeting of the Preparatory Committee of the Conference of the Caribbean Countries on the Problems of the Sea, Bogotá, February 1972. The Conference met in the Dominican Republic in June 1972.

Chapter VI
Venezuela: The Country in the Caribbean

Chapter VI

VENEZUELA: THE COUNTRY IN THE CARIBBEAN

Isidro Morales Paul

INTRODUCTION

Several geographic factors have contributed to the maritime importance of Venezuela: the longest coastline (2,718 kilometers; 1,689 miles) on the Caribbean, numerous natural harbors, and a strategic location providing a link between North and South America. Maritime transportation and transnational economic activity in general are both facilitated and stimulated by these characteristics.

Venezuela also possesses a sizable continental shelf, rich in oil and other potential mineral resources. It has been estimated that the so-called "new areas," among the most important of which are the Gulfs of Venezuela and la Vela, the basins of Margarita and of Falcon, and the Orinoco delta, contain approximately 30,000 million cubic meters of oil.[1] Venezuelan coastal waters are also endowed with plentiful living resources largely due to the confluence of equatorial currents.[2]

The existence of these enormous resources has determined Venezuela's position in the contemporary debate on the law of the sea and, particularly, its support of the Latin American position on the so-called "patrimonial sea."

THE TERRITORIAL SEA

Historically, until 1956, Venezuela supported the traditional three-mile rule on the breadth of the territorial sea.[3] In 1956, however, the Law on the Territorial Sea, Continental Shelf, Protection of Fisheries and Air Space provided for a twelve-mile territorial sea:

"Article 1. The territorial sea of the Republic of Venezuela shall extend over the entire length of its continental and insular coasts to a width of twenty-two kilometers and 224 meters [twelve nautical miles], measured from the baselines referred to in Article 2 of this Act."

This breadth has since been embodied in the Constitution of 1961.

125

It is apparent, therefore, that Venezuela is one of the few Latin American countries to have maintained a fairly conservative position on the question of the breadth of the territorial sea. It is also one of the few Latin American countries to have ratified the four Geneva Conventions on the Law of the Sea of 1958, albeit with reservations. As far as the Convention on the Territorial Sea is concerned, Venezuela has made reservations to Article 12 and Article 24 (2) and (3).

Where the coasts of two States are opposite or adjacent to each other, Articles 12 and 24 (3) adopt the median line principle for the delimitation of the territorial sea and contiguous zone. The Convention permits an exception in the case of historic title or other special circumstances. Venezuela deemed it necessary to make a formal reservation to protect its historic title to the Gulf of Venezuela and the continental shelf adjacent to the island of Curaçao.

Article 24 (2) of the Convention provides that the contiguous zone may not extend beyond twelve miles from the baseline from which the breadth of the territorial sea is measured. That provision was incompatible with the 1956 Law on the Territorial Sea, Article 3 of which established a contiguous zone of three miles in addition to the twelve miles of territorial sea.

Foreign vessels are accorded the right of innocent passage through the Venezuelan territorial sea in accordance with Article 14 of the Geneva Convention. Although the coastal State may determine what constitutes innocent passage, in the case of straits used for the purpose of international navigation between two ports of the high seas, a special regime prevails. In this situation the coastal State has no right to prohibit passage in time of peace.

This regime applies to the two entrances of the Gulf of Paria, the Boca de Serpiente and the Boca de Dragon, which separate Trinidad from the eastern coast of Venezuela.

Venezuela has also entered into a number of bilateral agreements reciprocally granting freedom of navigation in both territorial and internal waters to vessels of several nations (Belgium, Germany, El Salvador, Spain).[4]

Finally, special mention should be made of an anomolous situation which has developed in regard to the territorial sea in the disputed area of Guyana. By Decree 1152 of July 9, 1968, Venezuela reserved its rights over the territorial sea in the area between the mouths of the Essequibo and the Guainía rivers but the decree, in error, refers to a three-mile instead of a twelve-mile breadth.

THE CONTIGUOUS ZONE

The Law on the Territorial Sea of July 23, 1956, is not entirely compatible with the relevant provisions of the Geneva Convention on the Territorial Sea and the Contiguous Zone. As set forth in Article 3 of the law, the stated purposes of the Venezuelan contiguous zone include not only the usual fiscal, sanitary, and police measures, but also the security of the nation and the protection of its interests.

"Article 3. For the purposes of maritime control and vigilance, to guard the security of the nation and to protect its interest, a contiguous zone of five kilometers and 556 meters [three nautical miles] shall be established."

It is clear that the latter provisions are broader than those contemplated by the Geneva Convention, and it will be recalled that the International Law Commission rejected the "security" component of the contiguous zone as being too open-ended and clearly subjective.

The Venezuelan law also departs from the Geneva Convention with respect to the limits of the contiguous zone. As already observed, Venezuela made a reservation to Article 24 (2) and (3) of the Convention which would have implicitly restricted the extension of its contiguous zone (and thereby its territorial sea) to a maximum of twelve miles. The Venezuelan law provides for a three-mile contiguous zone in addition to the twelve-mile territorial sea.

THE CONTINENTAL SHELF

The treaty of February 26, 1942, between Venezuela and the United Kingdom delimiting the submarine area in the Gulf of Paria, although it did not mention the "continental shelf," was the forerunner of the Truman Proclamation of 1945 and the genesis of an entirely new doctrine.

The Gulf of Paria is approximately seventy miles long and thirty miles wide. The treaty delimited the submarine areas, seabed, and subsoil of the Gulf proportionally, giving Venezuela approximately two-thirds of the total area. It should be emphasized that the 1942 treaty did not affect the legal status of the superjacent waters but was confined to the submarine areas of the Gulf.

In the wake of the Truman Proclamation and the rapid expansion of shelf claims by other Latin American States, Venezuela adopted a Constitutional amendment in 1953 by which it declared the authority and jurisdiction of the State over "the seabed and subsoil of the areas which constitute the continental shelf." The 1956 Law on the Territorial Sea fixed the outer limit of the shelf at the 200-meter isobath or beyond that limit to where the depth of the waters permits exploitation. The law also provided that:

"Channels, depressions, or irregularities in the seabed of the continental shelf shall not constitute a break in the continuity of the shelf; and banks which by position or natural conditions are related to the continental shelf shall be comprised therein."

Insofar as delimitation of the shelf with adjacent countries is concerned, Venezuela has consistently opposed the equidistance method on the ground that it is not a rule of conventional or customary international law. A declaration to this effect was made by Venezuela upon signing the Geneva Convention on the Continental Shelf and by appending a reservation to Article 6 of the Convention.

Venezuela's position is that the proper criterion for delimitation is whether the shelf area in question constitutes a natural prolongation of the territory of the coastal State. In the delimitation of the Gulf of Paria, the United Kingdom recognized the validity of the concept of the *continuity* of the continental shelf in relation to the coast, and on that basis agreed to grant two-thirds of the area to Venezuela. The continuity criterion must be supplemented, of course, by proportionality in the relationship between the length of the coast and the extension of the continental shelf.

These considerations of prolongation and proportionality, in the absence of any generally subscribed international agreement on delimitation, are particularly relevant in the case of the Gulf of Venezuela, concerning which bilateral negotiations with Colombia are presently taking place.

THE GULF OF VENEZUELA

No account of Venezuela and the contemporary problems of the law of the sea would be complete without some reference, however brief, to the problem of the Gulf of Venezuela. The Gulf, which separates the peninsulas of Paraguaná and La Guajira in the westernmost part of Venezuela, covers an area of 27,000 square kilometers (10,425 square miles) and links Lake Maracaibo to the sea.

The difficulties surrounding the delimitation of the Gulf stem historically from the boundaries established between Colombia and Venezuela following the breakup of the Grand Colombian Republic. The Constitutions of Colombia (1830) and Venezuela (1831) applied the *uti possidetis* principle with regard to the frontiers of the new States, accepting as the basis of delimitation the administrative division between the territories under Spanish rule in 1810.

In 1891, after a prolonged and frustrating series of negotiations, the parties submitted their differences to arbitration. A mixed Colombian/Venezuelan commission, established by the arbitral award for the purpose of drawing the demarcation lines in the disputed areas of the Gulf, finished its work in 1901; and in 1941 the two countries signed an agreement which recognized as definitive and irrevocable the work of the Commission. The limits embodied in this agreement awarded approximately six percent of the coast of the Gulf of Venezuela to Colombia.

Despite this agreement, Venezuela continued to claim the Gulf of Venezuela as historic waters over which the country had exercised sovereign rights in an uninterrupted fashion since 1830. Venezuela justifies its claim on the fact that it has exercised uninterrupted authority over the maritime space concerned, the attitude of third States toward this exercise of authority, and, finally, on the basis of economic necessity, national security, and vital interests. According to Venezuelan authorities, the Gulf of Venezuela meets all of the international legal requirements of historic waters. It will be recalled that in the *Anglo-Norwegian Fisheries Case,* the International Court of Justice defined "historic waters" as "waters which are treated as internal waters but which would not have the character were it not for the existence of an historic title."[5]

Quite apart from these claims, the delimitation of the waters adjacent to the undisputed portion of the Colombian coast of the Gulf must still be clarified. From this point of view, there appear to be two zones in dispute. Firstly, in the southernmost sector of Colombian waters, Colombia claims that its portion of the sea penetrates as far as the interior portion of Venezuelan waters. The Colombian position in this regard is that such a delimitation is merely an application of the median line or equidistance principle. The Venezuelan thesis, however, is that the line to be applied should be that which prolongs the land territory, for otherwise the delimitation claimed by Colombia would partially obstruct the entrance to the Gulf and consequently to Lake Maracaibo.

Secondly, Colombia argues that the archipelago of the Monjes Islands does not possess internal waters, territorial sea, or a continental shelf. Venezuela, on its part, claims that it is entitled to assert its right to the internal waters, territorial sea, and continental shelf of the Island of Monjes as a matter of right.

VENEZUELA AND THE PATRIMONIAL SEA

Venezuela's conventional posture on the territorial sea, both before and after the 1958 and 1960 Geneva Conferences, placed it in an ideal position, both regionally and internationally, to mediate compromisory concepts.

Venezuela participated in the 1970 Lima meeting, but did not sign the declaration which issued from it. In a statement appended to the Final Act, Venezuela reiterated its position that it could not accept any extension of the territorial sea which would in any way affect its rights to the free navigation on or enjoyment of the high seas adjacent to its territory.

At the Santo Domingo Conference in June 1972, however, Venezuela played a much more articulate role in the elaboration of the declaration. In this declaration, it will be recalled, the Caribbean countries adopted a text defining both the territorial sea and the patrimonial sea (see Chapters IV and V).

Venezuela's new role is confirmed by its recent initiative in the United Nations Seabed Committee. On April 2, 1973, together with Colombia and Mexico, Venezuela cosponsored a series of draft articles, including the territorial sea and the patrimonial sea. The territorial sea is defined in accordance with the terms of the Geneva Convention, and it is proposed that its breadth "shall not exceed twelve nautical miles to be measured from the applicable baselines."[6]

The patrimonial sea is defined as an area adjacent to the territorial sea in which the coastal State exercises sovereign rights "over the renewable and non-renewable natural resources which are found in the waters, in the seabed, and in the subsoil" thereof (Article 4). The outer limit of this patrimonial sea "shall not exceed 200 nautical miles from the applicable baselines for measuring the territorial sea" (Article 8). An important qualification of the legal characteristics of the patrimonial sea is provided by Article 9:

> "In the patrimonial sea, ships and aircraft of all States, whether coastal or not, shall enjoy the right of freedom of navigation and overflight with no restrictions other than those resulting from the exercise by the coastal State of its rights within the area."

The coastal State's "sovereign" rights in the patrimonial area is further qualified by the freedom to lay submarine cables and pipelines (Article 10).

The "sovereign" rights, in addition to those over the renewable and nonrenewable natural resources, include the right to adopt "the necessary measures to ensure its sovereignty over the resources and prevent marine pollution" (Article 5); the right to regulate scientific research (Article 6); and the right to authorize and regulate the emplacement and use of artificial islands and any kind of facilities on the surface of the sea "in the water column and on the seabed and subsoil of the patrimonial sea" (Article 7).

The tripartite draft articles also contain provisions concerning the continental shelf. Abandoning the definition contained in the Geneva Convention, draft Article 13 defines the continental shelf as:

> "(a) the seabed and subsoil of the submarine areas adjacent to the coast, but outside the area of the territorial sea, to the *outer limits of the continental rise* [emphasis added] bordering on the ocean basin or abyssal floor;

> "(b) the seabed and subsoil of analogous submarine regions adjacent to the coasts of islands."

The coastal State shall exercise sovereign rights over the continental shelf "for the purpose of exploring it and exploiting its natural resources" (Article 14).

In that part of the shelf covered by the patrimonial sea, the patrimonial regime shall apply; that part which is beyond the patrimonial area shall be favored by the applicable regime established by international law (Article 15).

With its increasingly articulate participation in regional forums, and by joining forces in the United Nations with two other important maritime nations — Colombia and Mexico — Venezuela has created for itself a specific role in the forthcoming Conference on the Law of the Sea.

References

1. Anibal R. Martinez, *Recursos de Hidrocarburos de Venezuela* (Caracas: Edreca Editores, 1972).

130

2. Levi Marrero, *Venezuela y sus recursos* (Madrid: Editorial Mediterráneo, 1963), p. 401.
3. This may be contrasted with Uruguay, for example, where the three-mile rule has never been applied (see Chapter VIII). The three-mile rule was embodied in Article 21 of the Civil Code of October 28, 1862, and incorporated in the decree of September 15, 1939, which established the territorial limits of Venezuela for the purpose of neutrality.
4. Belgium, Treaty of Friendship, Commerce, and Navigation of 1884, modified in 1940; Germany, Treaty of Commerce and Navigation of 1909; El Salvador, Treaty of Friendship, Commerce, and Navigation of 1883; Spain, Treaty of Commerce and Navigation of 1882.
5. International Court of Justice Reports, 1951, p. 130.
6. United Nations Doc. A/AC.138/SC.II/L.21, p. 1.

Chapter VII
Brazil

BRAZIL

Vicente Marotta Rangel

INTRODUCTION

Brazil occupies almost one half of the entire South American continent and is the fourth largest country in the world in terms of non-interrupted land surface.[1] For every 1.3 kilometers of land frontier, there is one kilometer of sea coast. The coastline has a length of 9,200 kilometers[2] divided into five regions going from north to south as follows: (1) Amazonian or equatorial coast, from the mouth of the Oiapoque River to the eastern Maranhão; (2) the northeast coast, sometimes known as the barrier coast, as far as Bahia; (3) the eastern coast to south of Espírito Santo; (4) the southeast coast, also known as the Crystal Clear Cliffs, as far as Laguna; and (5) the southern or subtropical coast as far as Chuí Creek.[3]

The navigability of the coastal waters facilitated the settlement of the coastal regions. Beginning in the sixteenth century settlements were established on the coast but rarely, if ever, inland. They were, as one writer has described them, "fixed like crabs to the sand." Brazilian territory was overwhelmed by the sea and the opening up of the interior – a complex and not always successful process of penetration – has continued to the present time.[4]

Because of the high incidence of coastal settlement, which took advantage of the economic, environmental, and sociological conditions provided by the sea, Brazil was quite correctly designated a peripheral country.

An understanding of the Brazilian nation is possible only if the Atlantic Ocean is taken into account. The Atlantic is the "great designer of the coastline of the country; the Brazilian islands are located in it; and most of the rivers of the country flow into it."[5] It may be said that Brazil's present characteristics and unity have been achieved due to the advantages provided by the sea as a natural waterway; otherwise it would hardly have survived.

> "For a long time the country was a kind of archipelago in which a few islands, organized around the main centers of population and production, existed in total isolation from one another because of the immense and impenetrable deserts, forests, and other geographical obstacles. The voyage from Rio de Janeiro to Bahia, Pernambuco, or the far north was only possible by sea ... although today it might seem incredible, the voyage to the Mato Grosso could only be done up the River Plate via Buenos Aires."[6]

This explains why "the centers of population, overwhelmed by the sea, communicated with one another more by sea than by land until only a few years ago."[7]

It was realized gradually that the sea was not only a vital element for the transportation of persons and goods, but was also a source of natural wealth. The concept of the adjacent sea as an integral element of the Brazilian patrimony, and its role with regard to the basic needs of the country, has been emphasized as one of the values prevailing in the current legislation. This concept has acquired special significance in the public eye due to such things as lobster fishing by foreign vessels on the Brazilian continental shelf; trawling by these vessels, which destroys both lobsters and shrimps; exploration of mineral nodules lying on the shelf; the depletion of fish stocks; and the employment of sophisticated techniques by foreign vessels, which create unfair competition for the poor and rudimentary vessels of the coastal population.

THE BREADTH OF THE BRAZILIAN
TERRITORIAL SEA IN HISTORICAL PERSPECTIVE

The physical characteristic of the sea — its continual motion — is reflected in the nature of the law of the sea at the present time. The changing law of the sea is especially uncertain with regard to the delimitation of the boundary between territorial and international waters. Keeping this in mind, it is possible to under-stand the successive criteria that Brazilian legislation has adopted in this matter, which to a certain extent has been influenced by the transformations taking place in customary international law and in the legislation of other countries, particularly those of Latin America.

The examination of the rules on the delimitation of adjacent maritime areas enacted in Brazilian laws reveals five successive periods since the political independence of the country.

The earliest period corresponds to the Portuguese legislation in force at the time of the independence of Brazil. This is the period of the cannon-shot rule, enacted in Lisbon by means of a decree-law of March 4, 1805.[8] Thus, Brazil acceded to independence with a rule different from that in force in other American countries which had gained independence from Spain or England and for whom the rule of six or three nautical miles prevailed, at least since independence.

The cannon-shot rule was mentioned in Instruction No. 92 of July 31, 1850, addressed by the Brazilian Ministry of War to the Presidents of the maritime provinces. In 1876, when the rule was still in force, a law was enacted which authorized the captains of vessels or customs police to visit and arrest those ships suspected of smuggling, up to a distance of twelve miles from the coast.[9] This was the same year in which Great Britain abrogated the *Hovering Acts,* enacted in the early eighteenth century.

The second period corresponds to the three-mile rule, which was first provided for by Instruction No. 43 of the Ministry of Foreign Affairs of August 25, 1914. The rule was first enacted for the purposes of neutrality in World War I. It remained in force, however, for over thirty-six years, although not always strictly interpreted. The instructions given to the Brazilian delegation to the 1930 Hague Conference for the Codification of International Law advocated the enlargement of the territorial sea so that the needs of administrative law would coincide with the provisions of international law, thereby ensuring that the limits of the jurisdiction of the State over its sea and territories be identical "whether it is a case of international relations or of the application of administrative regulations." As a result of these instructions, the delegation of Brazil moved in favor of a six-mile territorial sea and against the institution of a contiguous zone. Notwithstanding this position, two years later the government established a contiguous zone of twelve miles measured from the coast, which was also applied to fishing (Fishing Code approved by Decree No. 23.672·of January 2, 1934, and confirmed by Decree-Law No. 794 of October 19, 1938, which amended the Code). In 1941 the Second Meeting of Consultation of Ministers of Foreign Affairs established a twelve-mile security zone. This was strongly supported by Brazil.

When World War II came to an end, and the process of revision of the rules of the law of the sea started, the Government of Brazil declared that its continental shelf was an integral part of the national territory. This was provided for in Decree No. 26.840 of November 8, 1950, which followed similar declarations by the United States, Mexico, Chile, Argentina, and Peru. In accordance with this decree, the incorporation of the shelf was not intended to imply an enlargement of the territorial sea, which continued to be governed by the three-mile formula.

The three-mile rule was gradually undermined by principles which Brazilian lawyers supported in international meetings. The Principles of Mexico on the legal regime of the sea, approved in 1956 by the Inter-American Council of Jurists, not only declared that three miles was insufficient as the limit of the territorial sea and that it was no longer a general rule of international law, but also supported the right of each State to fix the breadth of its territorial sea within reasonable limits. In the Geneva Conferences on the Law of the Sea, the joint United States-Canadian proposal was supported. Finally, the Inter-American Juridical Committee recommended in 1965, with the support of its President Raul Fernandes, that every American State "has the right to fix the breadth of its territorial sea up to a limit of twelve nautical miles measured from the applicable baseline."

A year later with the enactment of Decree-Law No. 44 of November 18, 1966, the period of a six-mile territorial sea was inaugurated. This decree also established an additional contiguous zone of six miles, for the purposes of customs, fiscal, sanitary, and immigration matters, but over which Brazil had "the same rights of fishing and exploration of the living resources of the sea" enjoyed in the territorial sea.

This period did not last long, for Decree-Law No. 553 of April 25, 1969, enlarged the territorial sea "to a belt of twelve nautical miles breadth, measured from the low-water line."

The twelve-mile period was even shorter. Less than a year later Decree-Law No. 1.098 of March 25, 1970, approved by Congress by means of legislative Decree No. 31 of May 27, 1970, proclaimed a 200-mile territorial sea. Brazil thus ceased to be the only country south of the equator which had not enacted a 200-mile maritime jurisdiction. This distance had been used three decades earlier by the Declaration of Panama with regard to hemispheric security, and twenty years earlier by the proclamations of Chile and Peru. Argentina, in 1967, and Uruguay, in 1969, had also adopted this limit.

THE BREADTH OF THE TERRITORIAL SEA
AND THE GENEVA CONVENTIONS

The recent evolution of Brazilian legislation on the territorial sea can only be understood if the Brazilian position with regard to the 1958 Geneva Conventions is taken into account.

In an article written shortly after the Geneva Conference, Hildebrando Accioly, who at that time served as legal consultant to the Ministry of Foreign Affairs, expressed surprise at the fact that some States had advocated an enlargement of the territorial sea beyond twelve miles, "because the ordinary limit of that maritime belt is still fixed at three miles in a majority of cases."[10] At that time, the three-mile rule was still in force in Brazil, and the government was willing to maintain it; it was not until 1966 that it was replaced by a six-mile rule. In a book published in 1964, when the three-mile rule was still in force, the present writer concluded that no territorial sea could be less than three or more than twelve miles, a principle which prevailed in the Geneva Conventions of 1958:

> "It is possible to conclude, therefore, that in accordance with these conventions it is lawful for a State to fix the breadth of its territorial sea within those limits. Hence, it also follows that if a State adopts a breadth short of twelve miles, it is lawful for it to establish a contiguous zone up to that limit, not necessarily restricted *rationale materiae* to Article 24 of the Convention on the Territorial Sea and the Contiguous Zone but also including other matters which are the result of the exercise of sovereignty, including those related to fishing."[11]

This explains the compatibility between the contiguous zone established in Brazilian legislation and that established by the Convention.

A fundamental issue of the Brazilian position on the law of the sea was the decision whether or not to sign the Geneva Conventions, particularly on the Territorial Sea and the Contiguous Zone. In 1968, two years after the Brazilian Legislature had established a six-mile territorial sea and a contiguous zone of six additional miles, the Executive introduced in Congress the four Geneva Conventions. The draft legislative-decree then prepared authorized the President of the Republic to order the accession of the government to those conventions, but with the following reservation: "The accession to the Convention on the Territorial Sea and the Contiguous Zone may only be ordered after a law will have extended the territorial sea of Brazil to twelve miles, eliminating the contiguous zone." As a matter of fact, this limit was adopted shortly thereafter, by means of Decree-Law No. 553 of April 25, 1969.

Notwithstanding this authorization, the Government of Brazil, taking into account the opinion of congressmen, officials, and others,[12] decided not to accede to the Geneva Conventions and in 1970 adopted the 200-mile territorial sea. The latter decision was legally feasible since Brazil was not bound by any treaty establishing an obligation to restrict its maritime territory to a shorter distance, nor was there in existence any rule of customary international law limiting its powers in this matter. Furthermore, a satisfactory legal base is in the process of crystallization in order to freely allow the adoption of this system by developing countries, taking into account the influence of geographical, economic, political, and biological factors.

THE BASES OF THE LEGISLATION IN FORCE

One of the criteria of Decree-Law No. 1.098 of March 25, 1970, reiterates section A-2 of Resolution XIII of the Third Meeting of the Inter-American Council of Jurists, held in Mexico in 1956, which declares that "Each State is competent to establish its territorial waters within reasonable limits, taking into account geographical, geological, and biological factors, as well as the economic needs of its population, and its security and defense." Another criterion further states that "the special interest of the coastal State in the preservation of the productivity of the living resources of the maritime areas adjacent to its coast is recognized by international law." The concern for productivity was a basic consideration in the decision which established a 200-mile territorial sea.

The need to protect the natural resources of the adjacent sea — a fact which was emphasized constantly — came to be of great importance as a result of the increasing exploitation of these resources by foreign vessels, and the discrepancy existing between their technology and the elementary technology of Brazilian vessels. The case of the numerous factory ships which fished twenty miles offshore, depleting the large stocks of the South Atlantic, is well known. As Paulo Irineu Roxo de Freitas puts it:

> "The devastation provoked by foreign fishing fleets in certain regions of the coast of Africa has already caused the extinction of ichthyological species, similarly to what had happened on the coasts of Peru and Ecuador and to what still happens on the coasts of Brazil. The shrimp of the southern and northern coasts, the lobsters (already notoriously decreased), the haddock and tuna of the coasts of the Northeast and East, the sardine, cod, anchovy, and other species of the southern coast, will certainly disappear as fish of industrial utilization if the intensive fishing of foreign fleets continues for some years, particularly in view of the hundreds of ships employed, the kind of fishing and nets used with no control, and the activity of factory ships which process and can their catch and transport it directly to their countries of origin."[13]

The government understood that a twelve-mile territorial sea, even if supplemented by fishing agreements, "could hardly lead to the modification of this negative outlook."[14]

Another element which influenced the acceptance of the 200-mile policy was the need to avoid a situation of isolating Brazil from its neighbors of the South Atlantic, which would have made it difficult to negotiate certain relevant problems, such as those of fishing, on a reciprocal basis. Strengthening the link of regional solidarity with other Latin American countries was considered to be of utmost importance. In order to avoid problems, it was argued that there should be no differences with the breadth fixed by Uruguay and Argentina "with the former, in fixing the lateral maritime limit, and with the latter in ratifying the agreement on fisheries which had been provisionally signed at the time that Argentina enlarged its territorial sea."[15]

The decision to adopt a 200-mile territorial sea was also influenced by strategic considerations, naturally related to the enlargement of the territorial ambit needed for the exercise of national security. From this point of view, the fact that both the Declaration of Panama of 1939 and the Inter-American Treaty of Reciprocal Assistance established a security zone, which to a certain extent corresponds to a 200-mile breadth, was duly taken into account.

Lastly, the importance of protecting the continental shelf and its natural resources was also taken into consideration.

In accordance with Decree-Law No. 1.098, national sovereignty is exercised over the territorial sea, the seabed and subsoil thereof, and the airspace above it. Ships of all nations enjoy the right of innocent passage through the territorial

140

sea. Innocent passage is defined as "the mere transit through the territorial sea, without exercising any activity unrelated to navigation and not stopping for purposes other than the needs of such navigation." In the territorial sea "all ships must observe the Brazilian regulations enacted to guarantee peace, public order, and security, and to avoid the pollution of waters and damage to the resources of the sea." This decree also provides for the preparation of bylaws on security matters, to be observed by foreign ships of war and other State ships. A prior decree of June 28, 1965, approved "the rules for the visit of foreign warships to the ports and territorial waters of Brazil in time of peace"; these visits can be official, non-official, and operational, each one having particular rules.

The fact that the 200-mile zone established by Decree No. 1.098 properly constitutes a territorial sea is beyond doubt, not only because it is expressly provided but also because the nature of the powers exercised by the coastal State over it correspond to that of the territorial sea as generally understood.

LANDWARD AND LATERAL DELIMITATION OF THE TERRITORIAL SEA

Decree-Law No. 1.098 provides that the territorial sea is measured "from the low-water line of the Brazilian continental and insular coasts which is adopted as reference in the Brazilian nautical charts." However, straight baselines shall be drawn "in those locations where the coastline is deeply cut into or where there is a fringe of islands along the coast and in its immediate vicinity" (Article 1, sole paragraph).

Both methods have been adopted by Brazilian legislation for many years, the former being the general rule. The regulations of the Department of Fishing and Coastal Sanitation, approved by Decree No. 16.183 of October 25, 1923, provided that the three-mile distance would be measured "seaward from the straight baselines that join the coastal points not more than ten miles distant from one another" (Article 2, sole paragraph). Section one of Article 17 of the Regulations on Maritime Transit, approved by Decree No. 5.798 of June 11, 1940, also provided that: "In those locations in which the coast, including the coasts of islands, is deeply cut into bays, shelters, etc., the three-mile belt of territorial waters shall be measured from the line joining the closest opposite points of the coast indenture which is twelve miles or less in distance." Decree-Law No. 553, which enlarged the territorial sea to twelve miles, changed the distance mentioned to that of "twenty-four miles or less," but this provision has been abrogated. The new law does not mention any particular distance to this effect.

With regard to the lateral limit between the territorial seas of Brazil and Uruguay, the Joint Declaration on the Limit of Maritime Jurisdiction, issued in Rio de Janeiro on May 10, 1969, refers to the median line, every point of which is equidistant from the closest points of the baseline, and which, beginning at the point where the boundary between both countries reaches the Atlantic Ocean, extends toward the zones of the adjacent sea.

THE CONTINENTAL SHELF

Referring to the continental shelf in the South Atlantic, Antônio Rocha Penteado comments that its extension is "far shorter than the general average of the oceans (ninety kilometers); it is very narrow in the African coasts, and in the South American region its broadest extension is to be found on the northern coast, between the Suriná and Maranhão rivers, and in the zone which extends south of Bahia to Patagônia. In the latter region it has an increasing extension following a northwest direction in the area known as Golfo de Santos or Santa Catarina, reaching its widest area on the Argentinian coast between Bahía Blanca and Terra del Fuego."[16]

João Dias da Silveira comments that the Brazilian continental shelf is variable:

"The continental shelf has a significant breadth in the equatorial region ... between Cape North and Punta de Mangoari it is still broader extending more than 300 kilometers. From there the shelf decreases towards the West; in the delta of the Parnaíba River it is 170 kilometers, in the coast of Ceara it is fifty kilometers or less, and in Cape São Roque it is very narrow. From there to the South of Bahia the shelf is very narrow, not exceeding thirty kilometers. To the South of Bahia and on the coast of Espíritu Santo the shelf again has a significant breadth, although it also has irregularities. Off Caravelas and São Mateo it is more than 200 kilometers wide. After new irregularities and decreasing in the *fluminense* coast, it again broadens: 103 kilometers at Itapemirim, 100 kilometers at São Tomé, 129 kilometers in the region of Isla Grande, 120 kilometers at Ubatuba, 132 kilometers at Punta del Buey, 163 kilometers at the mouth of the Icaparra River, 105 at Laguna, 84 kilometers at Cape Santa Marta, 180 kilometers at the mouth of Rio Grande and 160 at the mouth of Chuí Creek."[17]

Decree No. 26.840 of November 8, 1950, contained the first provisions on the Brazilian continental shelf. This decree followed similar proclamations by the United States, Mexico, Chile, Argentina, and Peru. As provided by this decree, the continental shelf of Brazilian continental and insular territory was "integrated to this territory, under the exclusive jurisdiction and dominium of the Federal Union." The Federal Constitution of January 24, 1967, also provided that the continental shelf be included in the property of the Union.

142

In accordance with this decree, "the exploration and exploitation of the natural wealth and resources" found in the continental shelf, is subject to the authorization or concession by the Federal Executive. "The rules on navigation through the waters overlying the shelf... without prejudice to those which are enacted, particularly with regard to fishing in the region" remained in force. Although the decree was in harmony with the Truman Proclamation of 1945, the latter provision on fishing implies – as Barry B. L. Auguste observes[18] – "a connection or relationship between the shelf and the superjacent waters." As a matter of fact, this relationship later came to be one of the prevailing reasons which led to the enlargement of the Brazilian territorial sea to 200 miles.

The fact that the decree was enacted eight years before the Geneva Convention on the Continental Shelf meant that the studies and reports subsequently carried out by the United Nations had no influence on it.[19] The interest of the government and of public opinion was concentrated on the need to preserve the natural resources of the shelf and to reserve its exploitation by the coastal State. It is estimated that the potential oil area is about four million square kilometers (one and one-half million square miles) in size, some wells already being exploited, as in Guaricema, Dourados, Carmópolis, and Caioba. It is also estimated that between 1971 and 1974, 132 wells of maritime exploitation will be drilled.[20] Of 800,000 square kilometers (about 308,880 square miles) of shelf, some 100,000 square kilometers (38,610 square miles) constitute an area of oil deposits of the highest yield.[21]

Since the whole of the Brazilian shelf is comprised within the 200-mile territorial sea, the country has no continental shelf in the legal meaning given to it by the Geneva Convention because this definition is only applicable to the submarine area outside the territorial sea.

THE FISHING ZONES
IN THE BRAZILIAN TERRITORIAL SEA

Decree No. 1.098 provided that the government would regulate fishing for three purposes: (1) the rational exploitation of the living resources of the sea; (2) the conservation of those resources; and (3) promotion of research and exploration. This decree establishes two zones in the territorial sea, according to whether or not they are exclusively reserved to Brazilian vessels. The outer zone is open to fishing by both national and foreign vessels, although the latter can carry on their activities only if they are duly registered and authorized, and always on condition that they observe the respective regulations.

Such regulations were established by Decree No. 68.459 of April 1, 1971, which among other objectives delimited with a greater precision the fishing zones of the territorial sea. The first zone comprises an area of 100 nautical miles, measured "from the low-water line of the Brazilian continental and insular coasts, adopted as a reference in the Brazilian nautical charts." The second zone extends beyond this limit to the 200-mile line. Fishing in the first zone is reserved, in general, to national vessels; foreign vessels can only fish in it when they have been leased to Brazilian legal entities. In the second zone, both national and foreign vessels can undertake fishing activities.

Notwithstanding this, the regulations provide for what could be called a third zone, in which the participation of foreign vessels is prohibited. This zone is not related to the waters of the sea but to the seabed of the territorial sea: "the exploitation of crustaceous and other living resources, which have a close relationship of dependency with the floor underlying the Brazilian territorial sea" is reserved to national fishing vessels, as provided by Article 1, No. 3, of these regulations.

CONCEPT AND NATIONALITY OF FISHING VESSELS

One basic concern of these regulations was to establish the concept of a fishing vessel. This has been defined as a vessel which is "exclusively and permanently dedicated to the catch, transformation, or research of the animal or vegetable beings which have in the waters or in the bed of the sea their natural or most frequent living environment." The definition is related not only to the activity of ships, but also to the fact that they are "registered and authorized" in the manner provided by the legislation in force (Regulations of Decree No. 68.459 of April 1, 1971, Article 2).

For the application of the decree regulating the 200-mile area, it is important to ask what are the conditions required by a fishing vessel to be considered Brazilian.

The Federal Constitution of 1946 provided that those vessels of which the owners, shippers, captains, and two-thirds of its crew were Brazilian born would be considered Brazilian vessels. The transportation of goods within Brazil was reserved to Brazilian ships, except in the case of public necessity (Article 155). An identical provision was contained in Article 15 of the Federal Constitution of January 24, 1967.

The Constitution in force introduced a new criterion in this matter — original Brazilian nationality no longer being required for national fishing vessels — subject to the regulations of Federal Law (Article 173, No. 2). To be considered a Brazilian fishing vessel, therefore, it is not necessary to meet the same conditions required for other kinds of ships. Decree-Law No. 221 of February 28, 1967, provides that "the registration of ownership of fishing vessels shall be granted by the Maritime Tribunal only to Brazilians by birth or naturalization or to corporations registered in the country" (Article 8). This provision conflicted with the Constitution of 1967, as admitted by the General Consultant of the Republic, Adroaldo Mesquita da Costa[22]; it was also subject to congressional criticism, from an economic and political point of view, as witnessed by the declarations of Senator Vasconcelos Torres in the Senate session of March 21, 1968.[23] Since the reasons underlying this provision have been recognized as valid, the regulations on the territorial sea refer to it expressly; and it is compatible with the Constitution in force.

In accordance with the fishing regulations of April 1, 1971, foreign fishing vessels are considered national vessels when leased to Brazilian legal entities with headquarters in the country. Leasing authorizations are granted by the Ministry of Agriculture for a period of up to one year, which can be extended. The situation and needs of the national construction of fishing vessels must be taken into account when granting an extension of leases. If an extension is not granted, the foreign vessel can operate only if it changes its registry to a Brazilian registration. However, vessels which are more than five years old, as shown by the date of their registration, are not allowed to have their nationality changed.

Foreign vessels not leased to Brazilian legal entities can operate only in the outer zone of the territorial sea. The pertinent permits are granted by the Ministry of Agriculture, in consultation with the Ministry of the Navy. The applications must be presented through a Brazilian legal entity which undertakes the legal and financial responsibility for the activities of the foreign vessel. Once the authorization has been granted, a registration fee of five hundred dollars and an operational fee of twenty dollars per deadweight ton of registry must be paid.

The captains of foreign vessels must know and observe the Brazilian laws and regulations, particularly those relating to fishing and the prevention of marine pollution. They are also under an obligation to notify the Ministry of the Navy about the date and hour of entry and exit of the Brazilian territorial sea. Official charts must be utilized and observed.

To transfer fish from one vessel to another in the territorial sea, and to disembark the catch of foreign ships in national ports, is subject to prior authorization by the Brazilian Government.

With regard to the fishing regulations, Dorival Teixeira Vieira comments:

> "... the fact that foreign vessels equipped with the most recent technological developments, including factory ships, operated near the Brazilian coast, and made fantastic catches of fish, contributed to a possible depletion of stocks. The registration and operational fees charged to foreign ships are not intended to provide the treasury with a higher income, but only that a part of the costs of supervision which are indispensible for the proper observance of the laws, be borne by the foreign fishermen. Furthermore, the registration of ships compels the captains and shippers to get acquainted with the laws and regulations related to their activities."

Among the short and long term objectives of the new law, the following is emphasized: "... to permit the conservation of the natural resources and the maintenance of the indispensable ecological balance of the maritime flora and fauna."[24]

If a foreign vessel exploits the living resources of the territorial sea without the authorization of the government, or in violation of the conditions of the authorization, authorities may order its attachment, as well as that of its equipment and cargo. The captain will also be responsible for infringement of the penal legislation in force (Article 11, No. 5).

INTERNATIONAL AGREEMENTS

Brazilian law has been supplemented by several treaties on the law of the sea. In particular, the following deserve mentioning: the Convention for the protection of submarine cables of 1884, the Convention for the unification of certain rules on the immunity of State ships of 1936, the Convention for the regulation of whale fishing of 1950, and the nuclear test ban treaty of 1963.

As was explained in detail above, Brazil has not signed or acceded to any of the 1958 Geneva Conventions on the Law of the Sea.

Decree-Law No. 1.098 of 1970 provides that by means of international agreements, special regimes of fishing, research, and exploration in the Brazilian territorial sea may be defined. In application of this provision, bilateral fishing agreements were concluded on August 4, 1971, with Trinidad and Tobago, and on August 19, 1971, with the Netherlands.[25] Other agreements were signed with the United States on May 9, 1972,[26] and again with Trinidad and Tobago on May 19, 1972; these agreements will be in force until January 1, 1974.

Among other matters, these agreements regulate the ichthyological species which may be fished; the number, capacity, and identification of vessels; the amounts due to the Brazilian Government as economic compensation and other reasons; the delimitation of the zones of the territorial sea covered by the agreement; and the period during which fishing may be undertaken. This is significant proof of how it is possible for governments to reconcile their interests in basic matters related to the exploitation of the biological resources of the sea, in spite of their different approaches to the question of the breadth of their maritime areas.

References

1. The country has an extension of 8,513,844 square kilometers (3,287,200 square miles) of noninterrupted lands. For an introduction to the human and physical characteristics of Brazil, see Pierre Deffontaines, *Geografia Humana do Brasil,* 2nd ed. (Rio: Livraria Editôra da Casa do Estudante do Brasil, 1952); C. Delgado de Carvalho, *Geografia do Brasil,* 9th ed. (Rio: Francisco Alves, 1938); Aroldo de Azevedo, "O 'Continente' Brasileiro," in *Brasil, a terra e o homen,* Vol. I (São Paulo: Companhia Editôra Nacional, 1964).

2. If bays and gulfs are not taken into account, the coast is approximately 7,198 kilometers (4,473 miles) in length. Moacier M. F. da Silva, *Geografia dos Transportes no Brasil* (IBGE, Biblioteca Geográfica Brasileira, 1949).
3. João Dias da Silveira, "Morfologia do Litoral," in *Brasil, a terra e o homen,* loc. cit., note 1 above, pp. 271 ff.
4. See Pasquale Petrone, "Povamento e Colonizacão," in *Brasil, a terra e o homen,* loc. cit., note 1 above, Vol. II (1970), pp. 127 ff.
5. Antônio Rocha Penteado, "O Atlântico Sul," in *Brasil, a terra e o homen,* loc. cit., note 1 above, Vol. I, pp. 307-309.
6. Senator Vasconcelos Torres, "Address in the Senate," in *Mar Territorial,* Vol. II (Ministry of the Navy, 1972), p. 689. Ney Rodrigues Innocencio expresses the view that "With regard to the conditions of transit along the coast, only the *Abrolhos* and *Canal de São Roque* can be considered geographical accidents capable of representing some problem," in *Atlas Nacional do Brasil* (IBGE, 1965), p. 27.
7. Antônio Rocha Penteado, "O Homen Brasileiro e o Meio," in *Brasil, a terra e o homen,* loc. cit., note 1 above, Vol. II, p. 22.
8. Eduardo H. Serra Brandão, "Aguas Jurisdicionais Portuguesas," in *Estudios de Derecho Internacional Maritimo* (Madrid, 1968), p. 79.
9. Hildebrando Accioly, "La Zone Contigue et le Droit de Poursuite en Haute Mer," in *Mélanges Gidel* (1961), p. 7.
10. Ibid., p. 1.
11. Vicente Marotta Rangel, *Natureza Jurídica e Delimitacão do Mar Territorial,* 2nd ed. (São Paulo, Editôra Revista dos Tribunais, 1970), pp. 227-228 (author's translation).
12. Among the draft laws introduced in favor of the 200-mile rule, the following may be mentioned: Draft No. 527 of 1967, by Representative Aroldo de Carvalho, and Draft No. 96 of 1968 by Senator Lino de Matos. In Draft No. 560 of 1967, introduced by Representative Flores Soares, a 100-mile territorial sea and a contiguous zone of 100 miles were proposed. The Brazilian Democratic Movement, one of the parties of the opposition, constantly came out in favor of a 200-mile territorial sea. See Nelson Carneiro, "Parecer do Relator da Comissão de Constituição e Justiça," in *Mar Territorial,* loc. cit., note 6 above, Vol. II, pp. 801 ff.
13. Paulo Irineu Roxo de Freitas, "Estudos sôbre a Ampliacão do Mar Territorial para Duzentas Milhas," in *Mar Territorial,* loc. cit., note 6 above, Vol. II, p. 524.
14. Carlos Calero Rodriguez, "O Problema do Mar Territorial," in *Mar Territorial,* loc. cit., note 6 above, Vol. I, p. 576.
15. Paulo Irineu Roxo de Freitas, "Estudos sôbre a Ampliacão do Mar Territorial para Duzentas Milhas," in *Mar Territorial,* loc. cit., note 6 above, Vol. II, p. 528.
16. Antônio Rocha Penteado, "O Atlântico Sul," in *Brasil, a terra e o homen,* loc. cit., note 1 above, Vol. I, p. 315.
17. João Dias da Silveira, "Morfologia do Litoral," in *Brasil, a terra e o homen,* loc. cit., note 1 above, Vol. I, p. 257.
18. Barry B. L. Auguste, *The Continental Shelf* (Geneva, 1960), p. 111.
19. Raymundo Nonnato L. de Castro, "Aspectos Fundamentais da Doutrina Brasileira sobre a Plataforma Continental," in *Boletim da Sociedade Brasileira de Direito Internacional,* No. 47-48 (1968), pp. 43-66. Also Celso de Albuquerque Mello, *Plataforma Continental* (Rio: Livraria Freitas Bastos, 1965); Raphael Valentino Sobrinho, "A Plataforma Continental," in *Revista Brasileira de Política Internacional,* No. 23 (1963); Gilda M. C. M. Russomano, "O Mar e o Direito," in *Boletim do Clube Naval,* No. 183 (1965); Vicente Marotta Rangel, "A quem pertence o Fundo do Mar," in *Problemas Brasileiros,* No. 44 (November, 1966), pp. 11-22.
20. Carlos Calero Rodriguez, "O Problema do Mar Territorial," in *Mar Territorial,* loc. cit., note 6 above, Vol. I., pp. 582-583.
21. Marco Maciel, "Mar de Duzentas Milhas e o Desenvolvimento Nacional," in *Mar Territorial,* loc. cit., note 6 above, Vol. II, p. 787.
22. *Official Gazette,* June 24, 1968.
23. *Mar Territorial e Marinha de Guerra* (Brasilia, 1970), pp. 219-222.

24. Dorival Teixeira Vieira, "Aspectos Econômicos do Mar de 200 Milhas," in *Problemas Brasileiros,* No. 92 (April 1971), pp. 17-18.
25. Texts of the agreement in *Mar Territorial,* loc. cit., note 6 above, Vol. I, pp. 337-343.
26. See agreement on the conservation of shrimp between Brazil and the United States, *International Legal Materials* (May 1972), pp. 453-467.

Chapter VIII
Uruguay

Chapter VIII

URUGUAY

Felipe H. Paolillo

INTRODUCTION

In recent years Uruguay's legislation and practice with regard to maritime sovereignty have undergone a remarkable and rapid evolution, culminating with the enactment of Law No. 13.833 in December 1969 which extended national sovereignty over a 200-mile wide maritime zone. This law had been preceded by an Executive Decree which claimed a 200-mile territorial sea. With these instruments Uruguay aligned itself with the group of States supporting a radical position, sometimes referred to as the "Latin American position," with regard to the breadth of the territorial sea. In addition to Uruguay, Argentina, Brazil, Chile, Costa Rica, Ecuador, Peru, Panama, El Salvador, and Nicaragua have asserted extensive claims of sovereignty or jurisdiction over the maritime domain.

This evolution has not been the result of an expansionist policy or of the search for narrow political advantage, but reflects the need to ensure a legal regulation of the rational exploitation of the oceans. Uruguay's destiny is closely linked to the sea, which serves as a means of communication, as a source of wealth, and as a strategic and political element. This link or dependence will certainly be increased in the future, particularly from an economic point of view. It is known that in the sea adjacent to the Uruguayan coast there is a considerable ichthyological wealth — the exploitation of which has only recently started — and there are also indications that oil and other mineral resources may be found in the subsoil. At the present time, however, Uruguay does not have the technological and financial means to undertake the exploitation of these immense natural resources although it has taken advantage of the legal instruments provided by international law in order to preserve what in law and in fact belongs to the country.

The present situation is a result of a continuing process of adaptation of municipal law to the changes which in recent years have taken place in the area of technology and in international politics and economics, but without contradicting in any way the principles and norms of international law. Disregarding the colonial legislation, which will be examined further below, one of the first cornerstones in this process is the decree of August 7, 1914, on rules of maritime neutrality. Article 2 of this decree provides that "waters up to the limit of five miles are considered territorial." Prior to this decree the Treaty of Montevideo on International Penal Law, to which Uruguay is a party, had established a five-mile limit for the purpose of criminal jurisdiction.

The 1960s witnessed a substantial escalation in the delimitation of the breadth of Uruguay's maritime territory; four different breadths were fixed during this period for the Uruguayan territorial sea:

(1) Until 1963 it remained five miles.

(2) The decree of February 21, 1963, following the trend which prevailed in the Geneva Conferences of 1958 and 1960 on the Law of the Sea:

- extended the territorial sea to six miles;

- declared that the area between six and twelve miles was a "contiguous zone" over which jurisdiction would be exercised for the prevention and punishment of violations of police, customs, fiscal, immigration, or sanitary laws committed in the national territory or territorial sea;

- declared that the national regulations on fishing and exploitation of the living resources of the territorial sea would also be in force within this zone.

(3) On May 16, 1969, Decree 235/69 doubled the breadth of the territorial sea, extending it to twelve miles. The contiguous zone was thereby eliminated (although Article 2 of the decree, which is superfluous, could lead to a different conclusion). In addition, exclusive rights for maritime fishing and hunting are proclaimed over the area between the outer limit of the territorial sea and the outer limit of the continental shelf (100 to 160 miles).

(4) Less than seven months after the previous decree had entered into force, the Executive Branch enacted Decree 604/969 of December 3, 1969, extending national sovereignty to a zone of 200 miles measured from the baselines. Shortly thereafter Law 13.833 came into force.

It is obvious from the foregoing that Uruguay never followed the three-mile rule. Indeed, since colonial times, this rule had been disavowed by the juridical order in force in the continent. As stated in a note of the Ministry of Foreign Affairs, delivered in reply to a *note verbale* of the Embassy of the United States expressing its disagreement in regard to the decree of February 21, 1963: ". . . as did all the former Spanish colonies, Uruguay became independent under the six-mile rule — two leagues — which was the Spanish regime as from the regulation of December 17, 1760."

This regulation was enacted by *Real Cédula* of the *Consejo de Hacienda* (reproduced in the *Novísima Recopilación* of the Laws of Spain of July 15,

1805), clarifying Article 11 of the Treaty of Utrecht, and established a limit of two marine leagues for the prevention of fiscal fraud. *The Real Orden* of May 1, 1775, also fixed the same limit with regard to the rules for the suppression of contraband.

Historically, then, the minimum breadth in force in Uruguay was five miles. As a consequence, in international forums, Uruguay was opposed to the restrictive approach of the great powers supporting the three-mile rule. In the Hague Conference of 1930 Uruguay supported the six-mile rule; and in the Geneva Conferences of 1958 and 1960 it accepted the compromise formula jointly proposed by the United States and Canada, that is, the "six-plus-six" formula.

The criteriological flexibility of the Uruguayan position has facilitated the adaptation of legislation to a changing reality which could not have been more volatile than in the law of the sea. This is why, when Uruguay accepted the "six-plus-six" formula, it clearly stated that it was on the understanding that this was a "minimum thesis." The head of the Uruguayan delegation to the second United Nations Conference on the Law of the Sea, Dr. Carlos M. Velasquez, stated in the general debate:

"... the discussions and voting at the first United Nations Conference on the Law of the Sea, and the statements and proposals at the present conference, leave no doubt that the majority of States now consider that the minimum breadth of the territorial sea cannot be less than six miles."

This being the official Uruguayan position, it has been repeatedly invoked.

In reply to the *note verbale* of the United States, referred to above, the view was expressed that:

"Such circumstances, as well as many others which are evidenced by the second Geneva Conference and numerous precedents of authors and international practice, prove beyond doubt that this widely accepted position is the minimum and as such is, precisely, one of the most important legal foundations of the Uruguayan decree of February 21, 1963."

In accordance with this position, Uruguay has always supported in the international sphere those initiatives which, within reasonable limits and in conformity with international law, have advanced wider limits of sovereignty or jurisdiction.

At the Second Meeting of the Consultation of Ministers of Foreign Affairs held in Havana in 1940, Uruguay supported the majority position with regard to a twelve-mile limit. In the Third Meeting of the Inter-American Council of Jurists held in Mexico in 1956, it again supported a twelve-mile limit as well as the following principle:

"Each State is competent to establish its territorial waters within reasonable limits, taking into account geographical, geological, and biological factors, as well as the economic needs of its population, and its security and defense."

It is interesting to note that in this meeting Uruguay proposed that it be declared an aspiration of the American nations to extend "... the maritime sovereignties of each country to a minimum distance of twenty-five miles from the respective coasts, as a definitive regime."

In May 1970 Uruguay sponsored a meeting in Montevideo of the 200-mile group of Latin American countries. Uruguay also attended the Lima meeting in August 1970, and actively participated in the drafting of the declarations approved in these two meetings which reiterate the right of States to fix, within certain limits, the breadth of the territorial sea.

The Declaration of Montevideo reaffirms as one of the basic principles of the law of the sea:

"The right [of States] to delimit their maritime sovereignty and jurisdiction in conformity with their own geographical and geological characteristics and consonant with factors that condition the existence of marine resources and the need for rational exploitation."

In Lima the same principle was defined with greater precision:

"The right of the coastal State to establish the limits of its maritime sovereignty or jurisdiction in accordance with reasonable criteria, having regard to its geographical, geological, and biological characteristics and the need to make rational use of its resources."

It should be pointed out that although Uruguay signed the Geneva Conventions on the Law of the Sea, it did not ratify them. Therefore, it is not bound by the provisions of these treaties, except of course to the extent that they embody rules of customary international law. In this case, however, the binding character of the norm derives from its customary nature.

Although there is no official explanation concerning the failure to ratify the Convention on the Territorial Sea and the Contiguous Zone, it is probably related to the evolving nature of the problem, in which the interaction of political, strategic, economic, and technological factors require a constant adaptation of legal provisions and principles. Indeed, the preamble of Decree 604/969 of December 3, 1969, refers to this as one of the reasons for extending the breadth of the territorial sea to 200 miles:

"The convenience and necessity of extending the territorial sea of the Republic, taking into account the evolution of the international practice of States with regard to the law of the sea and to maritime and ocean areas, with a view to assuring the defense of high national interests and

154

safeguarding the well-being of the Uruguayan people and their possibilities of development and progress."

Reference is then made to the tendency of States to claim broader maritime zones:

"... in recent years an increasing number of States have unilaterally extended their sovereign rights and exclusive competences, some of them incorporating in their territories considerable maritime areas."

This position was further confirmed by the *note verbale* of October 20, 1970, with which the Ministry of Foreign Affairs responded to the protest of the U.S.S.R.:

"The Ministry of Foreign Affairs therefore considers that in the present situation of rapid evolution of the law of the sea, State practice is so varied that it can only support, in a given period, conclusions of a mere statistical character and which, in any event, lack the other essential elements required by international law and recognized by the International Court of Justice in its most authoritative decisions as necessary to prove the existence of a norm of customary international law which limits the traditional power of States to extend the zones of their jurisdictions and sovereignty beyond the alleged maximum breadth of twelve miles invoked by the Government of the Soviet Union. In the South American continent, in particular, the multiplication in the last few years of acts extending jurisdiction or sovereignty to areas broader than the traditional ones can be considered, on the contrary, as an indication of the emergence of a regional custom, the content of which is clearly opposed to the restrictive thesis set forward in the note of the Ministry of Foreign Affairs of the Soviet Union."

BASES OF THE URUGUAYAN POSITION

The bases of the Uruguayan position in general are compatible with those of the "Latin American thesis." The 200-mile claim is supported by two basic principles: (1) that every coastal State is entitled to a belt of maritime territory over which it exercises its sovereignty in the same manner as over its continental or insular territory; and (2) that as yet there is no norm establishing the maximum breadth of that belt in a general and compulsory manner. Taken together these two principles establish the legal power of the State to fix the outer limit of the maritime area subject to its jurisdiction or sovereignty by means of a unilateral act, at least until a general agreement on the matter is reached.

While the first principle is uncontroverted, the second is the subject of much discussion. The major objection to the Latin American thesis is its supposed incompatibility with existing international law. A 200-mile territorial sea allegedly would violate the applicable legal rule. But what is the applicable legal rule? For some, the three-mile rule is still in force; for others, the maximum breadth is six miles; and an increasing number of States support a twelve-mile limit. Furthermore, several authors and the national legislation of a number of States advance intermediary distances. This diversity is the clearest proof of the absence of a generalized agreement concerning the existence of a rule of international law binding all States with regard to the maximum breadth of the territorial sea. The Geneva Conferences of 1958 and 1960 provided further evidence of the inexistence of such a rule, and were forced to abandon the attempt to establish a limit by means of a multilateral instrument.

Although the Geneva Conferences did not reach any agreement, at least it is possible to conclude that "... in the unanimous consensus [of States], twelve miles appears to be the maximum limit claimed for 'the line of respect.' "[2] Although conclusions of this nature may be valid in the light of the discussions and background of the conferences, they should be resorted to with the utmost caution. In the first place, if there was any consensus it was not unanimous. Even in 1958 the national legislation of several States had extended the powers of the State over areas beyond the twelve-mile limit, and these States reaffirmed their position during the Conference.[3] Jiménez de Aréchaga's conclusion may be considered valid (except as far as unanimity is concerned) to the extent to which it verifies a fact: the great majority of States as emerges from the proposals, discussions, and votes during the Conference were in favor of a twelve-mile limit for the territorial sea. This is not sufficient, however, to deduce the existence of an agreement with binding effect on States.

At present there is no general norm of international law, conventional or. customary, establishing a maximum breadth of the territorial sea. The most that can be said is that more than a decade ago the official opinion of the majority of States was expressed, and in the Geneva Conferences it was possible to determine to what extent the different proposals were supported. There is a considerable disparity, however, between the expression of this fact and the conclusion that there is a rule of law fixing the maximum breadth of the territorial sea.

In the *notes verbales* with which the Uruguayan Government replied to the States which opposed the extension of its territorial sea to 200 miles, it was stated:

"It is known, in effect, that there are at present no norms of positive international law in force, of a conventional or customary nature, which establish the permissible breadth of the territorial sea of States, or that in any clear and concrete manner limit the traditional powers of those States to freely and unilaterally determine that breadth.

"The negative results of the Hague Conference of 1930 and the Geneva Conferences of 1958 and 1960, with regard to these matters, leaves no room for doubt about the accuracy of the preceding statements. The

156

practice of States on every continent for the past forty years has also confirmed the validity of the position taken by Uruguay.

"Whether directly, by the unilateral extension of maritime areas of jurisdiction, or indirectly, by unilaterally drawing baselines from extreme points of reference, the fact is that many coastal States in every latitude and in every sea, have progressively extended their national powers over broad regions adjacent to their coasts formerly considered as belonging to the high seas. In the Latin American continent, on the other hand, the principles invoked by Uruguay have recently received the formal approval of several States, as evidenced by the Montevideo Declaration on the Law of the Sea of May 8, 1970, signed by nine countries, and by the Lima Declaration signed on August 8, 1970, by fourteen republics."

In addition, the Uruguayan position may also be justified on geographical, geological, biological, economic, and strategic grounds as in the "Latin American thesis."[4]

Economic considerations have prevailed over other motivations in recent Uruguayan legislation, although there is reference also to considerations of "security and protection." This is further evidenced by the fact that the 200-mile territorial sea was established by a law the purpose of which is to declare "in the national interest the exploitation, preservation, and study of the resources of the sea." On the other hand, Decree 604/969, the first legislative act providing for such a breadth, was based upon the need "to assure the defense of high national interests and to safeguard the well-being of the Uruguayan people and their possibilities of development and progress."

These economic considerations have been a constant factor in the formulation of the Latin American position with respect to the delimitation of the territorial sea or maritime zones of jurisdiction. The Meeting of the Inter-American Council of Jurists referred to the "economic needs" of the population; the meetings of Montevideo and Lima in 1970 implicitly based their conclusions upon the general principle of national sovereignty over natural resources, the rational exploitation of marine resources being one of the guidelines which justifies and at the same time imposes limitations upon the right to unilaterally establish jurisdiction or sovereignty over the maritime areas. This is another example of the influence of economic factors upon recent developments in the law of the sea. The exercise of certain rights over the continental shelf, exclusive fishing rights in areas beyond the territorial sea, as well as several norms related to the exploitation of living resources of the sea which grant broad powers to the coastal State over areas of the high seas (such as the right to unilateral regulation of fishing provided by the Geneva Convention), are additional examples of the influence of economic factors on the recent evolution of the law of the sea.

From this point of view, there can be no doubt that the conditions which a decade or more ago were conducive to the peaceful acceptance of a three- or six-mile territorial sea have been changed substantially. If a comparison is drawn between the Geneva Conferences and the present, other important differences become apparent. The increase in human needs, induced by the population explosion and, in some cases, by the improvement of the standard of living; the impressive progress of modern technology; the increasing gap which separates industrialized from developing countries and the growing conscience of the latter about such differences; the greater sophistication of national development policies in small countries; the knowledge about the damage, sometimes permanent, which the economic and military activities of industrialized countries have inflicted upon the human environment, particularly the marine environment and the need to preserve it for the future, are all factors which at the present time have a very different import than ten years ago. Since the old rules of three, six, and twelve miles lack economic or political foundation, these new factors justify the position of the developing countries which claim the right to unilaterally establish new rules until a general agreement is reached.

BREADTH AND DELIMITATION OF THE TERRITORIAL SEA

In December 1969 the breadth of the Uruguayan territorial sea was proclaimed to be 200 miles measured from the baseline. With regard to delimitation the law does not provide any details other than that the territorial sea extends "beyond the continental and insular territory and its internal waters." In this regard, it is implied, therefore, that the law refers to the principles of existing international law as embodied in the Geneva Convention on the Territorial Sea and the Contiguous Zone.

The drawing of baselines does not present difficulties in the continental and insular territory (that is, from the border with Brazil to Punta del Este). Beyond Punta del Este the baseline departs from the Uruguayan coast and is compatible with the outer limit of Rio de la Plata, as established by the joint Argentina-Uruguay declaration of January 30, 1961. This limit is a straight line joining Punta del Este in Uruguay with Punta Rosa of Cape San Antonio, Argentina. Section 2 of the declaration provides that this line shall be the baseline from which the territorial sea and adjacent contiguous zone of the respective countries shall be measured.

The delimitation of the Uruguayan territorial sea with regard to the adjacent territorial seas of Brazil and Argentina does present some problems, although each situation is quite different. For example, an agreement on limits has been signed and ratified with Brazil but not with Argentina. Although Uruguay and Argentina have jointly established the baseline from which the territorial sea adjacent to the mouth of the River Plate is measured, the determination of the lateral limit is still pending.

It should be pointed out that this situation is not necessarily a consequence of the fact that the limits between the two countries in the River Plate have not been defined either. Although both problems may be interrelated and may even be treated as interdependent, the lateral delimitation of the territorial sea could be agreed upon independently of the River Plate problem, not only from the point of view of substance but also from the point of view of timing; nothing prevents both countries from reaching an agreement with regard to the boundary line of their maritime territories before reaching a similar agreement about the river.

The maritime boundary between Uruguay and Brazil is regulated by the Joint Declaration on the Limit of Maritime Jurisdiction of May 10, 1969, which recognizes as the lateral limit of the respective maritime jurisdictions the median line, every point of which is equidistant from the closest points of the baseline, and which, beginning at the point where the boundary between both countries reaches the Atlantic Ocean, extends toward the zones of the adjacent sea.

This method, embodied in Article 12 of the Geneva Convention on the Territorial Sea, is known as the equidistance method. The Joint Declaration preceded the adoption of the 200-mile limit by both countries. The fact that the breadth of the maritime territory was subsequently altered has no effect upon the manner of delimitation. The declaration does not refer to any particular breadth nor to the legislation regulating the breadth of the territorial sea in either of the two countries. Since the equidistance rule was not made dependent on any particular breadth, it remained in force after the enactment of the acts by which Uruguay and Brazil extended their respective maritime territories.

The Joint Declaration did not end all the problems, however. The territorial boundary between the two countries, which the declaration refers to as the point where the boundary between both countries reaches the Atlantic Ocean and from where the lateral limit of the respective maritime jurisdictions is drawn, was somewhat uncertain. In accordance with the treaties of October 12, 1851 (Article 3, Section 1) and of May 15, 1852 (Article 1), the boundary at this point is compatible with the "mouth of the Chuí Creek." But the creek is geographically unstable, making it impossible to identify its precise location because of its variations and its tendency to move northwards. It was necessary, therefore, to establish precisely and definitively the coastal point from which the maritime boundary is drawn. This was done in an exchange of notes of July 21, 1972.

SCOPE OF THE CLAIMS

It is well-known that the content of the Latin American claims differ in nature and scope. To a certain extent it may be said that Uruguay has adopted the most radical position, since it has proclaimed sovereignty over the 200-mile

159

area and not merely exclusive rights as other States have done. To be more precise, the sovereignty over the territorial sea relates not only to the maritime waters of the area, but also to the air space above it and to the seabed and subsoil thereof.[5]

Within the national maritime territory, two zones measured from the baseline may be distinguished. Uruguayan sovereignty is exercised with greater force within a twelve-mile zone than within the zone lying between twelve and 200 miles. The coastal State and third States have different rights over these areas with regard to navigation, air navigation, and fishing.

Article 3 of the Uruguayan law grants the right of innocent passage to vessels of all nations within the twelve-mile zone in accordance with the Convention on the Territorial Sea and with well-established principles of international law. But this right is not granted with regard to aerial navigation.

The situation in the zone between twelve and 200 miles is quite different. The provisions of Law 13.833 do not affect freedom of navigation or overflight in this area. Notwithstanding the fact that the area is subject to Uruguayan sovereignty, these freedoms are safeguarded to the same extent as if the area formed part of the high seas.

In this respect Uruguayan legislation differs from the practice of other Latin American countries. In opting for a dual territorial sea regime, Uruguay departs both from the Declaration of Santiago of 1952, as well as from Argentinian and Brazilian legislation.

In accordance with the Declaration of Santiago of August 18, 1952, signed by Chile, Ecuador, and Peru, the jurisdiction or sovereignty of the coastal State is limited only by the right of innocent passage of vessels of third States, thereby implicitly excluding freedom of navigation which is inherent to the regime of the high seas.

Article V of the declaration reads:

> "This declaration shall not be construed as disregarding the necessary restrictions on the exercise of sovereignty and jurisdiction imposed by international law to permit the innocent and inoffensive passage of vessels of all nations through the [maritime] zone."

On the other hand, the Argentinian Law No. 17.094 of December 29, 1966, proclaims that freedom of navigation and overflight are in no way affected throughout the territorial sea, thereby establishing a more liberal regime than that of Uruguay where this freedom is only applicable beyond the first twelve miles.[6] The Brazilian Decree-Law No. 1.098 of March 25, 1970, proclaims a territorial sea of 200 miles granting vessels of all nations only the right of innocent passage. This position was reaffirmed by Brazil at the Montevideo meeting in a separate declaration appended to Article 6 of the Declaration of Montevideo.[7]

The regime established by Uruguayan legislation can be characterized as intermediate between Argentina and Brazil. In the first twelve miles, only the right of innocent passage is granted; between twelve and 200 miles, freedom of navigation and overflight is safeguarded.

Notwithstanding the existence of two sub-zones within the 200-mile area, each of them with a different legal regime, the whole area is unquestionably territorial sea. Both Decree 604/969 and Law 13.833 are very clear on this point, referring to the "territorial sea zone of 200 nautical miles," over which "the sovereignty of the Republic" is exercised. Furthermore, the sovereignty extends to the air space above the territorial sea, as well as to the seabed and subsoil thereof.

The fact that between twelve and 200 miles the principle of freedom of navigation and overflight is maintained does not alter the nature of the rights which the State exercises over the area. It is true that the concept of freedom of navigation has always been linked to the regime of the high seas, but in this case the principle of freedom of navigation originated in customary international law and subsequently became embodied in Article 2 of the Geneva Convention on the High Seas. However, the freedom of navigation and overflight permitted in the Uruguayan territorial sea beyond the twelve miles is not dependent upon a rule of international law but of municipal law, which as such may be revoked by another rule of municipal law. It would be difficult to object to the capacity of the coastal State to grant rights in favor of third States, rights which are broader than those granted by classical international law with respect to the uses of the national maritime territory. The possibility which every State possesses of imposing upon itself limitations upon the exercise of rights over the territorial sea stems, precisely, from its sovereign character.

If a State with a territorial sea of six or twelve miles decides, by means of a unilateral act, that it shall grant in this area freedom of navigation and overflight, should this be considered as a renunciation of its territorial sea? This interpretation would be erroneous and, in any event, it would be inadmissible if the same State continued to regard the area as forming part of its territory.

Recourse to new categorizations is unjustified merely because the claim does not follow a typical pattern. The full exercise of sovereignty is inherent in the claim itself. Thus, Uruguay could suspend or eliminate the regime of freedom of navigation beyond the twelve-mile limit by means of another unilateral act.

FISHERIES

The law also establishes different regimes with regard to fishing. Within the first twelve miles, commercial activities of marine fishing and hunting are reserved exclusively to duly registered vessels flying the national flag; although these activities might be permitted by vessels of other nationalities by virtue of international agreements based on reciprocity. Therefore the law has put an end to the abnormal situation which had developed over the years. Article 713 of the Civil Code established freedom of fishing in favor of nationals and aliens in the internal waters and territorial sea. The only limitation was provided by Law 3.135 of December 12, 1906, which prohibited the fishing and hunting of sea lions by foreign vessels. In spite of the fact that this regime was established by law, in practice the Uruguayan authorities followed the provisions of a decree of December 26, 1914, prohibiting "all foreign vessels and boats or their personnel" from fishing in Uruguayan jurisdictional waters.[8]

Since the latter provision was contrary to a superior hierarchial norm, the decree was certainly illegal, although its application did not raise major problems. Furthermore, the provisions of the decree were made applicable to the successive enlargements of the territorial sea and even beyond its outer limit. The decree of February 21, 1963, adopting the "six-plus-six" formula, provided that "the laws and regulations in force in the Republic for fishing and exploitation of the living resources of the territorial sea shall be applied in the contiguous zone." Fishing thereby was reserved to nationals not only in the maritime territory over which sovereignty was exercised, but also in the additional six miles of the contiguous zone.

The decree of May 16, 1969, extending the territorial sea to twelve miles, created an additional complication in the fishing regulations. Article 4 of the decree extended the zone of exclusive fishing and hunting to the outer limit of the continental shelf: "Exclusive fishing and marine hunting rights of the Republic are hereby declared in the maritime zone comprised between the outer limit of the territorial sea and the outer limit of the continental shelf, delimited in accordance with the provisions of this decree."

Although all these provisions have been abrogated by Law 13.833, it is useful to reemphasize that they were all illegal insofar as they reserved fishing exclusively to nationals, which was contrary to the law granting freedom of fishing. Law 13.833 resolves this situation and follows more rational standards than those contained in the decree of 1969. However, national ships unquestionably exercise exclusive fishing and hunting rights in internal waters and in the first twelve miles of the Uruguayan territorial sea.

Beyond twelve miles and up to the limit of 200 miles, the fisheries regime is not based entirely on the principle of freedom. The living resources of the area obviously appertain to Uruguay, but their exploitation can be undertaken by foreign vessels duly authorized by the Executive or by international agreements. The law provides several details for the granting of fishing permits in the area, further regulated by Decrees 540/971 of August 1971 and 711/71 of October 28, 1971, dealing with fishing in Uruguayan jurisdictional waters by foreign and national vessels respectively.

THE CONTINENTAL SHELF

There is very little Uruguayan legislation on the continental shelf. The decree of February 21, 1963, which inaugurated the cycle of intensive legislation on the law of the sea, does not regulate or even mention the continental shelf. The first national proclamation of rights over the shelf was contained in a decree of July 1963. The preamble of the decree refers to the need to determine the submarine areas over which the "Republic has exclusive and specific jurisdiction," and gives a detailed history of the legal situation which developed from the Proclamation by President Truman to the Geneva Convention. The provisions of the decree make clear that it is without prejudice to any other rights which the country might have over deeper areas, to the extent that their exploration or exploitation becomes possible. The Hydrographic Service of the Navy was entrusted with the task of drawing up charts of the maritime zone adjacent to the Uruguayan coast, beyond the territorial sea — which at that time was six miles — and up to the 200-meter isobath.

On the other hand, Consideration VII of the decree clearly stated that it was the government's intention to proceed in stages — first delimiting the area of the shelf reaching to the 200-meter depth, but without prejudice to the rights over the area lying at greater depths.

Several subsequent decrees referred to the exploitation and exploration of oil in the continental shelf: decrees of May 30, 1968, August 3, 1969, and November 1, 1969. The decree of May 16, 1969, establishing a twelve-mile territorial sea, embodies the definition of the continental shelf contained in the Geneva Convention and provides that the delimitation of the shelf which is adjacent to other countries shall be accomplished by means of international negotiations and in accordance with the principle of equidistance.

Although Uruguay has not yet ratified the Geneva Convention on the Continental Shelf, it has closely followed the basic concepts of that Convention. Article 2 of Law 13.833 follows the definition of the Geneva Convention both with regard to the continental shelf and the nature of the rights which the coastal State can exercise over it. Of course it is unnecessary to add that these rights of exploration and exploitation only apply beyond the 200-mile limit. Over the area comprised within the 200-mile zone — which covers most of what can geologically be considered the Uruguayan continental shelf — Uruguay exercises sovereign rights in accordance with Section 2, Article 2, of Law 13.833.

Due to the fact that Uruguay has accepted the Geneva definition of the continental shelf, which is based on the dual concept of depth and exploitability, the outer limit of the continental shelf has remained undefined. Contrary to the decree of May 1969 — now repealed — Law 13.833 does not provide for the delimitation of the continental shelf with adjacent countries. The agreement between Uruguay and Brazil with regard to the delimitation of the territorial sea does not refer to the continental shelf, but it constitutes, together with the provisions of the Geneva Convention and other international instruments, a precedent of great authority with regard to the criteria to be followed. There is, as yet, no agreement with Argentina.

PRESERVATION OF LIVING RESOURCES – POLLUTION

Law 13.833 provides rather general measures with regard to the conservation of the living resources of the sea in Articles 7, 13, and 19. The law envisages control of this problem either through national regulations or international agreements with the exception of the prohibitions contained in Articles 13 and 14.

Before Law 13.833 came into force, Uruguay had concluded with Brazil in December 1968 an agreement on fishing and conservation of living resources. This agreement does not provide for specific measures on conservation, but is confined to establishing the institutional machinery whereby such measures are to be worked out. A standing body – the Joint Commission on Fisheries and Preservation of the Living Resources of the Sea and Internal Waters – is created to:

"Study matters of common interest with regard to fishing and the preservation of the living resources in the waters of the sea adjacent to the coasts of both countries and in internal waters, as well as to elaborate in the shortest possible time an agreement to regulate, by means of the proper technical rules, the preservation of species, in order to obtain a constant maximum yield."

This Joint Commission is composed of four representatives of each side and shall meet every time that the national sections agree to convoke it; it is presided over by a representative of the country in which it meets.

With regard to pollution, Article 12 of the law provides that:

"Dumping of any substance which in any way might hinder the utilization or destroy the resources of the sea is prohibited; the dumping of oil, radioactive waste, industrial waste, or aniline is expressly prohibited.

"Regulations shall establish measures to prevent the pollution of the sea, and to this effect shall establish minimum distances from the coast within which dumping of substances mentioned in the preceding paragraph is prohibited."

Regulations on this matter have not yet been enacted, although their need is evident. Tourism is one of the principal sources of foreign currency in Uruguay, and pollution of the waters and beaches endangers not only the ichthyological resources and the fur industry based on sea lions but tourism also.

On December 9, 1970, the Executive enacted a law approving the International Convention for the Preservation of Pollution of the Sea by Oil of 1954, as amended in 1962.

References

1. For the doctrinal development of the "Latin American thesis," see Inter-American Council of Jurists, Third Meeting, Mexico, 1956, interventions by the delegates of Peru (Dr. Alberto Ulloa), Chile (Dr. Luis D. Cruz Ocampo), and Ecuador (Dr. Gonzalo Escudero), pp. 73-112; Felipe H. Paolillo, "Revolución en los Océanos. Problemas contemporáneos del Derecho del Mar," in *Revista Uruguaya de Derecho Internacional,* 1972, pp. 72 ff; Enrique García Sayán, Conferencia sobre Explotación y Conservación de las riquezas marítimas del Pacífico Sur: *Convenios y otros Documentos 1952-1969,* 3rd ed. (Lima, 1970), pp. 9 ff.
2. Eduardo Jiménez de Aréchaga, *Curso de Derecho Internacional Público* (Montevideo, 1961), Vol. II, pp. 559-560.
3. Alvaro Alvarez, *Los Nuevos Principios del Derecho del Mar* (Montevideo, 1969), pp. 52, 55, 83, 91.
4. See note 1 above.
5. This is provided by Article 2, Section 2, of Law 13.833.
6. However, in the Joint Declaration by the Presidents of Chile and Argentina of July 22, 1971, the two countries agreed to maintain freedom of navigation and overflight "beyond twelve miles and up to the limit of 200 miles." This declaration is more restrictive of freedom of navigation in the Argentinian territorial sea than Law No. 17.094.
7. For a more detailed analysis of the position of the Santiago group and the legislation of Argentina and Brazil, see the chapters in this book dealing with Argentina, Brazil, Chile, and Peru.
8. Jiménez de Aréchaga, op. cit., note 2 above, p. 524.

Chapter IX
Argentina and the Law of the Sea

Chapter IX

ARGENTINA AND THE LAW OF THE SEA

Frida M. Pfirter de Armas

INTRODUCTION

From an economic point of view the exploitation of the sea is essential for the Argentinian Republic. Its waters are rich in fauna, its coasts contain valuable algaes, and the subsoil is rich in oil, gas, and other minerals.[1] The coastal plains extend into the sea forming a broad continental shelf which at some points is more than 700 kilometers (435 miles) wide, as, for example, off Santa Cruz.[2]

The living resources of the sea provide food, fertilizers, and raw materials. The cold current of Malvinas provides ideal conditions for the development of plankton, essential for the nutrition of fish.[3] The submarine shelf has an abundance of ichthyological food. The Argentinian seas are also very rich in benthonic species.[4] Marine algaes, the exploitation of which has already begun, are of great importance in the production of chemicals which are used in the textile, canned food, and pharmaceutical industries. In recent years, scientific research has given a strong impetus to the exploitation of the mineral resources of the sea.

Since the oceans are an unrestricted means of communication, States have maritime interests at the local, regional, or world level which are vital for their commerce, economy, security, and culture. Thus, the sea must be considered an important element from the political and strategic points of view.

Commercial navigation routes are linked to land regions; those where traffic is concentrated are called "focal" regions.[5] In the case of Argentina, the focal maritime areas correspond to the regions of greatest economic value in the north and central parts of the country, namely the River Plate and Bahía Blanca. Although southern regions are less significant, the Gulf of San Jorge has an extensive traffic because of oil; and Antarctica is of major importance from the political and strategic points of view due to its position controlling interoceanic communications to the south of Cape Horn and the potential importance of the area in case of a general conflict.[6] It is also important to mention that 90 percent of Argentina's foreign trade is transported by sea.[7]

The foregoing considerations explain the strong interest of the country in the utilization of commercial routes, the exploitation of living resources of the sea, and the security of its territory — all of which require the exercise of jurisdiction over the sea and a naval power adequate to implement such jurisdiction.

Finally, it should be mentioned that Argentina participated in the 1958 and 1960 United Nations Conferences on the Law of the Sea. It signed the four 1958 Conventions but did not ratify any of them. The Optional Protocol for the Settlement of disputes was not signed by Argentina.

INTERNAL WATERS

The Constitution of Argentina, enacted in 1853, does not contain specific provisions on the law of the sea. There are some provisions of interest related to internal waters, however.

The right of navigation is granted to all inhabitants, both nationals and aliens; furthermore, aliens are granted the right to navigate through rivers and coastal areas. Navigation between provinces is free; there also is freedom of navigation through national rivers for ships of all flags, subject to the regulations enacted by proper authorities. The power to regulate freedom of navigation through national rivers, to establish ports and customs, regulate national and foreign maritime commerce, promote the construction of navigable channels, and regulate the exploration of national rivers is granted to Congress. Provinces are not empowered to enact laws on navigation, establish customs, or build warships; but they may promote the construction of navigable channels and the exploration of their rivers. Treaties on navigation are negotiated and signed by the President, but the approval of Congress is required before ratification.

The Civil Code, as amended in 1968, includes among other kinds of public property the internal seas, bays, entrances, ports, rivers, beaches, navigable lakes, islands, and bridges. In accordance with a decree of September 18, 1907,[8] the separation between the mouth of rivers, creeks, or lakes, and the sea, is established on the basis of lines determined by the appropriate authority.

Law No. 17.094[9] provides that in the Gulfs of San Matías, Nuevo, and San Jorge a straight baseline will be drawn between the capes located at their mouth, transforming the waters so enclosed into internal waters. A similar provision was established by Law No. 18.502 of December 24, 1969.[10] Several countries protested these provisions, considering them a violation of Article 7 of the Convention on the Territorial Sea because except for the Gulf of Nuevo[11] the width of the entrance exceeds twenty-four miles. However, Argentina is not a party to this Convention and the provision of Article 7 is not binding as a rule of customary international law. Since there was no agreement on the breadth of the territorial sea nor was there a customary rule on this matter, it cannot be argued that such rule exists for gulfs. The discussions of the International Law Commission and its successive changes of opinion are the best evidence that decisions were not taken on "solid ground."[12] The fact that the Gulf of San Jorge is of great importance to the country because of oil transportation also has to be taken into consideration.

THE TERRITORIAL SEA

Congress is empowered by the Constitution to fix the final limits of Argentinian territory and to approve or disapprove treaties concerning these limits. Treaties are negotiated and signed by the Executive. Since, broadly speaking, the territorial sea is in principle a part of the territory of the State, the fixing of its breadth must follow these provisions. However, in the event that Congress is unable to approve the treaty (e.g., when it is not in session) it may be given valid effect in terms of public international law through Executive action.

Landward Delimitation

An early reference to this problem was made by the Civil Code when providing that the adjacent sea is measured "from the low-water line." A decree of 1907, regulating fishing and hunting, provided that the limit between the territorial sea and river areas would be established by the Executive.

Presently, both Law No. 17.094 and Law No. 18.502 provide that the territorial sea is "measured from the line of the lowest tide, except in the cases of the San Matías, Nuevo, and San Jorge gulfs, where it will be measured from the line joining the promontories which form their mouth." Therefore, the general rule is that of the low-water line. In accordance with the Joint Declaration between Argentina and Uruguay of January 30, 1961, the territorial sea in the River Plate area is measured from a straight line joining Punta del Este in Uruguay with Punta Rosa of Cape San Antonio in Argentina.[13]

Although the relevant legislation does not specifically refer to islands, the provisions mentioned would appear to be so applicable under customary law. Despite the fact that Argentinian legislation provides for the low-water line as the landward limit of the territorial sea without distinguishing between different kinds of coasts, it may be suggested, following general rules and the precedent of gulfs, that straight baselines could be applied when the configuration of the coast so requires. Also, the Convention between Argentina and the Federal Republic of Germany on the entry of nuclear ships into Argentinian waters and their docking in Argentinian ports,[14] refers to 200 nautical miles measured from the baseline, not specifying whether it is the low-water line or a straight baseline.

Lateral Delimitation

Lateral delimitation presents two kinds of problems for Argentina: one with regard to Chile and the other with regard to Uruguay.

The meridian of Cape Horn seems to be the limit between the Pacific and Atlantic oceans[15] and, therefore, between Chile and Argentina. The area is currently under litigation because both States are not in agreement with regard to the eastern mouth of the Beagle Channel; the outcome of the current arbitration may have an influence on this situation. However, Article 2 of the Protocol between Chile and Argentina of 1893, supplementary to the Treaty on Limits of July 23, 1881, provides that "the sovereignty of each State over its respective coasts is absolute, so that Chile may not lay claim to any point toward the Atlantic Ocean, nor may Argentina lay claim to any point toward the Pacific."[16]

Since in this area the oceans meet, the limit between them is the line considered as a boundary by the majority of writers and specialized journals.[17] In the absence of natural obstacles, there is no reason to modify the already accepted traditional regime.

The lateral limit with regard to Uruguay is still unsettled and both countries have taken what may be extreme positions. The problem is related to the outer limit of the River Plate, which as already mentioned, is the straight line joining Punta del Este with Punta Rosa. The problem is related also to the limit within the river, a situation to which both States have different approaches. Uruguay favors the median line, while Argentina argues that the boundary runs along the deepest navigable channels or thalweg and that this is the norm imposed by general international law for navigable rivers.

The first question, therefore, is at what point should the lateral limit of the territorial sea begin? If the Argentinian position with regard to the delimitation within the river is accepted, the starting point would be where the thalweg meets the straight line joining Punta del Este with Punta Rosa. If, on the contrary, the Uruguayan position is accepted, the starting point would be in the middle of the straight line. A closely related question is what direction should the boundary of the territorial sea follow seaward? The following can be considered as alternatives: (a) a line perpendicular to the baseline of the territorial sea, e.g., the solution applied by Norway and Sweden in the Grisbadarma Case;[18] (b) the line equidistant to the baseline of the territorial sea as provided by the 1958 Geneva Convention, but not compulsory as a rule of customary international law[19] nor binding on Argentina since it has not ratified the Convention; (c) the line of the geographical parallel, followed by Chile, Peru, and Ecuador in the system of the South Pacific, and supported by Domingo Sabaté Lichtschein,[20] a solution apparently followed by the Ministry of Foreign Affairs of Argentina at present; and (d) the line of meridian passing through a point to be established on the landward limit of the territorial sea, which Uruguay supports.

Although from a political point of view and as a negotiating position the last two alternatives may be invoked, in fact both pretensions are unjust and inequitable, particularly if the special configuration of the Argentinian and Uruguayan coasts is taken into consideration, as well as their differences with the coasts of the Pacific which provided the basis for the application of one of the alternatives mentioned.

The equidistance or the perpendicular lines are more reasonable and just, for

172

both countries would then be granted a broad maritime front. This could not happen with Uruguay if the line of the parallel is followed, nor with Argentina if the line of the meridian is followed. A precedent which could have some influence is that of the Joint Declaration on the Limit of Maritime Jurisdiction of May 10, 1969, between Brazil and Uruguay providing for the median line, every point of which is equidistant from the closest points of the baseline, and which, beginning at the point where the boundary between both countries reaches the Atlantic Ocean extends toward the zone of the adjacent sea.[21]

Seaward Delimitation

The first provision on this matter was Article 2340 of the Civil Code which included in the property of the State "the seas adjacent to the territory of the Republic, to the distance of one marine league measured from the low-water line." However, with regard to security and the observance of fiscal laws, the police jurisdiction of the coastal State extended to four marine leagues (twelve miles).

A frequent error at the time was to consider the territorial sea the property of the State. Although this could be justified at the turn of the century, there is absolutely no justification for retaining the concepts of "dominium" and "property" in the amendments to the Civil Code introduced by Law No. 17.711, which failed to introduce the concept of "sovereignty." The legislation lacks uniformity with regard to the nature of the territorial sea which must be corrected in a future revision.

A decree of 1907 regulating maritime fishing and hunting enlarged the territorial sea to ten miles for the purpose of fishing and established that the Gulfs of San Matías, San Jorge, and Nuevo were territorial sea without regard to their extension or breadth. Decree No. 1386 of January 24, 1944,[22] declared to be temporary zones of mineral reserves "the coasts of oceans and the Argentinian epicontinental sea," that is, the waters superjacent to the continental shelf and the seabed and subsoil thereof.

Shortly thereafter, Decree No. 14.708 of October 11, 1946,[23] declared that the epicontinental sea and continental terrace appertained to the sovereignty of the nation, without impeding the freedom of navigation. This decree was enacted by a *de facto* government and was not ratified by Congress; although several writers have taken the view that it was validated at a later stage of constitutional rule, this is debatable.[24] Be that as it may, this situation is no longer of any relevance since the enactment of Law No. 17.094 on the adjacent sea and the continental shelf.

It is necessary to inquire, however, about the extent of that decree — did it presume to extend the territorial sea to the waters above the continental shelf or only to establish an exclusive fishing zone, as some writers argue?

By providing for a temporary zone of mineral reserves in the epicontinental sea,[25] Decree No. 1386 enlarged the territorial sea because mineral reserves can only be established in the territory of the State. With regard to minerals in the sea, territorial jurisdiction is given only in the case of the territorial sea or of the continental shelf. Although the wording of this decree lacks precision, the former interpretation is supported by Decree No. 14.708, which, referring to the territorial sea, reiterated the purpose of undertaking intensive scientific and technical studies for the exploitation of the wealth of this zone,[26] further stating that international law recognizes the power of each country to consider the epicontinental sea and continental terrace as part of the *national territory*.

Law No. 14.773 of November 10, 1958,[27] provided that the deposits of solid, liquid, or gas hydrocarbons existing in "the territory of the Republic and its continental shelf" are "the imprescriptible and inalienable property of the State."

Law No. 17.094 was enacted on December 29, 1966,[28] to regulate the adjacent sea and the continental shelf, but it referred to concepts that allow different and conflicting interpretations. Article 1 of this law reads:

> "The sovereignty of the Argentinian nation shall extend over the sea adjacent to its territory for a distance of 200 nautical miles measured from the line of the lowest tide, except in the cases of the San Matías, Nuevo, and San Jorge gulfs, where it will be measured from the line joining the promontories which form their mouth."

Article 2 reads:

> "The sovereignty of the Argentinian nation shall also extend over the seabed and the subsoil of the submarine zones adjacent to its territory up to a depth of 200 meters or, beyond this limit, up to that depth of the overlying waters which allows exploitation of the natural resources of those zones."

In accordance with these provisions, the territorial sea has a breadth of 200 miles, while the continental shelf follows the approach of the 1958 Geneva Convention. Article 3 further provides that "the provisions of this law shall not affect freedom of navigation or of air traffic."

Article 4 of this law also provides for the issuance of regulations establishing the terms under which foreign ships may conduct the exploration and exploitation of natural resources within the 200-mile zone. Provisional regulations were established by Decree No. 5106 of January 4, 1967,[29] which empowered the Naval Operations Command to issue fishing permits "in the Argentinian *territorial sea* [emphasis added], at a distance of no less than twelve miles from the coast." This decree divided the adjacent sea into two zones: the first twelve miles where exploitation is reserved to nationals, and beyond twelve miles where permits may be issued to foreign ships.

Article 1 of Law No. 17.500 of October 25, 1967, concerning the promotion of fisheries, provides that "The resources of the Argentinian territorial sea are the property of the national State, which shall authorize their exploitation in accordance with the provisions of this Act and the rules governing its application."[30] Article 2 confirms the area reserved exclusively for nationals, but also considers the possibility of enlarging this area:

> "Resources up to a distance of twelve nautical miles from the coast may be exploited only by vessels flying the national flag. In addition, the Executive Power shall each year select, within the Argentinian territorial sea, a specific zone whose exploitation shall be reserved for vessels flying the national flag."

This law also established incentives for the development of the national fishing industry, dividing the region into two zones – one to the north of Río Colorado, and the other to the south. Naturally, the latter region, being the less developed, obtained greater benefits.

The Presidential motion related to the approval of this law referred to the "political and economic position which is essential for the interests of the Nation concerning the sovereignty over the *territorial sea*" (emphasis added), as established by Law No. 17.094. The goals of this law were to foster a new aspect of the economy, particularly the creation of a strong and efficient fishing industry capable of providing new sources of work and foreign exchange.

Decree No. 8802 of November 22, 1967,[31] which abrogated Decree No. 5106 of January 4, 1967, approved the "provisional regulations governing the issue to foreign vessels of permits for the exploitation of the living resources of the Argentinian *territorial sea*" (emphasis added). These permits can only be granted beyond twelve miles from the coast. Foreign vessels operating in the area must be registered and hold a permit, the fees of which are higher in the case of factory and refrigerated ships. Foreign vessels must also comply with provisions on prohibited zones and periods, characteristics of equipment and gear, methods and techniques, nonexploitable species, conservation of species, and must not interfere with navigation or obstruct similar operations by vessels of Argentinian registration. The resources obtained from the sea shall not be sold on the Argentinian market except with express authorization. Other Articles refer to "the sea in waters under Argentinian jurisdiction" or to "Argentinian jurisdictional waters."

As explained further above, Law No. 17.711 of April 22, 1968, amended the Civil Code to read:

> "The following is public property: ... The *territorial seas* [emphasis added] to the distance that shall be fixed by special legislation, without regard to the jurisdictional power over the contiguous zone."

Law No. 18.502 of December 24, 1969,[32] settled the conflicts posed through the exercise of jurisdiction by the Argentinian provinces over the territorial sea adjacent to their coasts. The law provides: "Provinces shall exercise jurisdiction over the territorial sea adjacent to their coasts up to the distance of three nautical miles measured from the low-water line ..." and further provides that "The National State shall exercise exclusive jurisdiction over the *Argentinian territorial sea* [emphasis added] from the limit mentioned in the preceding Article and up to the limit fixed by Law No. 17.094." It was also provided that "The jurisdiction assigned to Provinces ... shall be exercised without prejudice to that corresponding to the National State in the whole extension of the *territorial sea*" [emphasis added]. The resources found in the three miles under the jurisdiction of provinces shall not be considered the property of the National State.

The Presidential motion reiterates that Law No. 17.094 "extended the *Argentinian territorial sea* [emphasis added] to the distance of 200 miles," and that the present law does not change this situation but only clarifies it with regard to the problems of federal and provincial jurisdiction.

Later, the National Fisheries Service enacted regulations No. 265/72[33] and 556/72,[34] gradually restricting the number of vessels allowed to operate in Argentinian waters. The first of these regulations referred to the "Argentinian territorial sea," "Argentinian territorial waters," and "jurisdictional waters," and fixed at sixty the number of vessels allowed to operate in the area; furthermore, it provided for two zones – in the zone south of parallel 39 operations may be carried out from a distance of twelve miles, but in the zone north of that parallel they can only be carried out seaward of seventy-five miles from the coast, thereby exclusively reserving the first seventy-five miles to nationals. The second regulation mentioned reduced to sixteen the number of vessels allowed to operate until the expiration of the permits issued by naval authorities, and referred to "the sea under Argentinian sovereignty" and "waters under Argentinian jurisdiction."

This restrictive approach found its clearest expression in the latest Law on Fishing, No. 20.136 of 1973,[35] which amended Law No. 17.500. The first amendment substituted the expression "maritime zones under Argentinian sovereignty" for "Argentinian territorial sea." Another amendment provides that the exploitation of living resources can only be undertaken by duly authorized Argentinian ships, and imposes severe penalties for violation, among them the retention of ships until the payment of fines.

In addition to this very complicated legislation, mention should be made also of the Joint Declaration by the Presidents of Chile and Argentina of July 22, 1971, making public the commencement of arbitral procedures for the Pacific settlement of the Beagle Channel dispute. With regard to the law of the sea, both Presidents declared that "in the zones of maritime sovereignty or jurisdiction beyond twelve miles and up to the limit of 200 miles, the principle of freedom of navigation and overflight shall be maintained for vessels and aircraft of any flag."[36]

Although this document has no legal force, it is an important source of interpretation. It should be noted also that the principle of freedom of navigation and overflight is *maintained* which must mean that it was already in existence. Even though the Declaration does not say so expressly, it is to be understood that in the first twelve miles that right of innocent passage applies. This approach is compatible with the statement by the Argentinian delegate to the United Nations Seabed Committee, Dr. Ernesto De la Guardia:

> "There is a principle of international law in force that prevents States from regulating navigation and overflight outside a maritime zone near to their coasts, while in the latter this regulation is justified on grounds of security and control of fiscal, customs, sanitary, and other laws."[37]

Both governments have chosen an interpretation by means of a Declaration and not by a formal act of national legislations, which in no way affects the legal validity of such interpretation and even strengthens it. Even though the Declaration is not a formal treaty, it has legal effects as evidenced by the fact that international law recognizes all sorts of international obligations as long as the intention of the parties is clear.

LEGAL NATURE OF THE ADJACENT ZONE

The laws that have been examined are not always clear in their meaning and, therefore, several interpretations are possible.

While the Civil Code of 1869, establishing a three-mile territorial sea and a twelve-mile contiguous zone, remained in force, the sovereignty of the nation was extended to 200 miles without affecting the freedom of navigation and overflight by the enactment of Law No. 17.094. Law No. 17.500 and other decrees regulated fishing in the 200-mile zone, reserving exclusively for nationals the first twelve miles and allowing foreign vessels in the remainder of this zone. In 1968 the Civil Code was amended to refer to a distance that would be established by special legislation, the latter being Law No. 17.094. Recently, Law No. 20.136 has reserved exclusively for nationals the exploitation of living resources in the whole of the 200-mile area. At the same time the President declared that freedom of navigation and overflight was guaranteed beyond twelve miles.

It is worthwhile to examine some of the interpretations that have been given to these unclear legal rules.

In two of his writings,[38] García Amador has identified the Argentinian claims with modern projections of specialized powers, namely fishing jurisdiction,[39] for freedom of navigation is not compatible with a regime of the territorial sea. He further believes that if the criteria established by Law No. 17.500 and other regulations is followed, "it would be possible to note other possible areas in which these instruments would bear upon the 200-mile maritime claim."[40]

One Argentinian writer, Juan Carlos Puig,[41] expresses the view that while the former Civil Code was in force the territorial sea had a three-mile breadth and the 200-mile zone established by Law No. 17.094 "was in practice a contiguous fishing zone,"[42] the first twelve miles of which were reserved exclusively for nationals in accordance with Law No. 17.500.[43] He further writes that since the amendment of the Civil Code by Law No. 17.711 "the Argentinian Republic lacks a territorial sea in its municipal legislation."[44]

Another writer, Ernesto Rey Caro, believes that the 200-mile zone is a territorial sea and does not qualify as "a *sui generis* maritime zone."[45] A critical examination of these interpretations should be undertaken. In the first place, it is necessary to emphasize that the Civil Code was amended by Law No. 17.094. As is well-known, the abrogation of a law might be tacit and a special law prevails over a general one;[46] between two contradictory rules, the most recent prevails. The Civil Code referred to the traditional concept of territorial sea, fixing its breadth at three miles. Law No. 17.094 proclaimed the sovereignty of the nation over 200 miles of sea adjacent to the territory, but at the same time granting freedom of navigation and overflight. Though the concept is different, it refers to the same adjacent maritime area.[47] Law No. 17.711 seems to confirm that there was a tacit abrogation of the Civil Code, for it refers to the distance fixed by special legislation, that is to say Law No. 17.094. Since the enactment of Law No. 17.711, the territorial sea no longer has a breadth of three miles.

It is difficult to accept the interpretation of Puig that Argentina lacks a territorial sea. To suppose that a coastal State has no territorial sea is contrary to international law according to which every State has a right to a belt of territorial waters.[48] As the International Court of Justice stated in the *Anglo-Norwegian Fisheries Case,* "It is the land which confers upon the coastal State a right to the waters off its coasts."[49] As was clearly stated by Judge McNair in his separate opinion in this case, no State can refuse its territorial waters for this is not an option but an obligation of international law.[50]

This concept is not new for already in the Grisbadarma Case the Permanent Court of Arbitration stated, in drawing the maritime limit between Norway and Sweden, that "in accordance with the fundamental principles of the law of nations, both old and new ... the *maritime territory* [emphasis added] is a necessary dependence of the land territory," further stating that "the automatic division of the territory in question should have been made in accordance with the general direction of the land territory, to which the maritime territory appertains."[51]

It is also inexact to state that Argentina claims in the 200-mile zone a contiguous fishing zone only. The powers claimed and exercised by Argentina are greater, for they also refer to the conservation of living resources, scientific research, and prevention of pollution.[52] One may conclude, therefore, that Argentina exercises over the area every sovereign right and the fact that presently only some of those rights are implemented does not imply that others have been renounced.

The Declaration of Latin American States on the law of the sea, approved in Lima in 1970,[53] is compatible with these claims for it affirms among other things the right of the coastal state to protect marine resources, prevent pollution, and regulate scientific research within the limits of the sovereignty or maritime jurisdiction of the signatory States.

One may also ask whether Argentina would permit naval confrontations, missile launching, gathering of information, naval blockades, or the operation of nuclear submarines in the 200-mile area. In spite of the absence of an official position, it may be suggested that it would not. The activities mentioned are only a few of the freedoms of the high seas that third States could undertake in the 200-mile area if the erroneous approach referred to is followed. As Emilio Oribe correctly pointed out,[54] the freedoms mentioned by the Geneva Convention on the High Seas do not exclude others which are recognized by the general principles of international law.

The opinion of García Amador seems to confirm the interpretation presented here. With regard to the Peruvian claims, he believes that they are not a territorial sea but only the exercise of powers related to the conservation, development, and exploitation of natural resources;[55] while in the case of Argentina he refers to other areas on which the claim might bear[56] and to the fact that such a claim is evidently of a complex nature and extent.[57] It is possible to deduce from this that the Argentinian legislation refers not only to fishing but other powers. However, if his position is that the area only involves specialized powers, this can be criticized on the ground that it is contrary to international law for a coastal State to renounce its territorial sea.

Several other instruments confirm that Argentina exercises broad powers over the area. The following may be mentioned: the Declarations of Montevideo and Lima on the Law of the Sea; the Joint Declaration by the Presidents of Argentina and Chile of July 22, 1971; the Joint Declaration with Venezuela of March 1, 1972,[58] with Peru of October 16, 1971,[59] and with Guatemala of February 18, 1972.[60]

The Agreement between Argentina and the Federal Republic of Germany on the entry of nuclear ships into Argentinian waters and their docking in Argentinian ports[61] is a good example of the sovereign rights exercised by Argentina. Although the Agreement states that the rights and points of view of the contracting parties with regard to their concepts of territorial sea and their competence on the high seas are not affected, in fact the Agreement embodies the exercise of powers that differ from those related exclusively to pollution. Both the operator of the ships and Germany are objectively responsible for any damage arising from a nuclear accident, which means not only pollution but also damage to property or people. The responsibility arises if the damage takes place in Argentinian waters — 200 miles — Argentinian territory, or even outside Argentinian waters if the ship was bound to or from an Argentinian port or waters. The jurisdiction of Argentinian courts may be invoked by the applicant, and municipal legislation is applicable on every point not governed by the Agreement; should the area be part of the high seas or one of specialized competence, the jurisdiction would be that of the flag State.

The only limitation on the powers exercised over the 200-mile area is the recognition of freedom of navigation and overflight, which is similar to the concept of a territorial sea. There are also some aspects, however, that separate the nature of this area from that of the territorial sea.

What then is the nature of this zone: an exclusive fishing zone, a zone where specialized powers are exercised, or a territorial sea in the traditional sense or in a new dynamic concept? The first argument has already been rejected. With regard to the other aspects, the approach of Rey Caro, who refers to a territorial sea with freedom of navigation, can also be criticized. Although the approach of García Amador is attractive because of its flexibility, it does not seem to respond to the reality of the Argentinian case.

The task of students of the law is not restricted to merely commenting upon and describing its provisions but must also aim to disclose its real meaning through the interpretation of texts, a method which is followed by modern codes.[62]

It is a well-known fact that government officials, and particularly the military, are somewhat fearful of referring to the "territorial sea" because of the implications that the concept might have in an eventual conflict with Brazil, a country that also claims 200 miles subject only to the right of innocent passage, a position which could result in prohibiting the northbound navigation of Argentinian ships through that area. A similar situation exists in the case of Chile and Peru. However, in accordance with the Geneva Convention on the Territorial Sea and Contiguous Zone, the coastal State can only regulate the passage of warships through the territorial sea, and suspensions of the right can only be temporary, in specified areas, nondiscriminatory and only when it is essential for the protection of its security.

Initiatives to extend the territorial sea are not new in Argentina. At the doctrinal level it was first suggested by Segundo R. Storni and José Leon Suárez, and this has been implemented by the several laws mentioned. At present, the 200-mile area embraces two concepts. The first twelve miles are, without doubt, a territorial sea in its most traditional sense, although this is not provided by any law for Law No. 17.500 which reserved the first twelve miles exclusively for nationals was abrogated by Law No. 20.136, which makes no such distinction. This is now clear as a result of the Joint Declaration with Chile[63] and of the Joint Argentinian-Uruguayan Act on the Law of the Sea of July 9, 1971. The latter referred to freedom of navigation and overflight in the 200-mile zone "beyond the external limit of the territorial sea,"[64] thereby assuming that there was a territorial sea different from the 200-mile zone. The former Declaration[65] and other official statements[66] have also indicated that freedom of navigation is guaranteed beyond twelve miles, which obviously is relevant from the point of view of international law.

The legal nature of the zone extending from twelve to 200 miles is by no means clear in the different Argentinian laws. Although Law No. 17.094 does not refer to the concept of territorial sea, the Presidential motion clearly indicated "that the precise delimitation of the extension of the national territory has a fundamental importance..." because laws are not clear about "the definition of the aforesaid limits." On the other hand, it does refer to the "adjacent sea," which in Argentina is equivalent to the territorial sea.

The Law on Fishing, No. 17.500, refers to the "Argentinian territorial sea," and declares that the "resources of the Argentinian territorial sea are the property of the National State." As was mentioned earlier, the Civil Code refers to the *territorial seas*. Also Law No. 18.502, which regulates federal and provincial jurisdiction over the territorial sea, constantly refers to the territorial sea. Decree No. 5106 uses the expression "Argentinian territorial sea," while Decree 8802 refers both to the "Argentinian territorial sea" and to the "Argentinian jurisdictional waters." Similar expressions are used by Regulation 265/72 issued by the National Fisheries Service.

All these provisions seem to confirm the existence of a 200-mile territorial sea. However, the nature of the area is still unclear since Law No. 17.094 declares that it does not affect the freedom of navigation and overflight. Furthermore, Regulation 556/72 of the National Fisheries Service no longer use the expression "territorial sea," and Law No. 20.136 amended Law No. 17.500 to substitute the expression "maritime zones under Argentinian sovereignty" for "Argentinian territorial sea."

Recently the Inter-American Juridical Committee has approved a resolution on the law of the sea whereby the 200-mile area is divided into two zones just as in the case of Argentina: a twelve-mile zone where the right of innocent passage is granted, and a zone extending from twelve to 200 miles, where freedom of navigation, overflight, and laying of submarine cables and pipelines is guaranteed.[67] In this particular resolution the use of the expression "territorial sea" is avoided altogether.

The recognition of the freedom of navigation and overflight, and the tendency that is evidenced by Law No. 20.136, reveals that the zone under

Argentinian jurisdiction extending beyond twelve miles has special characteristics, reconciling both the interests and rights of a developing country and that of the international community; the latter being principally the need to assure the freedom of communication and commerce.

The *ius communicationis* as mentioned by Vitoria,[68] Grotius, and others, and as Cavaré points out, continues in full force:

> "In fact there is here an essential human right. It is the right of freedom of communication, developed by Vitoria in the sixteenth century and later taken up by numerous writers. That right is the fundamental social argument that can be invoked in support of the freedom of the high seas."[69]

Therefore, the principle of freedom of navigation must be retained in the interest of the free communication between States.

The combination of both interests is the strongest foundation that can be given to the claims of coastal States to extend their jurisdiction. On the one hand, there is beyond doubt a legitimate interest of Argentina and other countries in a similar situation to extend their sovereignty to the 200-mile limit, for it is both compulsory and urgent to protect national interests in their broad meaning. In this case the national interest is "not the antithesis of a value ... it is one of the many values aimed at by international relations."[70] The need to take into consideration the influence of developing nations in the rules of international law is therefore evident.

On the other hand, it is also evident that these rights are to be implemented in such a manner that they will not affect the freedom of international communications. Argentina, with its lengthy international tradition of respect for the principles of the community of nations, has sought a compatibility of both interests, which has resulted in a 200-mile territorial sea where freedom of communication is safeguarded.

Once again it is necessary to insist[71] that the concept of the territorial sea cannot be given the same meaning today that it had centuries ago, for the conditions of the world and the position of States have changed. The concept, as many others of the law of the sea, is undergoing an evolution that does not imply its abrogation; without losing its essence it is incorporating new characteristics, just as is the case with the high seas and their adaptation to contemporary realities.[72] The evolution of the rules on the landward limit of the territorial sea, the seabed, and subsoil, the freedom of navigation and fishing, is the best evidence of this changing situation.

While freedom of navigation and overflight shall be respected, there is no reason to oppose the exercise of sovereign rights by the coastal State over a 200-mile area. As Friedmann wrote: "... Latin American values and attitudes toward international law have, because of a chronic economic and political position of inferiority, led to the articulation of certain doctrines not inconsistent with general international law, as an expression of national policies dictated by interest, not by any specific system of values."[73]

In conclusion, the following positions may be mentioned with regard to the legal nature of the zone extending beyond the twelve-mile territorial sea:

• Some writers believe that this area belongs to the high seas, and the coastal State exercises only specified powers. The freedom of the high seas is not affected, except in the matters falling under national jurisdiction. The area is sometimes considered as a "contiguous zone," or as a zone of "specialized powers."[74] It should be mentioned, however, that because of the restrictive meaning of the contiguous zone in the Geneva Convention and the doctrine of international law, this concept is less and less resorted to by States[75] and some writers believe that it is a "decadent notion."[76]

• Other writers believe that the zone is nothing but a territorial sea in its traditional meaning and that only the right of innocent passage is admissible.

• The zone has a special nature that differs from the foregoing categories. Some believe that it is an exclusive or reserved fishing zone. Others, particularly Edmundo Vargas, have developed the concept of a patrimonial sea which accords to the coastal State the exclusive right to explore, preserve, and exploit the natural resources of the sea, the seabed, and subsoil, but does not affect other freedoms of the high seas.[77] This concept is embodied in the Declaration of Santo Domingo on the Law of the Sea of June 9, 1972, which also recognizes powers with regard to scientific research and the prevention of pollution. The concept is to some extent similar to what García Amador has described as "zones of exclusive exploitation."[78]

However, whereas Vargas considers that only the freedom of fishing is affected by the concept, other aspects are also affected, namely maritime hunting and all the activities related to the exploration and exploitation of natural resources of every kind. Furthermore, this policy is not founded only on economic and social grounds but it has other motives as well which explains why scientific research is also covered by these claims. Because of this broader meaning, we are unable to agree with Francisco Villagrán Kramer when he states that meteorological stations would not fall under the regulation of the coastal State.[79]

• Other writers believe that the zone is a territorial sea but within a modern and dynamic concept which determines that the rights of the coastal State are limited by the interest of the international community particularly with regard to the freedom of navigation and overflight, and, as suggested by the Inter-American Juridical Committee, the laying of submarine cables and pipelines.[80] It is very clear that the zone cannot be considered a territorial sea in its traditional meaning, for it has special characteristics that make it different. The laws and other declarations on the law of the sea in Argentina do not permit consideration of a patrimonial sea, a concept that is not mentioned at all; furthermore, the Argentinian powers in the area are broader than a mere economic content such as that suggested by the concept of patrimonial sea.

Neither can the zone be considered a part of the high seas, for in accordance with the Geneva Convention no State can claim sovereignty over the high seas — a rule of general international law[81] — and in the case of Argentina such sovereignty is in fact exercised; furthermore, sovereignty and exclusive jurisdiction are characteristics of a territorial domain. The fact that the freedom of navigation and overflight have been recognized does not mean that the area is a part of the high seas, for other freedoms are not recognized, such as fishing and many others that can be related implicitly to the high seas, particularly the operation of submarines, launching of missiles, scientific research, naval operations, gathering of information, and others.

This is a situation, therefore, that is not governed by the rules of general international law nor precisely categorized by doctrine. The different expressions used by the Argentinian legislation, such as "jurisdictional sea" or "maritime zones under Argentinian jurisdiction," correspond to terminological or even political positions rather than to a different content. It is possible to conclude that in accordance with the evolution of the law of the sea, the zone is a territorial sea within a modern and dynamic concept that pursues the compatibility of the interests of the coastal State and those of the international community.

THE CONTINENTAL SHELF

Two Argentinian writers, Segundo R. Storni[82] and José Leon Suárez,[83] were the first to elaborate on this new concept of the law of the sea. The latter advocated an extension of the territorial sea on grounds of security, commerce, fishing, and hunting, taking as a reference the continental "terrace." The Civil Code does not refer to the continental shelf, but Decree No. 1386 of 1944 included among the zones of mineral reserves the "Argentinian epicontinental sea," which undoubtedly included the shelf and subsoil. Decree No. 14.708 of 1946 was more precise on this matter for it proclaimed the Argentinian sovereignty over the continental "terrace." Also Law No. 14.773 on the nationalization of oil declares that the "submarine shelf" is the exclusive property of the Republic. At present Law No. 17.094 follows with regard to the continental shelf the concept and definition of Article 1 of the Geneva Convention.

Both the Geneva Convention and the Argentinian law are unclear with regard to the outer limit of the continental shelf, thereby making possible an unlimited extension of sovereignty in application of the exploitability test. However, Argentinian representatives to international organizations have stated that "it is our interpretation that such rules grant to coastal States sovereign rights over the entire submerged continental territory, that is, up to the outer edge of the continental margin,"[84] and José María Ruda has pointed out that "the base of the continental slope provides us with an adequate criteria, particularly if its geological equivalence with the continent is taken into account."[85] Recently the Inter-American Juridical Committee has favored the outer edge of the continental rise as the limit of national jurisdiction.[86]

References

1. Rodolfo N. Panzarini, "Sobre el Océano," in *Estrategia,* No. 15 (March-April, 1972), p. 82.
2. Ibid., p. 76.
3. Julio Lima, "Financiamiento del desarrollo pesquero en América Latina," in *Revista de Estudios del Pacífico,* No. 4 (March 1972), p. 42. Also M. Grant Gross, *Oceanografía* (Barcelona, 1971), p. 123.
4. Teresa Flouret, *La Doctrina de la Plataforma submarina* (Madrid, 1952), p. 20.
5. Rodolfo N. Panzarini, op. cit., note 1 above, p. 83.
6. Ibid., pp. 92-98.
7. Julio Ques, "Política Naviera Nacional," in *Temas de Economía y Legislación sobre navagación y puertos,* Vol. II (Buenos Aires, 1964), p. 274.
8. *Registro Nacional de la Republica Argentina, 1907* (Buenos Aires, 1915).
9. *Official Bulletin,* January 10, 1967.
10. Ibid., January 7, 1970.
11. Domingo Sabaté Lichtschein, "El Caso de los submarinos del Golfo Nuevo ante el Derecho Internacional," *Revista de Derecho Internacional y Ciencias Diplomáticas* (Rosario, 1961), No. 19-20, p. 99.
12. Alvaro Alvarez, *Los Nuevos Principios del Derecho del Mar* (Montevideo, 1969), p. 151.
13. Julio A. Barberis and Eduardo A. Pigretti, *Régimen Jurídico del Río de la Plata* (Buenos Aires, 1969), p. 151.
14. Ministerio de Relaciones Exteriores, *Boletín Informativo,* No. 5 (May 1971), pp. 99-103.
15. Domingo Sabaté Lichtschein, *La soberanía argentina sobre las Islas Picton, Lennox y Nueva* (Buenos Aires, 1959), p. 134.
16. Isidoro Ruiz Moreno, *Historia de las Relaciones Exteriores Argentinas, 1810-1955* (Buenos Aires, 1961), pp. 229-232.
17. Federico A. Daus, "Caracteres geográficos del límite entre los Océanos Atlantico y Pacifico," Bulletin No. 32, CAEA (June 1966), pp. 2-4; Luis A. Capurro, "Los límites del Océano Atlantico Sur," ibid., pp. 9-14. Other citations in Domingo Sabaté Lichtschein, op. cit., note 15 above, pp. 133-134; and Alfredo Rizzo Romano, *La cuestión de límites con Chile en el Canal de Beagle* (Buenos Aires, 1968), pp. 175-180.
18. Permanent Court Arbitration, "The Grisbadarma Case," in Manley O. Hudson, *Cases and Other Materials on International Law* (St. Paul, Minn., 1929), pp. 407-408.
19. This was the criteria followed by the International Court of Justice in the *North Sea Continental Shelf Case* of February 20, 1969.
20. Domingo Sabaté Lichtschein, "El límite entre los mares de la Argentina y del Uruguay," *La Prensa* (Buenos Aires, February 2, 1970), p. 6.
21. Felipe H. Paolillo, see chapter VIII.
22. *Official Bulletin,* March 17, 1944.
23. Ibid., January 5, 1946.
24. César Díaz Cisneros, *Derecho Internacional Público,* Vol. I (Buenos Aires, 1966), p. 581.
25. Article 2 reads: "The zones of international frontiers of the national territories and those of the ocean coasts, as well as the Argentinian epicontinental sea, shall be temporary zones of mineral reserve."
26. Paragraph 5 of the Preamble of the Decree.
27. *Official Bulletin,* November 13, 1958.

28. Ibid., January 10, 1967.
29. Ibid., January 13, 1967.
30. Ibid., October 31, 1967.
31. Ibid., November 24, 1967.
32. Ibid., January 7, 1970.
33. Ibid., August 8, 1972.
34. Ibid., January 11, 1973.
35. Ibid., February 15, 1973.
36. *La Nación* (Buenos Aires), July 23, 1971.
37. Ibid., August 12, 1971.
38. F. V. García Amador, "La Jurisdicción Especial sobre las Pesquerías: Legislaciones Nacionales y Propuestas de los Gobiernos" (mimeo paper), Provisional Edition (Washington, D.C.: Pan American Union, 1972) and by the same author, "América Latina y el Derecho del Mar" (mimeo paper) (Washington, D.C., 1972).
39. García Amador, "América Latina y el Derecho del Mar," loc. cit., note 38 above, p. 6.
40. Ibid., p. 21. Also García Amador, "La Jurisdicción Especial sobre las Pesquerías," loc. cit., note 38 above, p. 64.
41. Juan Carlos Puig, "La Jurisdicción Marítima Argentina Según la ley No. 17,094 y los Acuerdos con Brasil de 1967," in *Estudios de Derecho y Política Internacional* (Buenos Aires, 1970).
42. Ibid., p. 237.
43. Ibid., p. 238.
44. Ibid.
45. Ernesto Rey Caro, "Paso inocente y libertad de navegación en el ordenamiento jurídico del mar territorial de algunos Estados americanos," in *La Ley*, No. 203 (Buenos Aires, October 24, 1972), p. 7.
46. Jorge Joaquín Llambías, *Tratado de Derecho Civil*, Vol. I (Buenos Aires, 1967), pp. 62-63. Raymundo M. Salvat and José María López Olaciregui, *Tratado de Derecho Civil Argentino*, Vol. I (Buenos Aires, 1964), pp. 237-239.
47. "Territorial sea," "jurisdictional sea," "adjacent sea," "coastal sea," are expressions used interchangeably. César Díaz Cisneros, op. cit., note 24 above, p. 570; Daniel Antokoletz, *Tratado de Derecho Internacional Público*, Vol. II (Buenos Aires, 1951), p. 169; Lucio Moreno Quintana, *Tratado de Derecho Internacional*, Vol. I (Buenos Aires, 1963), p. 343.
48. *Anglo-Norwegian Fisheries Case*, International Court of Justice Reports, 1951, pp. 119-121.
49. Ibid., p. 133.
50. Judge McNair, Dissenting Opinion, International Court of Justice Reports, p. 160.
51. The Grisbadarma Case, cit., note 18 above, pp. 407-408.
52. In a statement before the United Nations Seabed Committee, Ernesto De la Guardia said: "At present the Government of Argentina has interest in the regulation of specified activities undertaken in the 200-mile zone, in particular those related to the jurisdiction and control of fishing, conservation of living resources, and scientific research, and to adopt measures to prevent the noxious effects of marine pollution," in *La Nación* (Buenos Aires), August 12, 1971.
53. Latin American Meeting on Aspects of the Law of the Sea (Lima, August 4-8, 1970), *Final Act*.
54. Emilio Oribe, "Frente Marítimo de la Cuenca." Lecture delivered in the Second Meeting of Lawyers of the Cuenca del Plata, Cordoba, Argentina, April 1970.
55. García Amador, "La Jurisdicción Especial sobre las Pesquerías," loc. cit., note 38 above, p. 72.
56. García Amador, "América Latina y el Derecho del Mar," loc. cit., note 38 above, p. 21.
57. García Amador, "La Jurisdicción Especial sobre las Pesquerías," loc. cit., note 38 above, p. 62.
58. Ministerio de Relaciones Exteriores y Culto, *Boletín Informativo*, No. 3 (March 1972), pp. 46-48.

59. *Boletín Informativo,* No. 10 (October 1971), pp. 227-229.
60. Ibid., No. 2 (February 1972), p. 26.
61. Ministerio de Relaciones Exteriores, *Boletín Informativo,* No. 5 (May 1971), pp. 99-103.
62. Code of Portugal of 1966-1967.
63. *La Nación* (Buenos Aires), July 23, 1971.
64. Ministerio de Relaciones Exteriores, *Boletín Informativo,* No. 7 (July 1971), p. 152.
65. *La Nación,* July 23, 1971.
66. Ibid., August 12, 1971.
67. Ibid., February 11, 1973.
68. José Luis de Azcárraga, *Derecho Internacional Marítimo* (Barcelona, 1970), p. 76.
69. Louis Cavaré, *Le Droit International Public Positif,* Vol. II (Paris, 1969), p. 716.
70. Wolfgang Friedmann, *La nueva estructura del Derecho Internacional* (Mexico, 1967), p. 67.
71. See Frida M. Pfirter de Armas, Chapter XI.
72. Calixto A. Armas Barea and Frida M. Pfirter de Armas, "Pesca y Conservación de los recursos vivos en las aguas de la alta mar," First International Congress on the Law of the Sea, Pôrto Alegre, Brazil, April 1972, pp. 6-12.
73. Wolfgang Friedmann, op. cit., note 70 above, p. 366.
74. F. V. García Amador, *Introducción al Estudio del Derecho Internacional Contemporáneo* (Madrid, 1959), pp. 193-196.
75. Ibid., p. 196.
76. Alejandro Herrero y Rubio, "Una noción decadente: La zona contigua," in *Estudios de Derecho Internacional Marítimo* (Madrid, 1968), pp. 93-104. Calixto A. Armas Barea and Frida M. Pfirter de Armas, op. cit., note 72 above, pp. 7-8.
77. Edmundo Vargas, "Informe Preliminar sobre mar territorial y mar patrimonial," Inter-American Juridical Committee, April 1971, in Francisco Orrego Vicuña, *Chile y el Derecho del Mar* (Santiago: Editorial Andrés Bello, 1972), pp. 137-150.
78. F. V. García Amador, op. cit., note 74 above, pp. 197-203.
79. Francisco Villagrán Kramer, *El mar patrimonial como base de consenso regional. El caso del Mar Caribe* (Guatemala, 1972), p. 21.
80. *La Nación* (Buenos Aires), February 11, 1973.
81. Alvaro Alvarez, op. cit., note 12 above, p. 283.
82. Segundo R. Storni, *Intereses Argentinos en el mar* (Buenos Aires, 1916), p. 38.
83. José Leon Suárez, "El mar territorial y las industrias marítimas" in *Diplomacia Universitaria Americana* (Buenos Aires, 1918).
84. Ernesto De la Guardia, *La Nación* (Buenos Aires), August 12, 1972.
85. José María Ruda, "El límite exterior de la plataforma continental," in *Estudios de Derecho Internacional Público y Privado* (Universidad de Oviedo, 1970), p. 655.
86. *La Nación* (Buenos Aires), February 11, 1973.

Chapter X
Chile

Chapter X

CHILE

Francisco Orrego Vicuña

INTRODUCTION

The geographical characteristics of Chile have strongly influenced the interest of the country in the problems of the law of the sea. From the northern boundary with Peru to Cape Horn, Chile has a length of 4,275 kilometers (2,656 miles), which added to the Chilean Antarctic territory gives a total length of 8,050 kilometers (5,002 miles). The average width of the country is only 178 kilometers (110 miles). These factors create a natural link with the marine environment.

In addition, if important historical, political, economic, and strategic factors are taken into consideration, the continuing preoccupation of the country with the sea becomes evident — a preoccupation which led in the nineteenth century to the occupation of Easter Island, in the 1940s to the legal consolidation of an Antarctic policy, and in the 1950s to the construction of an international system of the South Pacific. This historical perspective reveals an important continuity in purpose, based upon deriving the greatest possible advantage from the maritime environment.

The relevant legislation and practice of Chile is voluminous,[1] and to a certain extent divergent, due to the different historical periods in which it has emerged and the different doctrinal and technical conceptions upon which it has been based. This legal framework has been enriched immensely by the international instruments to which Chile is a party. The legislative panorama is by no means unproblematic, particularly from the point of view of interpretation, nor has it reached a degree of coherence which can be considered satisfactory. Notwithstanding its deficiencies, however, it also reveals a certain maturity which should be emphasized.

THE BREADTH OF THE TERRITORIAL SEA
AND THE ZONE OF EXCLUSIVE EXPLOITATION

One of the most serious problems posed by the present legislation is the breadth of the territorial sea; the clarification of this point is of utmost significance because of its international implications.

The Basic Legislation

The basic legislation with regard to the territorial sea is contained in Article 593 of the Civil Code of 1855, which provides that:

> "The adjacent sea, to a distance of one marine league, measured from the low-water line is territorial sea and of national domain, but the right of police, with regard to the security of the country and the observance of fiscal laws, extends to a distance of four marine leagues measured in the same manner."

Thus, Article 593 established a three-mile territorial sea and a contiguous zone of nine additional miles. In observance of this provision, Chile clearly followed the three-mile rule. Difficulties arose, however, as early as 1914.

By Decree No. 1.857 of the Ministry of Foreign Affairs of November 5, 1914, it was declared that "the adjacent sea to the distance of three nautical miles measured from the low-water line is a jurisdictional or neutral sea in the coasts of the Republic, for the purpose of safeguarding the rights and fulfilling the duties which derive from the neutrality declared by the Supreme Government in case of international conflicts." This provision was compatible with Article 593 of the Civil Code. Shortly thereafter, Decree No. 1.896 of December 15, 1914, was enacted to cover the particular situation of the Straits of Magellan and the southern channels; this decree considered as "territorial or neutral sea the internal waters of the Straits of Magellan and of the southern channels, even in those parts in which the coasts are more than three miles distant."

A liberal interpretation of the Civil Code would have sufficed to include neutrality among the purposes of national security contemplated for the contiguous zone. Inadvertently, however, the expression "territorial sea" was preferred which led to a departure from the classical three-mile rule. It is also important to mention that in the 1930 Hague Conference for the Codification of International Law, Chile was the only country which supported a three-mile territorial sea with a contiguous zone, or, as an alternative, a six-mile territorial sea.[2]

The 200-mile Claim

The first significant departure from the traditional conception was the Official Declaration of President Gabriel Gonzalez Videla, of June 23, 1947, which formed part of the series of declarations which followed that by President Truman of September 28, 1945. On this occasion, national sovereignty was confirmed and proclaimed over the continental terrace[3] at whatever depth, and over the adjacent seas regardless of depth and to the extent necessary to preserve, protect, and exploit the natural resources and wealth of every kind. This measure did not "disregard the similar legitimate rights of other States on a basis of reciprocity, [nor did it] affect the rights of free navigation on the high seas."[4] The breadth of the zone claimed was fixed at 200 miles, without prejudice to future enlargements or modifications.

With the background of this and other similar acts,[5] the First Conference on the Exploitation and Conservation of the Maritime Resources of the South Pacific met in Santiago in August 1952, with the participation of Chile, Ecuador, and Peru. At this meeting a Declaration on the Maritime Zone was approved, on August 18, 1952, proclaiming, among other things, "exclusive sovereignty and jurisdiction over the area of sea adjacent to the coast of each country and extending not less than 200 nautical miles from the said coast," including jurisdiction over the seabed and subsoil corresponding to this zone. It should be noted that in this case 200 miles is the minimum distance. This proclamation "shall not be construed as disregarding the necessary restrictions on the exercise of sovereignty and jurisdiction imposed by international law to permit the innocent and inoffensive passage of vessels of all nations through the zone aforesaid."

Problems of Interpretation

Both the Presidential Declaration of 1947 and the Declaration of 1952 introduced a certain confusion with regard to the breadth of the territorial sea, particularly because of the expressions "sovereignty" and "exclusive jurisdiction" that were used. In addition, the 1952 Declaration referred to innocent passage, which relates to the concept of the territorial sea; the Declaration of 1947, on the other hand, referred to freedom of navigation, which relates to the regime of the high seas.

The enactment of Law No. 8.944 of February 11, 1948, the Water Code, provoked a first difficulty. Article 3 of this law established a territorial sea of fifty kilometers (thirty-one miles) and a contiguous zone of 100 kilometers (sixty-two miles). Shortly thereafter this law was suspended and finally abrogated,[7] being in force only between June 11 and August 19, 1948. During this period, Article 593 of the Civil Code was deprived of its force, although all of its provisions were later re-established. The Water Code, the legislative history of which does not provide any explanation about its origin, contributed to the confusion at the international level because it was mentioned in the documents prepared by the United Nations for the 1958 Conference on the Law of the Sea.

The presidential motion of July 26, 1954, submitting to the approval of Congress the Agreement Supplementary to the Declaration of Sovereignty Over the Maritime Zone of 200 Miles (hereinafter cited as Supplementary Agreement) and other Conventions of the system of the South Pacific, stated in one of its paragraphs:

> "The breadth of the territorial waters has been enlarged, replacing the obsolete concept of three nautical miles . . . by a new legal and philosophical conception which is more in agreement with the vital requirements of our people and which . . . has already been incorporated in similar proclamations or declarations of several countries."[8]

This interpretation soon presented the problem of whether the 1952 Declaration had abrogated Article 593 of the Civil Code, replacing the three-mile territorial sea by a 200-mile one. The Council for the Defense of the State was requested by the Ministry of Foreign Affairs[9] to deliver a legal opinion on the situation and status of the territorial sea with a view to responding to the request of the Secretary General of the United Nations for information on national legislation on the law of the sea. In its Opinion No. 119 of March 6, 1956,[10] the Council stated, after some confusing introductory remarks, that "it should be concluded that the said provision of the Civil Code is no longer in force and that presently the territorial sea of our country is of 200 nautical miles." The Council also suggested the need to amend Article 593 of the Civil Code. Seven years later, on November 19, 1963, a group of socialist senators — among them the present President of Chile — introduced a motion in the Senate proposing the following draft law:

> "Sole Article. Replace Article 593 of the Civil Code … by the following provision: 'The adjacent sea, to a distance of 200 miles, measured from the low-water line, is territorial sea; the seabed and subsoil and the natural resources existing in said zone are of national domain, without prejudice to the authorizations which shall be granted to private parties for its use, transit, and for the innocent passage of ships of all nations.' "

Legal Nature of the Zone

The interpretation given by the instruments cited above departs from the true purposes and nature of the zone. To assimilate the 200-mile zone of the territorial sea seriously hampers and distorts the essential purpose that inspired the claim. In particular, freedom of navigation and overflight are gravely restricted. An interpretation of this nature would certainly not be admitted by the international community; and, furthermore, it represents serious disadvantages for the interests and security of the country, for the application of similar criteria by States to the north of Chile would restrict the freedom of navigation of Chilean ships.

If the essential purpose of the instruments proclaiming 200 miles is examined in the light of their own considerations and foundations, it will be noticed that they refer exclusively to the protection, conservation, and exploitation of natural resources within the area. This is one of the characteristics of the territorial sea, but not its totality. It must be concluded, therefore, that this is not a case of absolute jurisdiction for every purpose but for only one concrete effect: the protection, conservation, and exploitation of the resources of the sea.

Dr. García Amador's analysis clearly reveals the conceptual problems involved in this matter:

> "… is this properly a territorial sea, as has been argued, or is it a contiguous zone only for the purpose of the conservation of resources, as has also been designated, or is it rather a *sui generis* maritime area? Its assimila-

tion to the institution of the territorial sea must be disregarded, among other reasons, because the purpose expressly declared is not to extend the whole of the powers of the coastal State, but only to extend one in particular, for certain effects, to the limit indicated. The purpose of this specialized jurisdiction is not limited to the mere 'conservation' or protection of the marine resources, which is the characteristic of a contiguous zone with regard to fisheries, because it also covers its use and exploitation. . . . Therefore, in spite of the links which it has with the concept of other maritime areas..., the 200-mile zone undoubtedly corresponds to the category of 'zones of exclusive exploitation'. . . ."[12]

This interpretation has been accepted also by Chilean and regional practice. The legal advisor of the Ministry of Foreign Affairs has stated that: "It is well-established that the purpose of the Presidential Declaration of June 23, 1947, and of the Tripartite Pacts of August 1952, is to maintain the integrity and the conservation of the maritime wealth, whatever its nature."[13] The delegate of Chile to the United Nations Conference on the Law of the Sea of 1960 also stated:

"Although from a strictly legal point of view sovereignty over the sea and territorial sea are equivalent expressions, opinions have not been coincident in determining the real legal nature of the 200-mile maritime zone established in the Declaration of Chile and Peru of 1947 and in the Agreements of Santiago in 1952. These documents, it is true, declared sovereignty over the sea, but only for a specific purpose."[14]

Even more precisely, the Joint Report of the delegations of Chile, Ecuador, and Peru to the preparatory meeting of the United Nations Conference on the Law of the Sea, held in Quito in January and February 1958, made the following observation: "The Delegation of Ecuador commented that the three countries agree that the rights proclaimed with regard to the conservation and exploitation of resources did not constitute, in the meaning of the Declaration of Santiago, an alteration of the territorial sea. . . ."[15] Statements in the same vein were made by the Minister of Foreign Affairs of Chile before the General Assembly of the United Nations in 1971; and it is also the interpretation officially communicated by the Chilean Government to the United Nations bodies.[16]

Thus, the preceding considerations indicate that the following maritime areas are established by Chilean legislation: (a) territorial sea with a breadth of three miles (Article 593 of the Civil Code); (b) contiguous zone for the purposes of security and the observance of fiscal laws of nine additional miles (Article 593 of the Civil Code); and (c) zone of exclusive exploitation of the resources of the sea with an extension of 200 miles (Presidential Declaration of 1947 and Declaration on the Maritime Zone of 1952). This means that Article 593 of the Civil Code has not been abrogated.

Delimitation of the Territorial Sea and Maritime Frontier

In accordance with Article 593 of the Civil Code, the breadth of the territorial sea is measured from the low-water line. However, the deeply indented coast extending southwards of the Channel of Chacao permits the delimitation by means of straight baselines in accordance with the conditions of the Convention on the Territorial Sea of 1958. Although Chile considers the waters of the southern archipelagoes to be internal waters,[17] apparently the straight baselines have not been drawn yet. The Declaration of 1952 provides that the delimitation of the jurisdictional zone shall be done "from the coasts."

To prevent conflicts arising from the involuntary violation of the boundary waters, the three South Pacific States — Chile, Ecuador, and Peru — signed the Convention on the Special Zone Maritime Frontier in Lima on December 4, 1954.[18] This Convention creates a special zone which begins twelve marine miles offshore and extends in width for ten miles on each side of the parallel which constitutes the maritime limit between Chile and Peru and between Peru and Ecuador. The accidental presence of vessels of either of the neighboring countries in this zone shall not be considered a violation of territorial waters.

The Chilean Antarctic territory expressly includes the "respective territorial sea."[19] Therefore, the preceding considerations are applicable *mutatis mutandis* to the territorial sea and the national maritime jurisdiction over the area. The 200-mile jurisdictional zone is also applicable to islands, which is particularly interesting in the case of Easter Island.

International Conflicts

The Chilean legislation, contrary to the case of Ecuador and Peru, has not provoked major international conflicts. In addition to minor conflicts arising from the penetration of Chilean or Peruvian vessels into the jurisdictional waters of the neighboring country, there has been only one conflict of any importance with American vessels. On December 12, 1957, a fleet of fishing vessels operating in the territorial sea, and to a distance of thirty miles offshore, refused to observe Chilean legislation. After diplomatic negotiations between the Governments of Chile and the United States, an Agreement was signed on January 2, 1958, between the Under Secretary of Foreign Affairs and a representative of the American Tunaboat Association; the latter undertook to request the pertinent fishing permits, pay the corresponding royalties, and applicable fees.[20]

INTERNATIONAL LEGISLATION AND DOCTRINE

The practice and legislation of Chile has been influenced considerably by international legislation and doctrine which have gradually tended towards a broader jurisdiction by the coastal State. In this connection, mention should be made of the Convention between Chile and the United States on transportation of intoxicating liquors by Chilean ships, signed in Washington on May 28,

1930,[21] as part of the series of "Liquor Treaties" promoted by the Government of the United States. In this Convention "the Government of Chile agrees that it will raise no objection to the boarding of private vessels under the Chilean flag outside the limits of territorial waters by the authorities of the United States. . . ." With regard to security matters, a similar tendency may be noted in the Declaration of Panama of 1939 and the Inter-American Treaty of Reciprocal Assistance.

Within this process of broadening the jurisdiction of coastal States, the participation of Chile in the system of the South Pacific and in the Geneva Conferences of 1958 and 1960 deserves special attention.

The System of the South Pacific

The institutional framework of the system of the South Pacific was established at the First Conference on the Exploitation and Conservation of the Maritime Resources of the South Pacific, which met in Santiago in August 1952. The Conference adopted the Declaration on the Maritime Zone and a number of basic instruments, including a Joint Declaration on the problems of fisheries in the South Pacific and the constituent text of the Permanent Commission of the South Pacific States.[22]

The Permanent Commission has gradually evolved a voluminous regional legislation consisting of conventions, agreements, and resolutions.[23] In addition to the Convention of 1952, Chile has ratified the Regulations of Permits for the Exploitation of the Resources of the South Pacific, signed in Quito, Ecuador, on December 12, 1955,[24] and the Supplementary Agreement of 1954 cited above.

The agreements and resolutions of the system are binding on member countries. In accordance with Article 4 of the Convention on the Organization of the Permanent Commission of the Conference:

> "The resolutions approved by the Permanent Commission shall be valid and binding in each of the member countries from the date of their approval except those which are objected to by any of the member countries in the following ninety days; in this case the resolution or resolutions in question will not be in force in the country raising the objection as long as it does not withdraw such objections. . . ."

The compatibility of this procedure with the Chilean constitutional system has been confirmed by the *Contraloría General de la Republica* not only with regard to the Resolutions mentioned in Article 4 but also with regard to Conventions.[25]

The work of the Permanent Commission has been conducted mainly at the technical level and only very exceptionally has it dealt with political problems. The influence of the regional system is particularly evident in the Chilean legislation on fisheries.

The Position of Chile in the Geneva Conferences

The Governments of Chile, Ecuador, and Peru agreed to support a common position in the United Nations Conference on the Law of the Sea of 1958. The joint position was agreed upon at a preparatory meeting held in Quito in January and February 1958.[26] They agreed to postpone consideration of the problem of the breadth of the territorial sea until the questions relating to fisheries, the contiguous zone, and the continental shelf had been clarified by the Conference. At the same time, they agreed to support the principle of the freedom of each State to fix the breadth of its territorial sea in accordance with its particular conditions.

Upon the failure of the Conference to reach an agreement on the breadth of the territorial sea,[27] the chief delegates of Chile, Ecuador, and Peru issued a Joint Declaration reaffirming the basic principles of the system of the South Pacific and declaring the need to pursue the search for equitable solutions with regard to the special rights of coastal States.[28]

The results of the Second United Nations Conference (1960) were not much better. Chile, Ecuador, and Peru voted against the joint proposal of the United States and Canada for a six-mile territorial sea and a fishing zone of six additional miles. Chile opposed this proposal on the ground that it would have granted rights to vessels which had been carrying out fishing activities in the fishing zone during the five-year period prior to January 1, 1958, for an additional ten years.[29]

Chile is not a party to any of the Geneva Conventions, although it signed the Convention on the Continental Shelf.

THE CONTINENTAL SHELF AND THE OCEAN FLOOR

Both the Presidential Declaration of 1947 and the Declaration on the Maritime Zone of 1952 expressly referred to jurisdiction over the submarine area, although the proclamation contained in each of these instruments is different. The Declaration of 1947 proclaimed sovereignty over "all the continental shelf adjacent to the continental and island coasts . . . whatever may be their depth," thus basing itself on geological considerations independently of criteria of distance or depth. The 200 miles relates to "especially all fisheries and whaling activities." The Declaration of 1952, on the other hand, is unequivocal with regard to the criterion of distance of 200 miles, both over the maritime zone proper and over the "seabed and subsoil thereof." The latter, then, is broader since the jurisdiction is extended over submarine areas which do not belong to the continental shelf, provided that they are comprised within the 200-mile area.

This approach is justified on the ground that Chile, for all practical purposes, does not have a continental shelf. Because of this, the Declaration of 1952 has not made the jurisdiction over the sea dependent upon the jurisdiction over the submarine area which is the general approach followed by other claims; on the contrary, the jurisdiction over the submarine area is a consequence of jurisdiction over the superjacent waters.

Even though Chile has no shelf, it followed with particular interest the process of elaboration of the Geneva Convention on the Continental Shelf.[30] The concern of the government was satisfied by the adoption of the exploitability concept by the Convention and the provision of Article 7 with regard to the rights of the coastal State to exploit the subsoil by means of tunnels.[31] Chile signed the Convention on October 31, 1958, and submitted it to the approval of Congress on March 4, 1959.[32] Notwithstanding the fact that both Committees on Foreign Relations of the House of Representatives and of the Senate favorably recommended its approval,[33] the Convention was never considered by the plenary sessions and the Executive withdrew it from Congress in December 1971.

In all probability this action was related to the current situation in the United Nations Seabed Committee. Chile favors the establishment of an international regime, provided that some prior conditions are met. The first of these is the recognition of the right of the coastal State to fix the limits of its national jurisdiction in accordance with its particular characteristics and economic needs. A second condition is that prior to the delimitation of the international seabed area, an agreement must be reached concerning the legal regime of this area beyond the limits of national jurisdiction, a regime which must be based not on the freedom of exploitation but on the general interest of the international community and, particularly, of the developing countries. Chile also supports the view that a new conference on the law of the sea must undertake a comprehensive examination of the problems which have not yet been solved, rather than dealing with isolated issues only.[34]

THE STRAITS OF MAGELLAN

The legal regime of the Straits of Magellan as an international waterway was established by the treaty between Chile and Argentina of July 23, 1881, Article 5 of which provides that: "... it is perpetually neutralized and the freedom of navigation ensured for the flags of all nations. In the interests of ensuring this freedom and neutrality, fortifications or military defenses which might contradict this purpose shall not be built on its coasts."[35]

This liberal regime would not appear to conflict with the current discussion on the freedom of navigation in international straits, the waters of which could become territorial waters of the coastal State as a consequence of the enlargement of the breadth of the territorial sea.

LEGAL REGIME OF NAVIGATION

The legal regime of navigation is established in the Commercial Code and in the Law of Navigation,[36] which also regulates the nationality of ships. Navigation of foreign merchant vessels through the Chilean territorial sea is subject to the principle of innocent passage which, to a certain extent, has been restricted in the interest of safety of navigation, particularly with regard to the obligation of using pilots and experts for the navigation of the southern channels.[37] The President of Chile is empowered to order the temporary closure for commerce of one or more major ports in special circumstances such as international war or because of sanitary requirements.[38]

The entry of foreign warships into the territorial sea is subject to prior notification and in some cases to prior authorization.[39] In 1960 the Governments of Chile and Argentina signed a controversial agreement concerning the innocent passage of Argentinian warships in the southern channels, an agreement which was not ratified by Chile.[40]

The Presidential Declaration of 1947 ensures freedom of navigation on the high seas which form part of the jurisdictional zone of 200 miles. Although the Declaration on the Maritime Zone of 1952 refers to "innocent passage" in the 200-mile zone, this constitutes a technical error since the nature of the zone itself ensures freedom of navigation. This interpretation has been confirmed by Chilean practice and upheld by the jurisprudence of the Supreme Court.[41]

THE LEGAL SYSTEM OF CHILE AND INTERNATIONAL LAW

The legal provisions which have been examined and which are supplemented by many other provisions on fishing and related institutions[42] have been systematically and sometimes violently criticized by foreign governments and scholars[43] as violations of international law.

A principal criticism is that the claims refer both to the resources of the submarine area and of the superjacent waters, which in the opinion of some critics is invalid *ab initio* because it would be incompatible with the principle of the freedom of the seas.[44] This argument starts from a base which is historically and legally false, that is, that the principle of the freedom of the seas prevents the exercise of jurisdiction by the coastal State over the resources of the adjacent sea. If this were the case, the exercise of jurisdiction over the submarine area would also be incompatible, for it is only another manner of exploiting the wealth of the sea.

If the contents and the evolution of this principle are examined with impartiality, it will become evident that its real meaning is different. As originally formulated the principle comprised, on the one hand, the freedom of navigation and, on the other, the freedom to exploit the resources of the sea, which were then limited to fishing. With the technological evolution, the foundations of the principle proved to be no longer valid, particularly with regard to the fact that the resources of the sea could be overexploited and exhausted. At the same time, this evolution opened up the possibility of exploiting the resources of the submarine area. Upon this evidence the principle evolved from its original negative content – prohibition to interfere – to a positive content, that is, the exploitation would be subordinated to the equal rights of others; thus, measures of conservation were gradually admitted and the abuse of rights was controlled. Furthermore, the concept of the exploitation of the resources in the general interest of the international community came into being.

If the principle was immutable, freedom of navigation could never have evolved to the point of comprising freedom of overflight – which Grotius did not foresee. Nor did Grotius foresee the exploitation of the resources of submarine areas. And if the jurisdiction of the State is admitted with regard to submarine areas, which constitutes a derogation from the principle of freedom of the seas, there is no valid reason for not admitting the jurisdiction of the State over the resources of the superjacent waters. Both aspects are only different applications of the same phenomenon, the exploitation of the resources of the sea, just as freedom of navigation and overflight are different applications of the *jus communicationis.*

This evolution of the principle has wrought an important change of perspective. From the very moment when the principle prohibited the abuse of the sea, which was clearly established by the beginning of this century when the dangers of overexploitation became evident, the act which is intrinsically contrary to international law is the one which leads to irrational exploitation, not the one designed to prevent it. The jurisdiction of the coastal State over fisheries prevents abusive use and overexploitation, which corresponds exactly to the purpose pursued by the Declarations of 1947 and 1952. Because these instruments prevent an act which is not compatible with the actual contents of the principle of the freedom of the seas, they are accomplishing a role identical to the one of protest in international law, that is, refusing to accept the effects of an act which is contrary to this legal system.

A second situation which has been criticized is the fact that jurisdiction over the submarine area extends to a distance of 200 miles.[45] Thus far, international law has not established a precise criterion for fixing the outer limit of the jurisdictional zone of the coastal State, as is clearly evidenced by the work of the United Nations on the international regime of the seabed and ocean floor. Furthermore, national practice throughout the world demonstrates that the criterion of depth has been used as much as the criterion of distance, apart from the use of a geological criterion which is the most variable. Nor has the Geneva Convention been any more precise in this regard, in addition to the fact that it does not establish a norm of customary international law generally binding.

The paradox of the existing law is that by applying the depth criterion a State may obtain jurisdiction over an area well in excess of 200 miles, whereas States whose coasts possess different geographical characteristics, and which extend their jurisdiction by reference to a distance criterion, are subject to objections.

Although Chile embraces a particular orientation, it is determined, nevertheless, to adopt a flexible attitude in the search for an international consensus. The 1973 United Nations Conference on the Law of the Sea will provide an opportunity for the great maritime powers to demonstrate their flexibility. An international consensus is becoming increasingly urgent in view of the polarization of positions of a radical nature which are not conducive to the development of a new law of the sea.

References

1. All pertinent texts have been compiled in Francisco Orrego Vicuña, *Chile y el Derecho del Mar* (Santiago: Editorial Andrés Bello, 1972).
2. Report of the Delegate of Chile, Mr. Miguel Cruchaga Tocornal, to the Conference of 1930, *Memoria del Ministerio de Relaciones Exteriores (Annual Report of the Ministry of Foreign Affairs),* 1930, pp. 245 ff.
3. "The zone around the continents, extending from the low-water line to the base of the continental slope, constitutes the 'continental terrace.'" F. V. García Amador, *The Exploitation and Conservation of the Resources of the Sea* (Leyden: Sijthoff, 1963), p. 87.
4. For the protest of the United States of July 2, 1948, see *Laws and Regulations on the Regime of the High Seas* (New York: United Nations Legislative Series, ST/LEG/ SER.B/.1, January 11, 1951), pp. 7-8. For a summary of the British protest of February 6, 1948, see Barry B. L. Auguste, *The Continental Shelf: The Practice and Policy of the Latin American States with Special Reference to Chile, Ecuador and Peru* (Geneva, 1960), p. 113.
5. In particular, Supreme Decree No. 781 of August 1, 1947, of the Government of Peru. See Conferencia sobre Explotación y Conservación de las riquezas marítimas del Pacífico Sur: *Convenios y otros Documentos 1952-1969,* 3rd ed. (Lima, 1970).
6. The Declaration was ratified in Chile by Decree No. 432 of the Ministry of Foreign Affairs of September 23, 1954. Published in the *Official Gazette* of November 22, 1954. The approval of Congress was communicated by Note of the Senate No. 495 of September 2, 1954.
7. The suspension was established by Laws No. 8.978, 9.288, 9.394, and 9.575. The abrogation was done by Law No. 9.896. The Water Code actually in force, approved by Law No. 9.909, is not applicable to maritime waters.
8. *Diario de Sesiones del Senado,* 1954, Session 15. *Anexo de documentos,* pp. 891 ff.
9. Ministry of Foreign Affairs, Note No. 00318, January 13, 1956.
10. Files of the Council of the Defense of the State, Santiago, Chile.
11. *Diario de Sesiones del Senado,* Session 13, November 19, 1963. *Anexo de documentos,* pp. 1314 ff.
12. F. V. García Amador, *Introducción al Estudio del Derecho Internacional Contemporáneo* (Madrid, 1959), pp. 202-203.
13. Opinion No. 15.639. April 22, 1960.
14. Francisco Orrego Vicuña, op. cit., note 1 above, p. 39.
15. *Memoria del Ministerio de Relaciones Exteriores,* 1958, Vol. I, pp. 381 ff.
16. *Limits and Status of the Territorial Sea, Exclusive Fishing Zones, Fishery Conservation Zones and the Continental Shelf* (United Nations Doc. A/AC.138/50, 1971 [August 1971]).
17. Guillermo Lagos Carmona, *Las Fronteras de Chile* (Santiago, 1966), p. 43.
18. Ratified in Chile by Supreme Decree of the Ministry of Foreign Affairs of September 21, 1967.
19. Supreme Decree No. 1.747 (November 6, 1940) of the Ministry of Foreign Affairs on Chilean Antarctic territory.
20. *Memoria del Ministerio de Relaciones Exteriores,* 1958, Vol. I, pp. 65 ff.

21. Ratified in Chile by Decree No. 1.739 of the Ministry of Foreign Affairs of December 30, 1930.
22. All these instruments have been ratified in Chile by Decree No. 432, cit. in note 6 above.
23. Texts of the Convention in Conferencia sobre Explotación y Conservatión de las riquezas marítimas del Pacífico Sur: *Convenios y ṭtros Documentos 1952-1969*, cit. in note 5 above.
24. Ratified in Chile by Decree No. 102 of the Ministry of Foreign Affairs of March 9, 1956. Published in the *Official Gazette* of April 7, 1956.
25. *Contraloría General de la Republica*, Opinion No. 50.227, September 10, 1957.
26. *Memoria del Ministerio de Relaciones Exteriores*, 1958, pp. 381 ff.
27. For the different proposals introduced in this Conference and Chile's voting record, see *Ministerio de Relaciones Exteriores:* Comentarios sobre las Conferencias de Ginebra de 1958 y 1960, February 6, 1963. Cited in Francisco Orrego Vicuña, op. cit., note 1 above, pp. 65 ff.
28. United Nations Doc. A/Conf. 13/L.50, April 27, 1958.
29. For the statements of the Delegate of Chile, Mr. Melo Lecaros, see Comentarios, op. cit., note 27 above.
30. See "Dictamen de la Asesoría Jurídica del Ministerio de Relaciones Exteriores sobre un proyecto [de la Comisión de Derecho Internacional de las Naciones Unidas] ... relativo a la plataforma continental...." *Memoria del Ministerio de Relaciones Exteriores*, 1952, pp. 228 ff.
31. This provision was of particular importance for the case of the coal mines of Lota, which penetrate the submarine subsoil by means of tunnels reaching a depth of 800 meters.
32. Presidential motion No. 7 of March 4, 1959. *Boletín de Sesiones Extraordinarias del Senado*, 1958-1959. Vol. II, Session 25, March 11, 1959, p. 1136.
33. Report of the Committee of Foreign Relations of the Senate, July 7, 1959. *Boletín de Sesiones Ordinarias del Senado*, 1959, Vol. I, Session 13, July 14, 1959, p. 787. Report of the Committee of Foreign Relations of the House, August 1, 1962. *Boletín de Sesiones Ordinarias de la Cámara de Diputados*, 1962, Vol. IV, Session 33, August 7, 1962, pp. 3,061 ff.
34. See statements by the Delegate of Chile in the United Nations Committee on the Seabed and Ocean Floor, United Nations Doc. A/AC.138/SC.1/SR.32, March 11, 1970; United Nations Doc. A/AC.138/SR.48, March 16, 1971.
35. See Julio Escudero Guzmán, *Situación Jurídica Internacional de las aguas del Estrecho de Magallanes* (Santiago, 1927).
36. *Official Gazette*, July 3, 1878.
37. *Reglamento de Practicaje y Pilotaje para la República.* Supreme Decree No. 1.836 of August 20, 1955; as amended by Decree No. 5.092 (December 15, 1956), Decree 710 (August 3,1968), and Decree 657 (August 3, 1970).
38. Customs Order. Decree No. 213 (July 22, 1953), Article 8.
39. *Reglamento de Admisión y Permanencia de Naves de Guerra Extranjeras en las aguas territoriales, puertos, bahías y canales de la República de Chile.* Supreme Decree No. 1.385 of October 18, 1951, as amended by Decree No. 2.623 of September 16, 1955.
40. Agreement on Navigation between Chile and Argentina, signed in Buenos Aires on June 12, 1960.
41. Supreme Court, *J. Lauritzen et al. v. the State*, December 1, 1955. Cited in Gonzalo Biggs, *Recopilación de la Legislación Pesquera y Marítima de Chile* (Santiago: Instituto de Fomento Pesquero, 1965), pp. 145 ff.
42. For the technical legislation on fishing and institutional legislation, see Francisco Orrego Vicuña, op cit., note 1 above.
43. In addition to the protests cited in note 3 above, see also H. Lauterpacht, "Sovereignty over Submarine Areas," *British Yearbook of International Law*, 1950; Richard Young, "Recent Developments with Respect to the Continental Shelf," *American Journal of International Law*, Vol. 42, October 1948.

44. Lauterpacht, *British Yearbook of International Law,* 1950, pp. 398, 412-414.
45. This criticism was made in particular in the protest of the United Kingdom, which objected to the extension "to the unprecedented distance of 200 nautical miles . . . without regard to the depth of the sea." See Barry B. L. Auguste, op. cit., note 4 above.

Chapter XI
Peru: The Road to the West

Chapter XI

PERU: THE ROAD TO THE WEST

Frida M. Pfirter de Armas

INTRODUCTION

"The road to the west" — the metaphorical phrase used by the Minister of Foreign Affairs, General Mercado Jarrín — succinctly describes the importance which Peru attaches to the sea. It should be stressed that the foundation of Peru's position with regard to the law of the sea is based on human and socio-economic considerations and not on defense or security considerations.[1]

The geographic and geological characteristics of Peru have created a rather unique situation. Although it has a very long coastline (1,400 miles), Peru does not have a continental shelf of any significant proportions. This has led some Peruvian writers to develop a theory of "compensation" designed to counter-balance the lack of a shelf, a theory they justify on grounds of economic development.[2] These writers have also insisted on the close relationship between the land territory and the sea, between the physical elements and the coastal people. As one writer stated: "No other people can have a better title over the sea surrounding their habitat, and every law must recognize this right in the nature of things."[3] From time immemorial the Peruvian people have exercised an exclusive right over their sea; it is inconceivable that foreigners should be capable of affecting these rights. Thus, in the opinion of Alberto Ulloa and Arias Schrieber, a "right of accession" has emerged.[4] The basis of this "right" according to these two writers has been created both by nature and by man, who taking advantage of the natural resources has created a proprietal relationship over the maritime domain.

It should be noted also that the abrupt decline of the Peruvian seabed generates wide differences in the temperature and conditions of the sea, causing both to vary according to depth. Cold waters from the bottom of the sea are constantly rising to the surface in a zone which should be warm. The combination of the Peruvian and the Humboldt currents, as well as the incidence of favorable winds, creates vast "plankton prairies" and an exceptionally rich source of ichthyological wealth.[5] The species of the Peruvian sea are mainly of the pelagic kind; in other words, some species do not live exclusively in the vicinity of the coast but may move seawards as far as 200 miles.[6] The guano birds, which feed on these species, produce an excellent natural fertilizer.[7]

The importance of fishing and the fishing industry in Peru is emphasized by climatological and geographic factors. The lack of rain, both on the coastal plain and in the mountain regions, means that the area of cultivatable land is small in relation to the size of the country. This has been influential in decreasing the number of people engaged in agriculture in comparison to the overall population growth of the country.

The exploitation of the resources of the sea, the protection of the ichthyological wealth, and the promotion of the fishing industry and related activities are fundamental to the economic development of the country, as well as to the improvement of nutrition and the standards of living of all the Peruvian people. For Peru, the protection of the resources of the sea is not only a legitimate interest which deserves priority, but it is also a duty. Successive Peruvian governments have viewed these tasks within the framework of the exercise of sovereignty which belongs to every State, and which enables it to legislate in accordance with its interests and to enact the provisions necessary to ensure the prosperity of the country.

These economic considerations have been the basis of every claim expounded by Peru since 1947. Control and protection of the natural resources are based on the most fundamental of humanitarian values – the right to live. The basic interests of the people – in the words of the Declaration of Santiago of 1952 – have determined that Peru must enact special legislation to prevent any activities which might endanger the existence of its natural resources.

PERUVIAN LEGISLATION AND THE MARITIME ZONE

The Peruvian position with regard to the law of the sea in general and to the territorial sea in particular has been the object of conflicting interpretations for a quarter of a century. To a great extent this is due to the contradictory nature of Peruvian legislation and pronouncements, as well as to an obvious preference of Peruvian legal advisers and legislators not to be bound by the traditional language and conceptions of the law of the sea. Thus, students of the Peruvian position must examine the relevant sources of Peru's legislation and practice and attempt to reach certain conclusions as to their legal import by reference to the traditional conceptions of the law of the sea embodied in customary and conventional international law.

A fundamental dichotomy in the analysis of the Peruvian position exists between those who interpret the 200-mile maritime zone as a *zone of specialized competence* and those who interpret it as a *territorial sea*. In the following pages an attempt will be made to clarify the applicable legislation and to review its implementation. On the basis of these findings some conclusions may be possible.

The foundation of Peru's "road to the west" is Supreme Decree No. 781 of

August 1, 1947. This decree, which was signed by President José Luis Bustamante y Rivero, a distinguished international lawyer who subsequently served as a Judge of the International Court of Justice from 1961 to 1970, and Enrique García Sayán, Minister of Foreign Affairs and subsequently Secretary General of the Permanent Commission of the South Pacific States, remains a pillar of the Peruvian position; and most subsequent legislation is organically related to it. The decree, as will be seen, is also the most important single source of confusion surrounding Peru's position.

The decree was inspired by a number of precedents, including the Truman Proclamation of 1945 and similar acts promulgated in Argentina, Chile, and Mexico. The most proximate and causal of these precedents was the Declaration of the President of Chile of June 23, 1947. The Truman Proclamation and the Argentinian and Mexican acts related exclusively to the question of national jurisdiction over the continental shelf (although it is true that the Argentinian decree referred also to the epicontinental sea); only the Chilean declaration extended national sovereignty to the adjacent sea.

Thus, Supreme Decree No. 781 appears to have been specifically inspired by Chile's action. Like the Chilean declaration, the Peruvian decree extended national sovereignty and jurisdiction to the submarine areas regardless of the depth of the superjacent waters (Article 1) and to the adjacent sea to the extent necessary for the reservation, protection, conservation, and exploitation of the natural wealth and resources therein (Article 2). Article 3 of the decree established a 200-mile zone within which the provisions of Articles 1 and 2 would be operative. Finally, Article 4 of the decree, in a provision that has created considerable doctrinal confusion, declared that: "The present declaration is without prejudice to the right of free navigation of the vessels of all nations, in accordance with international law." The injection of this provision, as will be shown below is confusing because it apparently contradicts the regime of "sovereignty and jurisdiction" established in Articles 1 and 2. If the zone created is a territorial sea, then the provision for free navigation would be incompatible with the traditional conception of a territorial sea embodied in customary and conventional international law.

Supreme Decree No. 781 functions as the basic norm of Peruvian legislation with respect to the law of the sea. The important Law No. 17,824 on Port Authorities, which has been in force since January 1, 1952, provides, for example, that the breadth of the territorial waters be fixed by reference to Decree No. 781.[8] Petroleum Law No. 11,780 of May 12, 1952, is also based on Decree No. 781. Article 14 of this law divided the national territory into four zones, one of which is the continental terrace, defined as "the zone between the western boundary of the coastal zone and an imaginary line drawn at a distance of 200 miles from the low-water mark."

On August 18, 1952, Chile, Ecuador, and Peru approved a Declaration on the

Maritime Zone, proclaiming as a norm of their international maritime policy exclusive sovereignty and jurisdiction over the adjacent sea to a distance of not less than 200 miles. This sovereignty and jurisdiction also extended to the seabed and subsoil. The Declaration, however, recognized as a limitation on the exercise of sovereignty and jurisdiction the rules of international law concerning innocent passage. This reference to innocent passage (as distinct from freedom of navigation) is important because it is an element which is characteristic of the territorial sea and would, therefore, tend to confirm the territorial sea nature of the maritime zone.[9] This interpretation of the Santiago Declaration by Peru has been expressed on numerous occasions in international conferences.[10]

The Declaration on the Maritime Zone of 1952 was followed in 1954 by a Supplementary Agreement[11] in which the signatories agreed to proceed jointly in the legal defense of the principle of sovereignty over the maritime zone to a distance of not less than 200 miles, including the seabed and subsoil thereof. They also agreed to consult each other and to collaborate closely in regard to claims or suits against any one of them, without prejudice to the individual right to enter into agreements which are not contrary to the common rules of the contracting parties.

Both the 1952 Santiago and 1954 Lima instruments were approved in Peru by Legislative Resolution No. 12,305 of May 6, 1955. Ecuador has also ratified both instruments, but Chile has only ratified the first.[12]

At the Conferences of Santiago in 1952 and of Lima in 1954, a number of important conventions were signed, including the Joint Declaration on the problems of fisheries in the South Pacific; regulations concerning maritime hunting activities in the South Pacific; convention on the system of sanctions; convention on measures of supervision and control in the maritime zones of the signatory countries; convention on the granting of permits for the exploitation of the resources of the South Pacific; and Convention on the Special Zone of the Maritime Frontier.[13]

Also at the Conference of 1952, the Convention on the Organization of the Permanent Commission of the Conference on the Exploitation and Conservation of the Maritime Resources of the South Pacific was signed and later ratified by all three countries.[14] In accordance with Article 4 of the Convention, the Permanent Commission is empowered to adopt resolutions which are binding on member States, unless any one of them objects to it within ninety days, in which case the resolution shall not be in force for the objecting country until it withdraws such objections. The Commission has approved several measures which are applicable in the three countries,[15] and in the opinion of García Sayán this Commission is part of the historical evolution leading to economic integration.[16]

One of the most important instruments of this regional system is the Convention on the Special Zone of the Maritime Frontier signed in Lima on

December 4, 1954. This zone begins twelve miles from the coast and extends ten miles on each side of the parallel which constitutes the maritime frontier between Chile and Peru and between Peru and Ecuador. The accidental presence of vessels of either of the neighboring countries in this zone shall not be considered a violation of the territorial waters comprised in the maritime zone.[17] This Convention has been ratified by all three countries, in the case of Peru by Legislative Resolution No. 12,305 of May 6, 1955.[18]

No person may engage in activities of hunting, fishing, extraction, or any other kind of exploitation of the resources of the 200-mile area, unless provided with the pertinent permit by Peru. The State has also reserved the right to regulate every aspect of these activities, including the granting of permits. These provisions have been established by the Convention on the Granting of Permits for the Exploitation of the Resources of the South Pacific, signed in Lima in 1954 and ratified in Peru by Law No. 12,305.[19] Peru has also enacted national legislation on this matter, which will be examined in more detail below.

The first reference to the air space above the territorial sea is found in the Convention on Measures of Supervision and Control of the Maritime Zones of the signatory countries, signed in Lima in 1954. Article 2 of this Convention provides: "The supervision and control referred to by Article 1 shall only be exercised by each country within its jurisdictional waters. However, its ships and aircraft may enter the maritime zone of the other signatory countries without special authorization when the said country expressly requests its cooperation."

This provision confirms and reinforces the interpretation that the zone is a territorial sea, for this is the only maritime space which does not permit the freedom of overflight. If it is provided that the aircraft of the signatory countries may enter the zone without authorization when their assistance is requested, it follows that if such assistance is not requested there will be no freedom of overflight.[20] In any case, third countries not parties to the Convention would not have such rights.

Mention should be made also of the significant Law No. 13,508, which is the General Organic Law of the Navy. Because this law is classified, its precise text is not known; however, the provisions of Article 4, which refers to the 200-mile breadth of the territorial sea, have been revealed through public debates.[21]

Article 2 of Law 15,720 on Civil Aviation provides that Peru exercises "exclusive jurisdiction over the space above its territory and its jurisdictional waters comprised within the 200 miles."

Decree-Law No. 17,752 of July 24, 1969, approving the General Water Law, provides in Article 1: "All waters, without exception, are the property of the State and the domain over them is inalienable and imprescriptible. There is neither private property nor acquired rights over waters. The use of waters which is justified and rational can be granted only in accordance with the social interest and the development of the country." Article 4 further provides: "The provisions of this law comprise the maritime, terrestrial, and atmospheric waters of the national territory and space, in all of their physical states, which principally but not exclusively are: (a) the waters of the sea extending to 200 miles; and (b) the waters of gulfs, bays, indentures, and creeks. . . ." Article 55 refers to the waters of the "territorial sea." The decree regulating this law provides that the rights of the State over the 200 miles adjacent to the national territory shall be exercised in accordance with Supreme Decree No. 781 and the Declaration of Santiago of 1952.

The General Mining Law of June 8, 1971, regulates the activities "related to the exploitation of the mineral substances of the soil and subsoil of the national territory, as well as of the sea, the continental margin, and the ocean floor and their respective subsoils to a distance of 200 nautical miles from the coast. . . ."

The General Fishing Law No. 18,810 of March 25, 1971, uses in several instances the expressions "jurisdictional sea" and "Peruvian sea." The State administers the hydrobiological resources and promotes and supervises fishing activities. For that purpose it sponsors a greater participation of Peruvians in this activity and determines the limits and zones where foreigners are allowed to participate. There is no exclusive fishing zone reserved for Peruvians: "Every person has the right to engage in activities of research, extraction, transformation, and commercialization of the hydrobiological resources, prior authorization, permit, license, or concession being granted by the Supreme Government as the case may be" (Article 7); this provision differs from the Convention on the Special Zone of the Maritime Frontier[22] which establishes that in the first twelve miles fishing and hunting are reserved exclusively to the nationals of each country.

From these provisions, which at first sight appear contradictory, one may conclude that only in the frontier zones with Chile and Ecuador is there a belt of twelve miles in which fishing and hunting is reserved to Peruvian nationals.

The law classifies fishing according to its objectives or uses in the following categories: (1) Fishing for human consumption (to satisfy the needs of the population in a direct manner), which is subdivided (Article 22) into (a) professional fishing, done by those "dedicated to extraction using in their activities small vessels and minor fishing equipment" or by those who use "large vessels, but own a condominium over such vessels and their fishing equipment" (Article 43); and (b) commercial fishing, undertaken by corporations of national or foreign ownership, the Public Corporation of Fishing Services, Joint Enterprises, and the Associated State Enterprises (Article 27). (2) Fishing for indirect human consumption, that is, industrial fishing which provides the raw materials for the production of fish meal and oil. (3) Fishing for research and scientific purposes. (4) Sport fishing.

Professional fishing for direct human consumption has been reserved to Peruvian nationals; the vessels employed in this activity are also required to be owned by Peruvians (Articles 26 and 43). Commercial fishing for direct human consumption is open to national enterprises — private, State owned, or mixed — as well as to foreign enterprises.

Fishing for indirect human consumption may be undertaken by existing enterprises, private or foreign owned, but the vessels, crews, and fishermen must be Peruvians (Article 28). This provision is also related to Articles 57-63 of the Regulations of Foreign Investments which provide that the present participation of foreign capital must not exceed 49 percent of the corporate capital. However, Article 58 provides that the incorporation of new fishing enterprises, with participation of foreign capital, shall not be authorized with respect to fishing for indirect human consumption, which apparently contradicts the provision of Article 28 mentioned above. Foreign investment is also prohibited in the fish meal and oil industries, as well as the transfer of shares from Peruvian nationals to foreigners or to enterprises with foreign capital.

Individuals may engage freely in sport fishing, but other legal entities require prior authorization. Persons or associations, both national and foreign, engaged in fishing for purposes of scientific research are required to observe the regulations in force.

The provisions which have been examined refer to individuals and enterprises with national or foreign capital incorporated in accordance with Peruvian law, and which operate with registered vessels flying the Peruvian flag. Foreign vessels can only fish in the 200-mile zone if they have been registered with, and obtain a special permit from, the Ministry of Fisheries (Article 21), which is a direct consequence of the supervision, protection, and control of fishing exercised by the State (Articles 105-107).[2][3]

DELIMITATION OF THE MARITIME ZONE

From where are the 200 miles of the Peruvian maritime zone measured? The legislation has followed different criteria on this matter. Supreme Decree No. 781 of 1947 fixes the distance by reference to geographic parallels. The petroleum law refers to the continental terrace comprised between the coast and a line drawn at a distance of 200 miles from the low-water mark.

The declarations of the South Pacific States have not established any rule with regard to measurement. Neither has Supreme Resolution No. 23 of 1955, which established the drawing of charts of the maritime zone.

In application, therefore, of the rules of customary international law embodied in the Geneva Convention, the 200 miles should be understood to be measured from the low-water mark when dealing with normal baselines, or from straight baselines when the configuration of the coast so requires.

On the other hand, such a drawing is not entirely compatible with a constant line parallel to the coast because of the fact that Peru also claims a maritime zone surrounding the islands, in application of the general rules of maritime jurisdiction. Therefore, at certain points the jurisdictional zone will extend seaward at distances longer than the normal projection from the coast.

With regard to the lateral delimitation with Ecuador and Chile, the Declaration on the Maritime Zone of 1952 refers to the parallel corresponding to the point where the land frontier between the States reaches the sea; also Article 1 of the Convention on the Special Zone of the Maritime Frontier refers to the "parallel which constitutes the maritime limit between the countries."[24]

LEGAL NATURE OF THE MARITIME ZONE

The majority of the authors who have studied the legal character of the maritime zone have concluded that the State exercises a limited sovereignty;[25] it is a zone of *specialized competences* and not a territorial sea with full sovereignty.[26] According to Raúl Ferrero, the zone "has not been established for defense considerations which normally determine the nature of the territorial sea."[27] In the opinion of Alberto Ulloa, defense has been the "primary foundation"[28] of the concept of the territorial sea,[29] but not the only one; this foundation is rapidly losing its significance and has been replaced by the idea of the economic exploitation of the wealth of the sea.[30]

Expressions in favor of the widening of the territorial sea are not novel. As long ago as 1918, José Leon Suárez — the Argentinian jurist — propounded this idea. He felt this was required not only for security reasons but was also important to commerce, hunting, and fishing.

The legislation of Peru is confused with regard to the nature of the maritime zone. Almost every document emphasizes the expression "exclusive sovereignty and jurisdiction," which has been reiterated in the statements of many government officials, particularly the Minister of Foreign Affairs,[31] the Ambassador to the United Nations, and others.[32]

From the traditional point of view, the idea of an exclusive sovereignty and jurisdiction can be considered as being limited only to the extent to which the "right of innocent and inoffensive passage" is taken into account, as is the case of the Declaration of Santiago and of Law No. 15,720 on Civil Aviation.

Also, as long as there is no clear indication that the word sovereignty is intended to mean certain specified competences only, the fact that it is exercised over the adjacent sea in an exclusive manner suggests that it is a territorial sea.[33] This would seem to be confirmed by the language of the Supplementary Convention to the 1952 Declaration of Santiago which expresses the purpose of the signatories to enter into "agreements or Conventions relating to the application of the principles governing that sovereignty, for the purpose in particular of regulating and protecting hunting and fisheries within the several maritime zones."[34] This means that the contracting parties consider that they have over the said area all the rights of sovereignty which correspond to the territorial sea, for they declare that they will exercise in particular (but not exclusively) one of those rights at that moment, enacting the pertinent regulations, and they do not renounce other rights.

However, Decree No. 781 and other legislation refer to freedom of navigation and overflight,[35] a situation which is not characteristic of the territorial sea. Nor do the decrees, laws, and agreements signed by Peru include the words "territorial sea" or "contiguous zone," except for the Declaration on the Maritime Zone which mentions them in paragraph 1. In general, the expressions "maritime zone" or "zone of exclusive jurisdiction" are used.

The Ministry of Foreign Affairs, in its replies to the notes of protest of the United States and of Great Britain, stated that the maritime zone did not have "the characteristics which apparently the protesting governments attribute to it," namely those of the territorial sea.[36]

Freedom of navigation and overflight correspond to the regime of the high seas. Is this, therefore, a zone of the high seas over which only an exclusive fishing zone has been established? The writer believes that this is not the case.

Alberto Ulloa has wielded a strong influence on the Peruvian position in this matter. He has stated repeatedly that if the concept of the territorial sea is not revitalized "to incorporate a new conception of international law,"[37] that concept would turn out to be nothing but "one of those wrecks which are found on the beaches."[38] This fact, together with doubts about the possibility of revitalizing the concept in accordance with present needs, which in turn has been hampered by the conflicting interests between the maritime powers and the coastal States, has led Peru to avoid mentioning the territorial sea in its legislation. This, however, is only a formalistic reaction to avoid being trapped by the language of the law. The concept of the territorial sea should not be abandoned. Potentially it offers many attractive advantages to the coastal State in the defense of its interests.

It is necessary also to examine the attitudes of the country when acting in accordance with its legislation. Although Decree No. 781 grants freedom of navigation, it also refers to exclusive sovereignty and jurisdiction which in general corresponds to the concept of the territorial sea. Sovereignty over the adjacent sea is considered as equal to the sovereignty over the continental shelf and terrace.

The kind of sovereign rights which Peru exercises over its adjacent or jurisdictional sea are clearly those which are regulated by the Geneva Convention on the Territorial Sea.

José Luis Bustamante y Rivero, former President of Peru, who enacted the Supreme Decree No. 781, considers that the 200-mile zone is a territorial sea. In a recent book he says: "States can only claim exclusive rights over their coastal waters if they consider them as territorial sea. International law does not permit otherwise. To divide those spaces into zones of a different nature and exert over them different competences is incompatible with the right of sovereignty. It has been argued recently that Article 3 (of Decree No. 781) only establishes a maritime zone of special jurisdiction, limited to the purposes of control and protection of the resources therein, including waters, soil, and subsoil, but that such jurisdiction does not imply an act of sovereignty on the part of the State. . . . In my opinion, this position is erroneous for the interpretation and the legal vocabulary used by the text of the Supreme Decree of August 1, 1947, most assuredly identifies the 200-mile zone with the territorial sea."[39]

Furthermore, the Declaration on the Maritime Zone of 1952 clearly states in paragraph 1 that "the former extent of the territorial sea and contiguous zone is insufficient"; therefore, the extension of exclusive sovereignty and jurisdiction over the 200-mile zone must refer to the widening of the territorial sea.

A note addressed to the Minister of Foreign Affairs of Panama by the Ambassador of Peru in 1954 refers expressly to the "Peruvian territorial waters" and "territorial sea," requesting the Government of Panama to instruct ships of Panamanian nationality to respect the sovereignty and jurisdiction of Peru over its territorial waters. It is also interesting to examine the decision given by the Captain of the Port of Paita, on November 26, 1954, in the Onassis whaling fleet case. In this decision, sanctions were applied to the captains and owners of the captured vessels for violations of the Regulations on Port Authorities and National Merchant Marine, approved by Supreme Decree No. 21 of October 31, 1951, and in force since January 1, 1952, on the ground that whale hunting had been undertaken without a permit in *territorial waters;* it was also mentioned that hunting in the *territorial sea* had been undertaken not only by those who had been captured, but also by those who had escaped and were later compelled to return.[40]

When the Supplementary Agreement was being discussed in 1954, a draft was introduced, providing in paragraph 1 that "Chile, Ecuador, and Peru shall proceed jointly in the legal defense of the principle of sovereignty over the 200-mile *territorial sea*" (emphasis added). The delegate of Peru requested that the latter expression be changed to *maritime zone,* arguing that there would be less resistance to this at the international level. The delegate of Chile declared that the concept of the territorial sea was identified completely with that of a maritime zone, for the contracting countries had also proclaimed their sovereignty over the latter zone. He consented to the change requested by Peru since it did not imply any modification of the basic principle. The Secretary General of the Permanent Commission also agreed with the Delegate of Peru, on the grounds that the change did not weaken the concept of the territorial sea and had some diplomatic advantages. As a result, the article was approved as follows: "Chile, Ecuador, and Peru shall proceed jointly in the legal defense of the principle of sovereignty over the maritime zone to a distance of not less than

200 nautical miles... ," but on the understanding that such amendment did not imply any change of concepts.[41]

When the Protocol of Accession to the Declaration on the Maritime Zone was signed in Quito in 1955, with a view to the accession of other American States, it was again repeated that "the extent of the territorial sea and contiguous zone is insufficient" to permit the conservation, development, and use of the resources to which the coastal States are entitled.[42]

If, in addition, the provisions of the Convention on measures of supervision and control of the maritime zones of the signatory countries are also taken into consideration, the picture becomes clear; for those provisions imply that there is neither freedom of overflight nor "innocent passage" for aircraft. This same interpretation is also applicable to Law No. 15,720 on Civil Aviation, which provides that Peru exercises "exclusive jurisdiction" over the 200-mile zone.

Furthermore, should the interpretation be adopted that the 200-mile zone is not a territorial sea but only a fisheries zone, or a zone of specialized competences, the absurd conclusion would follow that Peru has no territorial sea at all.[43] This would contradict international law, however, according to which every State has a right to a belt of territorial waters.[44] According to the dissenting opinion of Judge McNair in the International Court of Justice's *Anglo-Norwegian Fisheries Case,* the coastal State not only has the right but also the duty to have a territorial sea:

> "To every State whose land territory is at any place washed by the sea, international law attaches a corresponding portion of maritime territory consisting of what the law calls territorial waters (and in some cases national waters in addition). International law does not say to a State, 'You are entitled to claim territorial waters if you want them.' No maritime State can refuse them. International law imposes upon a maritime State certain obligations and confers upon it certain rights arising out of the sovereignty which it exercises over its maritime territory. The possession of this territory is not optional, not dependent upon the will of the State, but compulsory."[45]

THE CONTINENTAL SHELF

Supreme Decree No. 781 of 1947 separately and expressly claimed the submarine areas and the natural resources thereof, without regard to the depth of the superjacent waters. The limits of the zone were established by the Petroleum Law — both with regard to the continent and to islands[46] — by the General Law on Mining,[47] and by Supreme Resolution No. 23 of 1955;[48] all these instruments fix an outer limit of 200 nautical miles measured from the coast.

If the 200-mile zone claimed by Peru is considered to be a territorial sea, Peru does not claim or even have a continental shelf from the legal point of view, for in accordance with Article 1 of the Geneva Convention the continental shelf is defined as the submarine area *outside the area of the territorial sea*. All of the Peruvian claims would be *within* the 200-mile territorial sea.

CONCLUSIONS

The salient features of Peruvian legislation and practice may be summarized as follows:

(1) Although using contradictory expressions, Peru has established a 200-mile maritime zone over which it exercises "exclusive sovereignty and jurisdiction."

(2) Supreme Decree No. 781 recognized freedom of navigation in the 200-mile area, a fact which has been underscored by government officials presently holding office; however, the author of the decree, José Luis Bustamante y Rivero, asserts that the area is a territorial sea.

(3) In accordance with the Conventions of the South Pacific, only the "right of innocent passage" is granted in the 200-mile zone.

(4) Within this maritime zone, a twelve-mile area, measured form the coast and running along the parallel which constitutes the lateral maritime frontier between the countries of the South Pacific, an exclusive fishing and hunting area for nationals has been reserved. In the remaining area, fishing, hunting, or any other exploitation of natural resources may be undertaken with the pertinent permit or authorization; only small-scale fishing for direct human consumption has been reserved to nationals in this area.

(5) There is no freedom of overflight in this zone.

(6) The landward limit of the zone is the low-water line or straight baselines where applicable. Each island or group of islands has a maritime zone of its own. The lateral limit is the parallel corresponding to the point where the land frontier reaches the sea.

(7) The kind of sovereign rights which are exercised over the territorial sea have not been renounced with regard to the 200-mile zone, although particular attention is given to the problems related to the exploitation and conservation of natural resources.

(8) Peru does not have a contiguous zone.

(9) Peru does not claim the continental shelf in the legal meaning of the Geneva Convention, for all claims are comprised within the 200-mile area.

Two different interpretations may be derived from these provisions:

(A) *The 200-mile area is a special maritime zone* for the sole purpose of protection and regulation of fishing, hunting, or any other kind of exploitation of natural resources. The following arguments support this position:

218

- The provisions which have been examined only emphasize those aspects related to the fishing, hunting, or any other kind of exploitation of natural resources, making no express reference to other forms of exercise of sovereignty and jurisdiction over the territorial sea.

- Supreme Decree No. 781 recognizes freedom of navigation, which is not compatible with the idea of the territorial sea.

- The Peruvian replies to the protests of Great Britain and the United States indicate that the area does not have the characteristics of a territorial sea which those governments seem to attribute to it.

- The Declarations of the Minister of Foreign Affairs and diverse governmental representatives repeatedly refer to the freedom of navigation in the area.

(B) *The 200-mile area is a territorial sea,* an interpretation which is supported by the following arguments:

- Peru exercises exclusive sovereignty and jurisdiction over the area.

- As long as it is not specified that sovereignty is exercised only for certain purposes, it must be understood to comprise all the powers of the regime of the territorial sea.

- The Conventions to which Peru is a party refer to the "right of innocent passage," which corresponds to the regime of the territorial sea. Because these Conventions have come into force after the enactment of Decree No. 781, the latter is modified by them.

- Dr. José Luis Bustamante y Rivero, who signed Supreme Decree No. 781 as the President of the Republic, asserts that the area is a territorial sea. Although the intention of the legislator is not the most acceptable means of interpretation, it is significant nonetheless when coincident with other criteria suggested by the application of the provision, which is the case here.

- The Declaration on the Maritime Zone of 1952, and the Protocol of Accession to it, declare that the previous extent of the territorial sea is insufficient for the protection of natural resources.

- The interpretation of the Law on Port Authorities, which became effective on January 1, 1952, the Law on the Navy, and Law 15,720 on Civil Aviation, which does not permit freedom of overflight in the 200-mile area, confirms these views.

- The practice of Peruvian authorities in enforcing their jurisdiction over the 200-mile zone (e.g., the Onassis whaling fleet case).

- To pretend that the 200-mile area is a special maritime zone would deprive Peru of a territorial sea of its own, which is both absurd and contrary to international law.

On balance, therefore, the second interpretation is to be preferred.

It is evident that the present concept of the territorial sea is very different from that held in previous centuries, because conditions in the world and the position of States have changed. This institution, as well as many others of the law of the sea, is evolving, but this does not mean that it must disappear. Although new characteristics are shaping the institution, its essence continues to be the same. It is still a part of the territory of the State in its larger meaning, over which rights, jurisdiction, and exclusive sovereignty are exercised.

References

1. Alfonso Arias Schreiber, "Fundamentos de la Soberanía Marítima del Perú" in *Revista de Derecho y Ciencias Políticas.* Year XXXIV, No. I-II (Lima, 1970), p. 50. Also Edgardo Mercado Jarrín, "Conferencia sobre Soberanía Marítima," *Fundamentos de la posición Peruana* (Lima, May 11, 1970), p. 15.
2. Alberto Ulloa, *Derecho Internacional Público,* Vol. I, 4th ed. (Madrid, 1957), p. 565. Also by the same author, "El Neuvo Derecho del Mar" in *Estudios de Derecho Internacional Marítimo* (Madrid, 1968), p. 34.
3. Arias Schreiber, op. cit., note 1 above, p. 47.
4. Alberto Ulloa, "El Neuvo Derecho del Mar" in op. cit., note 2 above, p. 47.
5. Mercado Jarrín, op. cit, note 1 above, p. 6. Arias Schreiber, op. cit., note 1 above, p. 41.
6. Arias Schreiber, op. cit., note 1 above, p. 42.
7. Alberto Ulloa, "El Neuvo Derecho del Mar" in op. cit., note 2 above, p. 35.
8. Raúl Ferrero, *Derecho Internacional,* Vol. I (Lima, 1966), pp. 95, 129-132. Andrés Aramburú Menchaca, "Mar Territorial y Mar Patrimonial" in *El Comercio* (Lima, February 28, 1972).
9. This view is contrary to that expressed by F. V. García Amador who does not consider the maritime zone a territorial sea *stricto senso.* He bases his argument on the fact that since innocent passage is an integral element of the legal regime of the territorial sea it would be unnecessary to refer to it expressly if the maritime zone was intended to be a territorial sea. See F. V. García Amador, "América Latina y el Derecho del Mar" (mimeo paper) (Washington, D.C., 1972), p. 8.
10. See Declarations of the Delegation of Peru with regard to paragraph 6 of the Montevideo Declaration on the Law of the Sea of May 8, 1970, and with regard to the Lima Declaration of August 8, 1970. República Oriental del Uruguay, Presidencia de la República, *América Latina y la Extensión del Mar Territorial* (Montevideo, 1971), pp. 152 and 178.
11. Agreement Supplementary to the Declaration of Sovereignty Over the Maritime Zone of 200 Miles. Conferencia sobre Explotación y Conservación de las riquezas marítimas del Pacífico Sur: *Convenios y otros Documentos 1952-1969,* 3rd ed. (Lima, 1970), pp. 44 and 45.
12. Ibid., pp. 5-7, 91, 99, 100, and 117. See also Francisco Orrego Vicuña, *Chile y el Derecho del Mar* (Santiago: Editorial Andrés Bello, 1972). Introductory Study.
13. Conferencia sobre Explotación, op. cit., note 11 above, pp. 5-7.

14. Ibid., pp. 5, 35, 91, 114, and 117.
15. For example, Regulations on Permits for the Exploitation of the Resources of the South Pacific.
16. Enrique García Sayán, "Progresión de una Tesis," in Conferencia sobre Explotación, op. cit., note 11 above, p. 11.
17. Conferencia sobre Explotación, op. cit., note 11 above, p. 57.
18. Ibid., pp. 95, 100, 117, and 118.
19. Ratifications by Peru in ibid., pp. 6, 7, and 52.
20. Jaime Rivera Marfan, *La Declaración sobre Zona Marítima de 1952* (Santiago, 1968), pp. 82, 96.
21. Andrés Aramburú Menchaca, "El Mar y la Integración," in *La Crónica* (Lima, December 2, 1968). Also "El Libro Blanco sobre el Derecho del Mar," in *El Comercio* (Lima, March 12, 1972).
22. See p. 210.
23. General Fishing Law No. 18,810 of March 25, 1971.
24. Conferencia sobre Explotación, op. cit., note 11 above, pp. 32 and 58.
25. Alberto Ulloa, *Derecho Internacional Público,* loc. cit., note 2 above, p. 543.
26. Raúl Ferrero, op. cit., note 8 above, p. 98.
27. Ibid.
28. Alberto Ulloa, *Derecho Internacional Público,* loc. cit., note 2 above, p. 561.
29. Mercado Jarrín, op. cit., note 1 above, p. 15. In his opinion this was "the most important foundation in the classical concept of the territorial sea."
30. Alberto Ulloa, *Derecho Internacional Público,* loc. cit., note 2 above, p. 544.
31. Mercado Jarrín, op. cit., note 1 above, pp. 4, 8, 16, 19, and 20.
32. Arias Schreiber, op. cit., note 1 above, p. 57.
33. Rivera Marfan, op. cit., note 20 above, p. 92.
34. Conferencia sobre Explotación, op. cit., note 11 above, p. 45.
35. Mercado Jarrín, op. cit., note 1 above, p. 19. Also Felipe Portocarrero Olave, *Derecho Internacional Público* (Lima, 1966), p. 137.
36. Complete texts in Raúl Ferrero, op. cit., note 8 above, pp. 151 ff.
37. Alberto Ulloa, *Derecho Internacional Público,* loc. cit., note 2 above, p. 562.
38. Ibid.
39. Andrés Aramburú Menchaca, "Bustamante y Rivero y el Mar del Peru" in *El Comercio* (Lima, March 29, 1972). Book review of *La Doctrina Peruana de las 200 millas* by José Luis Bustamante y Rivero.
40. Raúl Ferrero, op. cit., note 8 above, pp. 128-132.
41. Rivera Marfan, op. cit., note 20 above, pp. 138-139.
42. Conferencia sobre Explotación, op. cit., note 11 above, p. 71.
43. F. V. García Amador, "América Latina y el Derecho del Mar," cit., note 9 above, p. 71.
44. *Anglo-Norwegian Fisheries Case,* International Court of Justice Reports, 1951, pp. 119-121.
45. Ibid., p. 160, dissenting opinion of Judge Arnold McNair.
46. See p. 210.
47. See p. 213.
48. See p. 212-213.

Annexes

Annex I   *Multilateral Instruments* 224

   The Geneva Conventions . . . .
  1. Convention on the Territorial Sea and the Contiguous Zone 224
  2. Convention on the High Seas 231
  3. Convention on Fishing and Conservation of the Living Resources
     of the High Seas 239
  4. Convention on the Continental Shelf 244

Annex II   *Regional Instruments and Declarations* 249

  1. Declaration of Santiago on the Maritime Zone, August 18, 1952 . . 249
  2. Agreement Supplementary to the Declaration of Santiago 1954 . . . 250
  3. Montevideo Declaration on the Law of the Sea 1970 251
  4. The Lima Declaration of the Latin American States on the
     Law of the Sea 1970 252
  5. The Declaration of Santo Domingo 1972 253

Annex III   *Bilateral Instruments and Declarations* 257

  1. Agreement on Fishing between Brazil and Argentina, signed at
     Buenos Aires on 29 December 1967 257
  2. Agreement on Fishing and Conservation of Living Resources
     between Brazil and Uruguay, signed at Montevideo on
     12 December 1968 258
  3. Agreement between the United States of America and the United
     Mexican States on Traditional Fishing in the Exclusive Fishery
     Zones Contiguous to the Territorial Seas of Both Countries.
     Effected by Exchange of Notes signed at Washington on
     27 October 1967 259
  4. Agreement between the Government of the United States of
     America and the Government of Canada on Reciprocal Fishing
     Privileges in Certain Areas off Their Coasts. Signed at Ottawa
     on 24 April 1970 264
  5. Agreement between the Government of the Federative Republic
     of Brazil and the Government of the United States of America
     Concerning Shrimp. Done at Brasilia May 9, 1972 266
  6. Treaty between the United Kingdom and Venezuela Relating to
     the Submarine Areas of the Gulf of Paria, February 26, 1942 270

ANNEX I

MULTILATERAL INSTRUMENTS

THE GENEVA CONVENTIONS

1. CONVENTION ON THE TERRITORIAL SEA AND THE CONTIGUOUS ZONE

The States Parties to this Convention
Have agreed as follows:

PART I

TERRITORIAL SEA

SECTION I. GENERAL

Article 1

1. The sovereignty of a State extends, beyond its land territory and its internal waters, to a belt of sea adjacent to its coast, described as the territorial sea.
2. This sovereignty is exercised subject to the provisions of these articles and to other rules of international law.

Article 2

The sovereignty of a coastal State extends to the air space over the territorial sea as well as to its bed and subsoil.

SECTION II. LIMITS OF THE TERRITORIAL SEA

Article 3

Except where otherwise provided in these articles, the normal baseline for measuring the breadth of the territorial sea is the low-water line along the coast as marked on large-scale charts officially recognized by the coastal State.

Article 4

1. In localities where the coastline is deeply indented and cut into, or if there is a fringe of islands along the coast in its immediate vicinity, the method of straight baselines joining appropriate points may be employed in drawing the baseline from which the breadth of the territorial sea is measured.
2. The drawing of such baselines must not depart to any appreciable extent from the general direction of the coast, and the sea areas lying within the lines must be sufficiently closely linked to the land domain to be subject to the régime of internal waters.

3. Baselines shall not be drawn to and from low-tide elevations, unless light-houses or similar installations which are permanently above sea level have been built on them.

4. Where the method of straight baselines is applicable under the provisions of paragraph 1, account may be taken, in determining particular baselines, of economic interests peculiar to the region concerned, the reality and the importance of which are clearly evidenced by a long usage.

5. The system of straight baselines may not be applied by a State in such a manner as to cut off from the high seas the territorial sea of another State.

6. The coastal State must clearly indicate straight baselines on charts, to which due publicity must be given.

Article 5

1. Waters on the landward side of the baseline of the territorial sea form part of the internal waters of the State.

2. Where the establishment of a straight baseline in accordance with article 4 has the effect of enclosing as internal waters areas which previously had been considered as part of the territorial sea or of the high seas, a right of innocent passage, as provided in articles 14 to 23, shall exist in those waters.

Article 6

The outer limit of the territorial sea is the line every point of which is at a distance from the nearest point of the baseline equal to the breadth of the territorial sea.

Article 7

1. This article relates only to bays the coasts of which belong to a single State.

2. For the purposes of these articles, a bay is a well-marked indentation whose penetration is in such proportion to the width of its mouth as to contain land-locked waters and constitute more than a mere curvature of the coast. An indentation shall not, however, be regarded as a bay unless its area is as large as, or larger than, that of the semi-circle whose diameter is a line drawn across the mouth of that indentation.

3. For the purpose of measurement, the area of an indentation is that lying between the low-water mark around the shore of the indentation and a line joining the low-water mark of its natural entrance points. Where, because of the presence of islands, an indentation has more than one mouth, the semi-circle shall be drawn on a line as long as the sum total of the lengths of the lines across the different mouths. Islands within an indentation shall be included as if they were part of the water area of the indentation.

4. If the distance between the low-water marks of the natural entrance points of a bay does not exceed twenty-four miles, a closing line may be drawn between these two low-water marks, and the waters enclosed thereby shall be considered as internal waters.

5. Where the distance between the low-water marks of the natural entrance points of a bay exceeds twenty-four miles, a straight baseline of twenty-four miles shall be drawn within the bay in such a manner as to enclose the maximum area of water that is possible with a line of that length.

225

6. The foregoing provisions shall not apply to so-called "historic" bays, or in any case where the straight baseline system provided for in article 4 is applied.

Article 8

For the purpose of delimiting the territorial sea, the outermost permanent harbour works which form an integral part of the harbour system shall be regarded as forming part of the coast.

Article 9

Roadsteads which are normally used for the loading, unloading and anchoring of ships, and which would otherwise be situated wholly or partly outside the outer limit of the territorial sea, are included in the territorial sea. The coastal State must clearly demarcate such roadsteads and indicate them on charts together with their boundaries, to which due publicity must be given.

Article 10

1. An island is a naturally formed area of land, surrounded by water, which is above water at high tide.
2. The territorial sea of an island is measured in accordance with the provisions of these articles.

Article 11

1. A low-tide elevation is a naturally formed area of land which is surrounded by and above water at low-tide but submerged at high tide. Where a low-tide elevation is situated wholly or partly at a distance not exceeding the breadth of the territorial sea from the mainland or an island, the low-water line on that elevation may be used as the baseline for measuring the breadth of the territorial sea.
2. Where a low-tide elevation is wholly situated at a distance exceeding the breadth of the territorial sea from the mainland or an island, it has no territorial sea of its own.

Article 12

1. Where the coasts of two States are opposite or adjacent to each other, neither of the two States is entitled, failing agreement between them to the contrary, to extend its territorial sea beyond the median line every point of which is equidistant from the nearest points on the baselines from which the breadth of the territorial seas of each of the two States is measured. The provisions of this paragraph shall not apply, however, where it is necessary by reason of historic title or other special circumstances to delimit the territorial seas of the two States in a way which is at variance with this provision.
2. The line of delimitation between the territorial seas of two States lying opposite to each other or adjacent to each other shall be marked on large-scale charts officially recognized by the coastal States.

226

Article 13

If a river flows directly into the sea, the baseline shall be a straight line across the mouth of the river between points on the low-tide line of its banks.

SECTION III. RIGHT OF INNOCENT PASSAGE

Sub-Section A. Rules applicable to all ships

Article 14

1. Subject to the provisions of these articles, ships of all States, whether coastal or not, shall enjoy the right of innocent passage through the territorial sea.
2. Passage means navigation through the territorial sea for the purpose either of traversing that sea without entering internal waters, or of proceeding to internal waters, or of making for the high seas from internal waters.
3. Passage includes stopping and anchoring, but only in so far as the same are incidental to ordinary navigation or are rendered necessary by *force majeure* or by distress.
4. Passage is innocent so long as it is not prejudicial to the peace, good order or security of the coastal State. Such passage shall take place in conformity with these articles and with other rules of international law.
5. Passage of foreign fishing vessels shall not be considered innocent if they do not observe such laws and regulations as the coastal State may make and publish in order to prevent these vessels from fishing in the territorial sea.

6. Submarines are required to navigate on the surface and to show their flag.

Article 15

1. The coastal State must not hamper innocent passage through the territorial sea.
2. The coastal State is required to give appropriate publicity to any dangers to navigation, of which it has knowledge, within its territorial sea.

Article 16

1. The coastal State may take the necessary steps in its territorial sea to prevent passage which is not innocent.
2. In the case of ships proceeding to internal waters, the coastal State shall also have the right to take the necessary steps to prevent any breach of the conditions to which admission of those ships to those waters is subject.
3. Subject to the provisions of paragraph 4, the coastal State may, without discrimination amongst foreign ships, suspend temporarily in specified areas of its territorial sea the innocent passage of foreign ships if such suspension is essential for the protection of its security. Such suspension shall take effect only after having been duly published.
4. There shall be no suspension of the innocent passage of foreign ships through straits which are used for international navigation between one part of the high seas and another part of the high seas or the territorial sea of a foreign State.

Article 17

Foreign ships exercising the right of innocent passage shall comply with the laws and regulations enacted by the coastal State in conformity with these articles and other rules of international law and, in particular, with such laws and regulations relating to transport and navigation.

Sub-section B. Rules applicable to merchant ships

Article 18

1. No charge may be levied upon foreign ships by reason only of their passage through the territorial sea.

2. Charges may be levied upon a foreign ship passing through the territorial sea as payment only for specific services rendered to the ship. These charges shall be levied without discrimination.

Article 19

1. The criminal jurisdiction of the coastal State should not be exercised on board a foreign ship passing through the territorial sea to arrest any person or to conduct any investigation in connexion with any crime committed on board the ship during its passage, save only in the following cases:

(a) If the consequences of the crime extend to the coastal State; or

(b) If the crime is of a kind to disturb the peace of the country or the good order of the territorial sea; or

(c) If the assistance of the local authorities has been requested by the captain of the ship or by the consul of the country whose flag the ship flies; or

(d) If it is necessary for the suppression of illicit traffic in narcotic drugs.

2. The above provisions do not affect the right of the coastal State to take any steps authorized by its laws for the purpose of an arrest or investigation on board a foreign ship passing through the territorial sea after leaving internal waters.

3. In the cases provided for in paragraphs 1 and 2 of this article, the coastal State shall, if the captain so requests, advise the consular authority of the flag State before taking any steps, and shall facilitate contact between such authority and the ship's crew. In cases of emergency this notification may be communicated while the measures are being taken.

4. In considering whether or how an arrest should be made, the local authorities shall pay due regard to the interests of navigation.

5. The coastal State may not take any steps on board a foreign ship passing through the territorial sea to arrest any person or to conduct any investigation in connexion with any crime committed before the ship entered the territorial sea, if the ship, proceeding from a foreign port, is only passing through the territorial sea without entering internal waters.

Article 20

1. The coastal State should not stop or divert a foreign ship passing through the

territorial sea for the purpose of exercising civil jurisdiction in relation to a person on board the ship.

2. The coastal State may not levy execution against or arrest the ship for the purpose of any civil proceedings, save only in respect of obligations or liabilities assumed or incurred by the ship itself in the course or for the purpose of its voyage through the waters of the coastal State.

3. The provisions of the previous paragraph are without prejudice to the right of the coastal State, in accordance with its laws, to levy execution against or to arrest, for the purpose of any civil proceedings, a foreign ship lying in the territorial sea, or passing through the territorial sea after leaving internal waters.

Sub-section C. Rules Applicable to government ships other than warships

Article 21

The rules contained in sub-sections A and B shall also apply to government ships operated for commercial purposes.

Article 22

1. The rules contained in sub-section A and in article 18 shall apply to government ships operated for noncommercial purposes.

2. With such exceptions as are contained in the provisions referred to in the preceding paragraph, nothing in these articles affects the immunities which such ships enjoy under these articles or other rules of international law.

Sub-section D. Rules applicable to warships

Article 23

If any warship does not comply with the regulations of the coastal State concerning passage through the territorial sea and disregards any request for compliance which is made to it, the coastal State may require the warship to leave the territorial sea.

PART II

CONTIGUOUS ZONE

Article 24

1. In a zone of the high seas contiguous to its territorial sea, the coastal State may exercise the control necessary to:

(a) Prevent infringement of its customs, fiscal, immigration or sanitary regulations within its territory or territorial sea;

(b) Punish infringement of the above regulations committed within its territory or territorial sea.

2. The contiguous zone may not extend beyond twelve miles from the baseline from which the breadth of the territorial sea is measured.

3. Where the coasts of two States are opposite or adjacent to each other, neither

of the two States is entitled, failing agreement between them to the contrary, to extend its contiguous zone beyond the median line every point of which is equidistant from the nearest points on the baselines from which the breadth of the territorial seas of the two States is measured.

PART III

FINAL ARTICLES

Article 25

The provisions of this Convention shall not affect conventions or other international agreements already in force, as between States Parties to them.

Article 26

This Convention shall, until 31 October 1958, be open for signature by all States Members of the United Nations or of any of the specialized agencies, and by any other State invited by the General Assembly of the United Nations to become a party to the Convention.

Article 27

This Convention is subject to ratification. The instruments of ratification shall be deposited with the Secretary-General of the United Nations.

Article 28

This Convention shall be open for accession by any States belonging to any of the categories mentioned in article 26. The instruments of accession shall be deposited with the Secretary-General of the United Nations.

Article 29

1. This Convention shall come into force on the thirtieth day following the date of deposit of the twenty-second instrument of ratification or accession with the Secretary-General of the United Nations.
2. For each State ratifying or acceding to the Convention after the deposit of the twenty-second instrument of ratification or accession, the Convention shall enter into force on the thirtieth day after deposit by such State of its instrument of ratification or accession.

Article 30

1. After the expiration of a period of five years from the date on which this Convention shall enter into force, a request for the revision of this Convention may be made at any time by any Contracting Party by means of a notification in writing addressed to the Secretary-General of the United Nations.
2. The General Assembly of the United Nations shall decide upon the steps, if any, to be taken in respect of such request.

Article 31

The Secretary-General of the United Nations shall inform all States Members of the United Nations and the other States referred to in article 26:

(a) Of signatures to this Convention and of the deposit of instruments of ratification or accession, in accordance with articles 26, 27 and 28;

(b) Of the date on which this Convention will come into force, in accordance with article 29;

(c) Of requests for revision in accordance with article 30.

Article 32

The original of this Convention, of which the Chinese, English, French, Russian and Spanish texts are equally authentic, shall be deposited with the Secretary-General of the United Nations, who shall send certified copies thereof to all States referred to in article 26.

IN WITNESS WHEREOF the undersigned plenipotentiaries, being duly authorized thereto by their respective governments, have signed this Convention.

DONE AT GENEVA, this twenty-ninth day of April one thousand nine hundred and fifty-eight.

2. CONVENTION ON THE HIGH SEAS

The States Parties to this Convention,

Desiring to codify the rules of international law relating to the high seas,

Recognizing that the United Nations Conference on the Law of the Sea, held at Geneva from 24 February to 27 April 1958, adopted the following provisions as generally declaratory of established principles of international law,

Have agreed as follows:

Article 1

The term "high seas" means all parts of the sea that are not included in the territorial sea or in the internal waters of a State.

Article 2

The high seas being open to all nations, no State may validly purport to subject any part of them to its sovereignty. Freedom of the high seas is exercised under the conditions laid down by these articles and by the other rules of international law. It comprises, *inter alia,* both for coastal and non-coastal States:

(1) Freedom of navigation;

(2) Freedom of fishing;

(3) Freedom to lay submarine cables and pipelines;

(4) Freedom to fly over the high seas.

These freedoms, and others which are recognized by the general principles of international law, shall be exercised by all States with reasonable regard to the interests of other States in their exercise of the freedom of the high seas.

Article 3

1. In order to enjoy the freedom of the seas on equal terms with coastal States, States having no sea-coast should have free access to the sea. To this end States situated between the sea and a State having no sea-coast shall by common agreement with the latter and in conformity with existing international conventions accord:

(a) To the State having no sea-coast, on a basis of reciprocity, free transit through their territory; and

(b) To ships flying the flag of that State treatment equal to that accorded to their own ships, or to the ships of any other States, as regards access to seaports and the use of such ports.

2. States situated between the sea and a State having no sea-coast shall settle, by mutual agreement with the latter, and taking into account the rights of the coastal State or State of transit and the special conditions of the State having no sea-coast, all matters relating to freedom of transit and equal treatment in ports, in case such States are not already parties to existing international conventions.

Article 4

Every State, whether coastal or not, has the right to sail ships under its flag on the high seas.

Article 5

1. Each State shall fix the conditions for the grant of its nationality to ships, for the registration of ships in its territory, and for the right to fly its flag. Ships have the nationality of the State whose flag they are entitled to fly. There must exist a genuine link between the State and the ship; in particular, the State must effectively exercise its jurisdiction and control in administrative, technical and social matters over ships flying its flag.

2. Each State shall issue to ships to which it has granted the right to fly its flag documents to that effect.

Article 6

1. Ships shall sail under the flag of one State only and, save in exceptional cases expressly provided for in international treaties or in these articles, shall be subject to its exclusive jurisdiction on the high seas. A ship may not change its flag during a voyage or while in a port of call, save in the case of a real transfer of ownership or change or registry.

2. A ship which sails under the flags of two or more States, using them according to convenience, may not claim any of the nationalities in question with respect to any other State, and may be assimilated to a ship without nationality.

Article 7

The provisions of the preceding articles do not prejudice the question of ships employed on the official service of an intergovernmental organization flying the flag of the organization.

232

Article 8

1. Warships on the high seas have complete immunity from the jurisdiction of any State other than the flag State.

2. For the purposes of these articles, the term "warship" means a ship belonging to the naval forces of a State and bearing the external marks distinguishing warships of its nationality, under the command of an officer duly commissioned by the government and whose name appears in the Navy List, and manned by a crew who are under regular naval discipline.

Article 9

Ships owned or operated by a State and used only on government non-commercial service shall, on the high seas, have complete immunity from the jurisdiction of any State other than the flag State.

Article 10

1. Every State shall take such measures for ships under its flag as are necessary to ensure safety at sea with regard *inter alia* to:

(a) The use of signals, the maintenance of communications and the prevention of collisions;

(b) The manning of ships and labour conditions for crews taking into account the applicable international labour instruments;

(c) The construction, equipment and seaworthiness of ships.

2. In taking such measures each State is required to conform to generally accepted international standards and to take any steps which may be necessary to ensure their observance.

Article 11

1. In the event of a collision or of any other incident of navigation concerning a ship on the high seas, involving the penal or disciplinary responsibility of the master or of any other person in the service of the ship, no penal or disciplinary proceedings may be instituted against such persons except before the judicial or administrative authorities either of the flag State or of the State of which such person is a national.

2. In disciplinary matters, the State which has issued a master's certificate or a certificate of competence or licence shall alone be competent, after due legal process, to pronounce the withdrawal of such certificates, even if the holder is not a national of the State which issued them.

3. No arrest or detention of the ship, even as a measure of investigation, shall be ordered by any authorities other than those of the flag State.

Article 12

1. Every State shall require the master of a ship sailing under its flag, in so far as he can do so without serious danger to the ship, the crew or the passengers:

(a) To render assistance to any person found at sea in danger of being lost;

(b) To proceed with all possible speed to the rescue of persons in distress if

informed of their need of assistance, in so far as such action may reasonably be expected of him;

(c) After a collision, to render assistance to the other ship, her crew and her passengers and, where possible, to inform the other ship of the name of his own ship, her port of registry and the nearest port at which she will call.

2. Every coastal State shall promote the establishment and maintenance of an adequate and effective search and rescue service regarding safety on and over the sea and — where circumstances so require — by way of mutual regional arrangements co-operate with neighbouring States for this purpose.

Article 13

Every State shall adopt effective measures to prevent and punish the transport of slaves in ships authorized to fly its flag, and to prevent the unlawful use of its flag for that purpose. Any slave taking refuge on board any ship, whatever its flag, shall, *ipso facto,* be free.

Article 14

All States shall co-operate to the fullest possible extent in the repression of piracy on the high seas or in any other place outside the jurisdiction of any State.

Article 15

Piracy consists of any of the following acts:

(1) Any illegal acts of violence, detention or any act of depredation, committed for private ends by the crew or the passengers of a private ship or a private aircraft, and directed:

(a) On the high seas, against another ship or aircraft, or against persons or property on board such ship or aircraft;

(b) Against a ship, aircraft, persons or property in a place outside the jurisdiction of any State;

2. Any act of voluntary participation in the operation of a ship or of an aircraft with knowledge of facts making it a pirate ship or aircraft;

3. Any act of inciting or of intentionally facilitating an act described in sub-paragraph 1 or sub-paragraph 2 of this article.

Article 16

The acts of piracy, as defined in article 15, committed by a warship, government ship or government aircraft whose crew has mutinied and taken control of the ship or aircraft are assimilated to acts committed by a private ship.

Article 17

A ship or aircraft is considered a pirate ship or aircraft if it is intended by the persons in dominant control to be used for the purpose of committing one of the acts referred to in article 15. The same applies if the ship or aircraft has been used to commit any such act, so long as it remains under the control of the persons guilty of that act.

234

Article 18

A ship or aircraft may retain its nationality although it has become a pirate ship or aircraft. The retention or loss of nationality is determined by the law of the State from which such nationality was derived.

Article 19

On the high seas, or in any other place outside the jurisdiction of any State, every State may seize a pirate ship or aircraft, or a ship taken by piracy and under the control of pirates, and arrest the persons and seize the property on board. The courts of the State which carried out the seizure may decide upon the penalties to be imposed, and may also determine the action to be taken with regard to the ships, aircraft or property, subject to the rights of third parties acting in good faith.

Article 20

Where the seizure of a ship or aircraft on suspicion of piracy has been effected without adequate grounds, the State making the seizure shall be liable to the State the nationality of which is possessed by the ship or aircraft, for any loss or damage caused by the seizure.

Article 21

A seizure on account of piracy may only be carried out by warships or military aircraft, or other ships or aircraft on government service authorized to that effect.

Article 22

1. Except where acts of interference derive from powers conferred by treaty, a warship which encounters a foreign merchant ship on the high seas is not justified in boarding her unless there is reasonable ground for suspecting:
   (a) That the ship is engaged in piracy; or
   (b) That the ship is engaged in the slave trade; or
   (c) That, though flying a foreign flag or refusing to show its flag, the ship is, in reality, of the same nationality as the warship.
2. In the cases provided for in sub-paragraphs *(a)*, *(b)* and *(c)* above, the warship may proceed to verify the ship's right to fly its flag. To this end, it may send a boat under the command of an officer to the suspected ship. If suspicion remains after the documents have been checked, it may proceed to a further examination on board the ship, which must be carried out with all possible consideration.
3. If the suspicions prove to be unfounded, and provided that the ship boarded has not committed any act justifying them, it shall be compensated for any loss or damage that may have been sustained.

Article 23

1. The hot pursuit of a foreign ship may be undertaken when the competent

authorities of the coastal State have good reason to believe that the ship has violated the laws and regulations of that State. Such pursuit must be commenced when the foreign ship or one of its boats is within the internal waters or the territorial sea or the contiguous zone of the pursuing State, and may only be continued outside the territorial sea or the contiguous zone if the pursuit has not been interrupted. It is not necessary that, at the time when the foreign ship within the territorial sea or the contiguous zone receives the order to stop, the ship giving the order should likewise be within the territorial sea or the contiguous zone. If the foreign ship is within a contiguous zone, as defined in article 24 of the Convention on the Territorial Sea and the Contiguous Zone, the pursuit may only be undertaken if there has been a violation of the rights for the protection of which the zone was established.

2. The right of hot pursuit ceases as soon as the ship pursued enters the territorial sea of its own country or of a third State.

3. Hot pursuit is not deemed to have begun unless the pursuing ship has satisfied itself by such practicable means as may be available that the ship pursued or one of its boats or other craft working as a team and using the ship pursued as a mother ship are within the limits of the territorial sea, or as the case may be within the contiguous zone. The pursuit may only be commenced after a visual or auditory signal to stop has been given at a distance which enables it to be seen or heard by the foreign ship.

4. The right of hot pursuit may be exercised only by warships or military aircraft, or other ships or aircraft on government service specially authorized to that effect.

5. Where hot pursuit is effected by an aircraft:

(a) The provisions of paragraphs 1 to 3 of this article shall apply *mutatis mutandis;*

(b) The aircraft giving the order to stop must itself actively pursue the ship until a ship or aircraft of the coastal State, summoned by the aircraft, arrives to take over the pursuit, unless the aircraft is itself able to arrest the ship. It does not suffice to justify an arrest on the high seas that the ship was merely sighted by the aircraft as an offender or suspected offender, if it was not both ordered to stop and pursued by the aircraft itself or other aircraft or ships which continue the pursuit without interruption.

6. The release of a ship arrested within the jurisdiction of a State and escorted to a port of that State for the purposes of an inquiry before the competent authorities may not be claimed solely on the ground that the ship, in the course of its voyage, was escorted across a portion of the high seas, if the circumstances rendered this necessary.

7. Where a ship has been stopped or arrested on the high seas in circumstances which do not justify the exercise of the rights of hot pursuit, it shall be compensated for any loss or damage that may have been thereby sustained.

Article 24

Every State shall draw up regulations to prevent pollution of the seas by the discharge of oil from ships or pipelines or resulting from the exploitation and exploration of the seabed and its subsoil, taking account of existing treaty provisions on the subject.

Article 25

1. Every State shall take measures to prevent pollution of the seas from the dumping of radio-active waste, taking into account any standards and regulations which may be formulated by the competent international organizations.
2. All States shall co-operate with the competent international organizations in taking measures for the prevention of pollution of the seas or air space above, resulting from any activities with radio-active materials or other harmful agents.

Article 26

1. All States shall be entitled to lay submarine cables and pipelines on the bed of the high seas.
2. Subject to its right to take reasonable measures for the exploration of the continental shelf and the exploitation of its natural resources, the coastal State may not impede the laying or maintenance of such cables or pipelines.
3. When laying such cables or pipelines the State in question shall pay due regard to cables or pipelines already in position on the seabed. In particular, possibilities of repairing existing cables or pipelines shall not be prejudiced.

Article 27

Every State shall take the necessary legislative measures to provide that the breaking or injury by a ship flying its flag or by a person subject to its jurisdiction of a submarine cable beneath the high seas done wilfully or through culpable negligence, in such a manner as to be liable to interrupt or obstruct telegraphic or telephonic communications, and similarly the breaking or injury of a submarine pipeline or high-voltage power cable shall be a punishable offence. This provision shall not apply to any break or injury caused by persons who acted merely with the legitimate object of saving their lives or their ships, after having taken all necessary precautions to avoid such break or injury.

Article 28

Every State shall take the necessary legislative measures to provide that, if persons subject to its jurisdiction who are the owners of a cable or pipeline beneath the high seas, in laying or repairing that cable or pipeline, cause a break in or injury to another cable or pipeline, they shall bear the cost of the repairs.

Article 29

Every State shall take the necessary legislative measures to ensure that the owners of ships who can prove that they have sacrificed an anchor, a net or any other fishing gear, in order to avoid injuring a submarine cable or pipeline, shall be indemnified by the owner of the cable or pipeline, provided that the owner of the ship has taken all reasonable precautionary measures beforehand.

Article 30

The provisions of this convention shall not affect conventions or other international agreements already in force, as between States parties to them.

237

Article 31

This Convention shall, until 31 October 1958, be open for signature by all States Members of the United Nations or of any of the specialized agencies, and by any other State invited by the General Assembly of the United Nations to become a Party to the Convention.

Article 32

This Convention is subject to ratification. The instruments of ratification shall be deposited with the Secretary-General of the United Nations.

Article 34

1. This Convention shall come into force on the thirtieth day following the date of deposit of the twenty-second instrument of ratification or accession with the Secretary-General of the United Nations.
2. For each State ratifying or acceding to the Convention after the deposit of the twenty-second instrument of ratification or accession, the Convention shall enter into force on the thirtieth day after deposit by such State of its instrument of ratification or accession.

Article 35

1. After the expiration of a period of five years from the date on which this Convention shall enter into force, a request for the revision of this Convention may be made at any time by any Contracting Party by means of a notification in writing addressed to the Secretary-General of the United Nations.
2. The General Assembly of the United Nations shall decide upon the steps, if any, to be taken in respect of such request.

Article 36

The Secretary-General of the United Nations shall inform all States Members of the United Nations and the other States referred to in article 31:
(a) Of signatures to this Convention and of the deposit of instruments of ratification or accession, in accordance with articles 31, 32 and 33;
(b) Of the date on which this Convention will come into force, in accordance with article 34;
(c) Of requests for revision in accordance with article 35.

Article 37

The original of this Convention, of which the Chinese, English, French, Russian and Spanish texts are equally authentic, shall be deposited with the Secretary-General of the United Nations, who shall send certified copies thereof to all States referred to in article 31.

IN WITNESS WHEREOF the undersigned plenipotentiaries, being duly authorized thereto by their respective governments, have signed this Convention.

DONE AT GENEVA, this twenty-ninth day of April one thousand nine hundred and fifty-eight.

3. CONVENTION ON FISHING AND CONSERVATION OF THE LIVING RESOURCES OF THE HIGH SEAS

The States Parties to this Convention,

Considering that the development of modern techniques for the exploitation of the living resources of the sea, increasing man's ability to meet the need of the world's expanding population for food, has exposed some of these resources to the danger of being over-exploited,

Considering also that the nature of the problems involved in the conservation of the living resources of the high seas is such that there is a clear necessity that they be solved, whenever possible, on the basis of international co-operation through the concerted action of all the States concerned,

Have agreed as follows:

Article 1

1. All States have the right for their nationals to engage in fishing on the high seas, subject *(a)* to their treaty obligations, *(b)* to the interests and rights of coastal States as provided for in this Convention, and *(c)* to the provisions contained in the following articles concerning conservation of the living resources of the high seas.

2. All States have the duty to adopt, or to co-operate with other States in adopting, such measures for their respective nationals as may be necessary for the conservation of the living resources of the high seas.

Article 2

As employed in this Convention, the expression "conservation of the living resources of the high seas" means the aggregate of the measures rendering possible the optimum sustainable yield from those resources so as to secure a maximum supply of food and other marine products. Conservation programmes should be formulated with a view to securing in the first place a supply of food for human consumption.

Article 3

A State whose nationals are engaged in fishing any stock or stocks of fish or other living marine resources in any area of the high seas where the nationals of other States are not thus engaged shall adopt, for its own nationals, measures in that area when necessary for the purpose of the conservation of the living resources affected.

Article 4

1. If the nationals of two or more States are engaged in fishing the same stock or stocks of fish or other living marine resources in any area or areas of the high seas, these States shall, at the request of any of them, enter into negotiations with a view to prescribing by agreement for their nationals the necessary measures for the conservation of the living resources affected.

2. If the States concerned do not reach agreement within twelve months, any of the parties may initiate the procedure contemplated by article 9.

Article 5

1. If, subsequent to the adoption of the measures referred to in articles 3 and 4, nationals of other States engage in fishing the same stock or stocks of fish or other living marine resources in any area or areas of the high seas, the other States shall apply the measures, which shall not be discriminatory in form or in fact, to their own nationals not later than seven months after the date on which the measures shall have been notified to the Director-General of the Food and Agriculture Organization of the United Nations. The Director-General shall notify such measures to any State which so requests and, in any case, to any State specified by the State initiating the measure.

2. If these other States do not accept the measures so adopted and if no agreement can be reached within twelve months, any of the interested parties may initiate the procedure contemplated by article 9. Subject to paragraph 2 of article 10, the measures adopted shall remain obligatory pending the decision of the special commission.

Article 6

1. A coastal State has a special interest in the maintenance of the productivity of the living resources in any area of the high seas adjacent to its territorial sea.

2. A coastal State is entitled to take part on an equal footing in any system of research and regulation for purposes of conservation of the living resources of the high seas in that area, even though its nationals do not carry on fishing there.

3. A State whose nationals are engaged in fishing in any area of the high seas adjacent to the territorial sea of a State shall, at the request of that coastal State, enter into negotiations with a view to prescribing by agreement the measures necessary for the conservation of the living resources of the high seas in that area.

4. A State whose nationals are engaged in fishing in any area of the high seas adjacent to the territorial sea of a coastal State shall not enforce conservation measures in that area which are opposed to those which have been adopted by the coastal State, but may enter into negotiations with the coastal State with a view to prescribing by agreement the measures necessary for the conservation of the living resources of the high seas in that area.

5. If the States concerned do not reach agreement with respect to conservation measures within twelve months, any of the parties may initiate the procedure contemplated by article 9.

Article 7

1. Having regard to the provisions of paragraph 1 of article 6, any coastal State may, with a view to the maintenance of the productivity of the living resources of the sea, adopt unilateral measures of conservation appropriate to any stock of fish or other marine resources in any area of the high seas adjacent to its territorial sea, provided that negotiations to that effect with the other States concerned have not led to an agreement within six months.

2. The measures which the coastal State adopts under the previous paragraph shall be valid as to other States only if the following requirements are fulfilled:

(a) That there is a need for urgent application of conservation measures in the light of the existing knowledge of the fishery;

(b) That the measures adopted are based on appropriate scientific findings;

(c) That such measures do not discriminate in form or in fact against foreign fishermen.

3. These measures shall remain in force pending the settlement, in accordance with the relevant provisions of this Convention, of any disagreement as to their validity.

4. If the measures are not accepted by the other States concerned, any of the parties may initiate the procedure contemplated by article 9. Subject to paragraph 2 of article 10, the measures adopted shall remain obligatory pending the decision of the special commission.

5. The principles of geographical demarcation as defined in article 12 of the Convention on the Territorial Sea and the Contiguous Zone shall be adopted when coasts of different States are involved.

Article 8

1. Any State which, even if its nationals are not engaged in fishing in an area of the high seas not adjacent to its coast, has a special interest in the conservation of the living resources of the high seas in that area, may request the State or States whose nationals are engaged in fishing there to take the necessary measures of conservation under articles 3 and 4 respectively, at the same time mentioning the scientific reasons which in its opinion make such measures necessary, and indicating its special interest.

2. If no agreement is reached within twelve months, such State may initiate the procedure contemplated by Article 9.

Article 9

1. Any dispute which may arise between States under articles 4, 5, 6, 7 and 8 shall, at the request of any of the parties, be submitted for settlement to a special commission of five members, unless the parties agree to seek a solution by another method of peaceful settlement, as provided for in Article 33 of the Charter of the United Nations.

2. The members of the commission, one of whom shall be designated as chairman, shall be named by agreement between the States in dispute within three months of the request for settlement in accordance with the provisions of this article. Failing agreement they shall, upon the request of any State party, be named by the Secretary-General of the United Nations, within a further three-month period, in consultation with the States in dispute and with the President of the International Court of Justice and the Director-General of the Food and Agriculture Organization of the United Nations, from amongst well-qualified persons being nationals of States not involved in the dispute and specializing in legal, administrative or scientific questions relating to fisheries, depending upon the nature of the dispute to be settled. Any vacancy arising after the original appointment shall be filled in the same manner as provided for the initial selection.

3. Any State party to proceedings under these articles shall have the right to name one of its nationals to the special commission, with the right to participate

fully in the proceedings on the same footing as a member of the commission, but without the right to vote or to take part in the writing of the commission's decision.

4. The commission shall determine its own procedure, assuring each party to the proceedings a full opportunity to be heard and to present its case. It shall also determine how the costs and expenses shall be divided between the parties to the dispute, failing agreement by the parties on this matter.

5. The special commission shall render its decision within a period of five months from the time it is appointed unless it decides, in case of necessity, to extend the time limit for a period not exceeding three months.

6. The special commission shall, in reaching its decisions, adhere to these articles and to any special agreements between the disputing parties regarding settlement of the dispute.

7. Decisions of the commission shall be by majority vote.

Article 10

1. The special commission shall, in disputes arising under article 7, apply the criteria listed in paragraph 2 of that article. In disputes under articles 4, 5, 6 and 8, the commission shall apply the following criteria, according to the issues involved in the dispute:

(a) Common to the determination of disputes arising under articles 4, 5 and 6 are the requirements:

(i) That scientific findings demonstrate the necessity of conservation measures;

(ii) That the specific measures are based on scientific findings and are practicable; and

(iii) That the measures do not discriminate, in form or in fact, against fishermen of other States;

(b) Applicable to the determination of disputes arising under article 8 is the requirement that scientific findings demonstrate the necessity for conservation measures, or that the conservation programme is adequate, as the case may be.

2. The special commission may decide that pending its award the measures in dispute shall not be applied, provided that, in the case of disputes under article 7, the measures shall only be suspended when it is apparent to the commission on the basis of *prima facie* evidence that the need for the urgent application of such measures does not exist.

Article 11

The decisions of the special commission shall be binding on the States concerned and the provisions of paragraph 2 of Article 94 of the Charter of the United Nations shall be applicable to those decisions. If the decisions are accompanied by any recommendations, they shall receive the greatest possible consideration.

Article 12

1. If the factual basis of the award of the special commission is altered by

substantial changes in the conditions of the stock or stocks of fish or other living marine resources or in methods of fishing, any of the States concerned may request the other States to enter into negotiations with a view to prescribing by agreement the necessary modifications in the measures of conservation.

2. If no agreement is reached within a reasonable period of time, any of the States concerned may again resort to the procedure contemplated by article 9 provided that at least two years have elapsed from the original award.

Article 13

1. The regulation of fisheries conducted by means of equipment embedded in the floor of the sea in areas of the high seas adjacent to the territorial sea of a State may be undertaken by that State where such fisheries have long been maintained and conducted by its nationals, provided that non-nationals are permitted to participate in such activities on an equal footing with nationals except in areas where such fisheries have by long usage been exclusively enjoyed by such nationals. Such regulations will not, however, affect the general status of the areas as high seas.

2. In this article, the expression "fisheries conducted by means of equipment embedded in the floor of the sea" means those fisheries using gear with supporting members embedded in the sea floor, constructed on a site and left there to operate permanently or, if removed, restored each season on the same site.

Article 14

In articles 1, 3, 4, 5, 6 and 8, the term "nationals" means fishing boats or craft of any size having the nationality of the State concerned, according to the law of that State, irrespective of the nationality of the members of their crews.

Article 15

This Convention shall, until 31 October 1958, be open for signature by all States Members of the United Nations or of any of the specialized agencies, and by any other State invited by the General Assembly of the United Nations to become a Party to the Convention.

Article 16

This Convention is subject to ratification. The instruments of ratification shall be deposited with the Secretary-General of the United Nations.

Article 17

This Convention shall be open for accession by any States belonging to any of the categories mentioned in article 15. The instruments of accession shall be deposited with the Secretary-General of the United Nations.

Article 18

1. This Convention shall come into force on the thirtieth day following the date of deposit of the twenty-second instrument of ratification or accession with the Secretary-General of the United Nations.

2. For each State ratifying or acceding to the Convention after the deposit of the twenty-second instrument of ratification or accession, the Convention shall enter into force on the thirtieth day after deposit by such State of its instrument of ratification or accession.

Article 19

1. At the time of signature, ratification or accession, any State may make reservations to articles of the Convention other than to articles 6, 7, 9, 10, 11 and 12.

2. Any contracting State making a reservation in accordance with the preceding paragraph may at any time withdraw the reservation by a communication to that effect addressed to the Secretary-General of the United Nations.

Article 20

1. After the expiration of a period of five years from the date on which this Convention shall enter into force, a request for the revision of this Convention may be made at any time by any contracting party by means of a notification in writing addressed to the Secretary-General of the United Nations.

2. The General Assembly of the United Nations shall decide upon the steps, if any, to be taken in respect of such request.

Article 21

The Secretary-General of the United Nations shall inform all States Members of the United Nations and the other States referred to in article 15:

(a) Of signatures to this Convention and of the deposit of instruments of ratification or accession, in accordance with Articles 15, 16 and 17;

(b) Of the date on which this Convention will come into force, in accordance with article 18;

(c) Of requests for revision in accordance with article 20;

(d) Of reservations to this Convention, in accordance with article 19.

Article 22

The original of this Convention, of which the Chinese, English, French, Russian and Spanish texts are equally authentic, shall be deposited with the Secretary-General of the United Nations, who shall send certified copies thereof to all States referred to in article 15.

IN WITNESS WHEREOF the undersigned plenipotentiaries, being duly authorized thereto by their respective governments, have signed this Convention.

DONE AT GENEVA, this twenty-ninth day of April one thousand nine hundred and fifty-eight.

4. CONVENTION ON THE CONTINENTAL SHELF

The States Parties to this Convention
Have agreed as follows:

Article 1

For the purpose of these articles, the term "continental shelf" is used as referring *(a)* to the seabed and subsoil of the submarine areas adjacent to the coast but outside the area of the territorial sea, to a depth of 200 metres or, beyond that limit, to where the depth of the superjacent waters admits of the exploitation of the natural resources of the said areas; *(b)* to the seabed and subsoil of similar submarine areas adjacent to the coasts of islands.

Article 2

1. The coastal State exercises over the continental shelf sovereign rights for the purpose of exploring it and exploiting its natural resources.

2. The rights referred to in paragraph 1 of this article are exclusive in the sense that if the coastal State does not explore the continental shelf or exploit its natural resources, no one may undertake these activities, or make a claim to the continental shelf, without the express consent of the coastal State.

3. The rights of the coastal State over the continental shelf do not depend on occupation, effective or notional, or on any express proclamation.

4. The natural resources referred to in these articles consist of the mineral and other non-living resources of the seabed and subsoil together with living organisms belonging to sedentary species, that is to say, organisms which, at the harvestable state, either are immobile on or under the seabed or are unable to move except in constant physical contact with the seabed or the subsoil.

Article 3

The rights of the coastal State over the continental shelf do not affect the legal status of the superjacent waters as high seas, or that of the air space above those waters.

Article 4

Subject to its right to take reasonable measures for the exploration of the continental shelf and the exploitation of its natural resources, the coastal State may not impede the laying or maintenance of submarine cables or pipelines on the continental shelf.

Article 5

1. The exploration of the continental shelf and the exploitation of its natural resources must not result in any unjustifiable interference with navigation, fishing or the conservation of the living resources of the sea, nor result in any interference with fundamental oceanographic or other scientific research carried out with the intention of open publication.

2. Subject to the provisions of paragraphs 1 and 6 of this article, the coastal State is entitled to construct and maintain or operate on the continental shelf installations and other devices necessary for its exploration and the exploitation of its natural resources, and to establish safety zones around such installations and devices and to take in those zones measures necessary for their protection.

3. The safety zones referred to in paragraph 2 of this article may extend to a distance of 500 metres around the installations and other devices which have been erected, measured from each point of their outer edge. Ships of all nationalities must respect these safety zones.

4. Such installations and devices, though under the jurisdiction of the coastal State, do not possess the status of islands. They have no territorial sea of their own, and their presence does not affect the delimitation of the territorial sea of the coastal State.

5. Due notice must be given of the construction of any such installations, and permanent means for giving warning of their presence must be maintained. Any installations which are abandoned or disused must be entirely removed.

6. Neither the installations or devices, nor the safety zones around them, may be established where interference may be caused to the use of recognized sea lanes essential to international navigation.

7. The coastal State is obliged to undertake, in the safety zones, all appropriate measures for the protection of the living resources of the sea from harmful agents.

8. The consent of the coastal State shall be obtained in respect of any research concerning the continental shelf and undertaken there. Nevertheless, the coastal State shall not normally withhold its consent if the request is submitted by a qualified institution with a view to purely scientific research into the physical or biological characteristics of the continental shelf, subject to the proviso that the coastal State shall have the right, if it so desires, to participate or to be represented in the research, and that in any event the results shall be published.

Article 6

1. Where the same continental shelf is adjacent to the territories of two or more States whose coasts are opposite each other, the boundary of the continental shelf appertaining to such States shall be determined by agreement between them. In the absence of agreement, and unless another boundary line is justified by special circumstances, the boundary is the median line, every point of which is equidistant from the nearest points of the baselines from which the breadth of the territorial sea of each State is measured.

2. Where the same continental shelf is adjacent to the territories of two adjacent States, the boundary of the continental shelf shall be determined by agreement between them. In the absence of agreement, and unless another boundary line is justified by special circumstances, the boundary shall be determined by application of the principle of equidistance from the nearest points of the baselines from which the breadth of the territorial sea of each State is measured.

3. In delimiting the boundaries of the continental shelf, any lines which are drawn in accordance with the principles set out in paragraphs 1 and 2 of this article should be defined with reference to charts and geographical features as they exist at a particular date, and reference should be made to fixed permanent identifiable points on the land.

Article 7

The provisions of these articles shall not prejudice the right of the coastal State to exploit the subsoil by means of tunnelling irrespective of the depth of water above the subsoil.

Article 8

This Convention shall, until 30 October 1958, be open for signature by all States Members of the United Nations or of any of the specialized agencies, and by any other State invited by the General Assembly of the United Nations to become a party to the Convention.

Article 9

This Convention is subject to ratification. The instruments of ratification shall be deposited with the Secretary-General of the United Nations.

Article 10

This Convention shall be open for accession by any States belonging to any of the categories mentioned in article 8. The instruments of accession shall be deposited with the Secretary-General of the United Nations.

Article 11

1. This Convention shall come into force on the thirtieth day following the date of deposit of the twenty-second instrument of ratification or accession with the Secretary-General of the United Nations.
2. For each State ratifying or acceding to the Convention after the deposit of the twenty-second instrument of ratification or accession, the Convention shall enter into force on the thirtieth day after deposit by such State of its instrument of ratification or accession.

Article 12

1. At the time of signature, ratification or accession, any State may make reservations to articles of the Convention other than to articles 1 to 3 inclusive.
2. Any contracting State making a reservation in accordance with the preceding paragraph may at any time withdraw the reservation by a communication to that effect addressed to the Secretary-General of the United Nations.

Article 13

1. After the expiration of a period of five years from the date on which this Convention shall enter into force, a request for the revision of this Convention may be made at any time by any contracting party by means of a notification in writing addressed to the Secretary-General of the United Nations.
2. The General Assembly of the United Nations shall decide upon the steps, if any, to be taken in respect of such request.

Article 14

The Secretary-General of the United Nations shall inform all States Members of the United Nations and the other States referred to in article 8:

(a) Of signatures to this Convention and of the deposit of instruments of ratification or accession, in accordance with articles 8, 9 and 10;

(b) Of the date on which this Convention will come into force, in accordance with article 11;

(c) Of requests for revision in accordance with article 13;

(d) Of reservations to this Convention, in accordance with article 12.

Article 15

The original of this Convention, of which the Chinese, English, French, Russian and Spanish texts are equally authentic, shall be deposited with the Secretary-General of the United Nations, who shall send certified copies thereof to all States referred to in article 8.

IN WITNESS WHEREOF the undersigned plenipotentiaries, being duly authorized thereto by their respective governments, have signed this Convention.

DONE AT GENEVA, this twenty-ninth day of April one thousand nine hundred and fifty-eight.

ANNEX II

REGIONAL INSTRUMENTS AND DECLARATIONS

1. DECLARATION OF SANTIAGO ON THE MARITIME ZONE, AUGUST 18, 1952

"1. Governments are bound to ensure for their peoples access to necessary food supplies and to furnish them with the means of developing their economy.

"2. It is therefore the duty of each Government to ensure the conservation and protection of its natural resources and to regulate the use thereof to the greatest possible advantage of its country.

"3. Hence it is likewise the duty of each Government to prevent the said resources from being used outside the area of its jurisdiction so as to endanger their existence, integrity and conservation to the prejudice of peoples so situated geographically that their seas are irreplaceable sources of essential food and economic materials.

"For the foregoing reasons the Governments of Chile, Ecuador and Peru, being resolved to preserve for and make available to their respective peoples the natural resources of the areas of sea adjacent to their coasts, hereby declare as follows:

"(I) Owing to the geological and biological factors affecting the existence, conservation and development of the marine fauna and flora of the waters adjacent to the coasts of the declarant countries, the former extent of the territorial sea and contiguous zone is insufficient to permit of the conservation, development and use of those resources, to which the coastal countries are entitled.

"(II) The Governments of Chile, Ecuador and Peru therefore proclaim as a principle of their international maritime policy that each of them possesses sole sovereignty and jurisdiction over the area of sea adjacent to the coast of its own country and extending not less than 200 nautical miles from the said coast.

"(III) Their sole jurisdiction and sovereignty over the zone thus described includes sole sovereignty and jurisdiction over the sea floor and subsoil thereof.

"(IV) The zone of 200 nautical miles shall extend in every direction from any island or group of islands forming part of the territory of a declarant country. The maritime zone of an island or group of islands belonging to one declarant country and situated less than 200 nautical miles from the general maritime zone of another declarant country shall be bounded by the parallel of latitude drawn from the point at which the land frontier between the two countries reaches the sea.

"(V) This Declaration shall not be construed as disregarding the necessary restrictions on the exercise of sovereignty and jurisdiction imposed by international law to permit the innocent and inoffensive passage of vessels of all nations through the zone aforesaid.

"(VI) The Governments of Chile, Ecuador and Peru state that they intend to sign agreements or conventions to put into effect the principles set forth in this Declaration and to establish general regulations for the control and protection of hunting and fishing in their respective maritime zones and the control and coordination of the use and working of all other natural products or resources of common interest present in the said waters."

2. AGREEMENT SUPPLEMENTARY TO THE DECLARATION OF SANTIAGO 1954

The Governments of the Republics of Chile, Ecuador and Peru, in conformity with the provisions of resolution X of 8 October 1954, signed at Santiago de Chile by the Standing Committee of the Conference on the Exploitation and Conservation of the Maritime Resources of the South Pacific,

Having noted the proposals and recommendations approved in October of this year by the said Standing Committee,

Have appointed the following plenipotentiaries:

. . .

AND WHEREAS

Chile, Ecuador and Peru have proclaimed their sovereignty over the sea adjacent to the coasts of their respective countries to a distance of not less than two hundred nautical miles from the said coasts, the sea-bed and the subsoil of this maritime zone being included:

The Governments of Chile, Ecuador and Peru, at the First Conference on the Exploitation and Conservation of the Maritime Resources of the South Pacific, held at Santiago de Chile in 1952, expressed their intention of entering into agreements or conventions relating to the application of the principles governing that sovereignty, for the purpose in particular of regulating and protecting hunting and fisheries within their several maritime zones:

NOW THEREFORE THE SAID PLENIPOTENTIARIES HEREBY AGREE AS FOLLOWS:

1. Chile, Ecuador and Peru shall consult with one another for the purpose of upholding, in law, the principle of their sovereignty over the maritime zone to a distance of not less than two hundred nautical miles, including the sea-bed and the subsoil corresponding thereto. The term "nautical mile" means the equivalent of one minute of the arc measured on the Equator, or a distance of 1,852.8 metres.

2. If any complaints or protests should be addressed to any of the Parties, or if proceedings should be instituted against a Party in a court of law or in an arbitral tribunal, whether possessing general or special jurisdiction, the contracting countries undertake to consult with one another concerning the case to be presented for the defence and furthermore bind themselves to co-operate fully with one another in the joint defence.

3. In the event of a violation of the said maritime zone by force, the State affected shall report the event immediately to the other Contracting Parties, for the purpose of determining what action should be taken to safeguard the sovereignty which has been violated.

4. Each of the Contracting Parties undertakes not to enter into any agreements, arrangements or conventions which imply a diminution of the sovereignty over the said zone, though this provision shall not prejudice their rights to enter into agreements or to conclude contracts which do not conflict with the common rules laid down by the contracting countries.

5. All the provisions of this Agreement shall be deemed to be an integral and supplementary part of, and not in any way to abrogate, the resolutions and decisions adopted at the Conference on the Exploitation and Conservation of the Maritime Resources of the South Pacific, held at Santiago de Chile in August 1952.

3. MONTEVIDEO DECLARATION ON THE LAW OF THE SEA 1970

The States represented at the Montevideo Meeting on the Law of the Sea,

Recognizing that there exists a geographic, economic and social link between the sea, the land, and its inhabitant, Man, which confers on the coastal peoples legitimate priority in the utilization of the natural resources provided by their marine environment,

Recognizing likewise that any norms governing the limits of national sovereignty and jurisdiction over the sea, its soil and its subsoil, and the conditions for the exploitation of their resources, must take account of the geographical realities of the coastal States and the special needs and economic and social responsibilities of developing States,

Considering that scientific and technological advances in the exploitation of the natural wealth of the sea have brought in their train the danger of plundering its living resources through injudicious or abusive harvesting practices or through the disturbance of ecological conditions, a fact which supports the right of coastal States to take the necessary measures to protect those resources within areas of jurisdiction more extensive than has traditionally been the case and to regulate within such areas any fishing or aquatic hunting, carried out by vessels operating under the national or a foreign flag, subject to national legislation and to agreements concluded with other States,

That a number of declarations, resolutions and treaties, many of them inter-American, and multilateral declarations and agreements concluded between Latin American States, embody legal principles which justify the right of States to extend their sovereignty and jurisdiction to the extent necessary to conserve, develop and exploit the natural resources of the maritime area adjacent to their coasts, its soil and its subsoil,

That, in accordance with those legal principles the signatory States have, by reason of conditions peculiar to them, extended their sovereignty or exclusive rights of jurisdiction over the maritime area adjacent to their coasts, its soil and its subsoil to a distance of 200 nautical miles from the baseline of the territorial sea,

That the implementation of measures to conserve the resources of the sea, its soil and its subsoil by coastal States in the areas of maritime jurisdiction adjacent to their coasts ultimately benefits mankind, which possesses in the oceans a major source of means for its subsistence and development,

That the sovereign right of States to their natural resources has been recognized and reaffirmed by many resolutions of the General Assembly and other United Nations bodies,

That it is advisable to embody in a joint declaration the principles emanating from the recent movement towards the progressive development of international law, which is receiving ever-increasing support from the international community,

Declare the following to be Basic Principles of the Law of the Sea:

1. The right of coastal States to avail themselves of the natural resources of the sea adjacent to their coasts and of the soil and subsoil thereof in order to promote the maximum development of their economies and to raise the levels of living of their peoples;

2. The right to establish the limits of their maritime sovereignty and jurisdiction in accordance with their geographical and geological characteristics and with the factors governing the existence of marine resources and the need for their rational utilization;

3. The right to explore, to conserve the living resources of the sea adjacent to their territories, and to establish regulations for fishing and aquatic hunting;

4. The right to explore, conserve and exploit the natural resources of their continental shelves to where the depth of the superjacent waters admits of the exploitation of such resources;

5. The right to explore, conserve and exploit the natural resources of the soil and subsoil of the sea-bed and ocean floor up to the limit within which the State exercises its jurisdiction over the sea;

6. The right to adopt, for the aforementioned purposes, regulatory measures applicable in areas under their maritime sovereignty and jurisdiction, without prejudice to freedom of navigation by ships and overflying by aircraft of any flag.

Furthermore, the signatory States, encouraged by the results of this Meeting, express their intention to co-ordinate their future action with a view to defending effectively the principles embodied in this Declaration.

This Declaration shall be known as the "Montevideo Declaration on the Law of the Sea."

4. THE LIMA DECLARATION OF THE LATIN AMERICAN STATES ON THE LAW OF THE SEA 1970

The Latin American Meeting on Aspects of the Law of the Sea,
Considering:

That there is a geographical, economic and social link between the sea, the land, and man who inhabits it, which confers on coastal populations a legitimate priority right to utilize the natural resources of their maritime environment;

That in consequence of that priority relationship, the right has been recognized of coastal States to establish the extent of their maritime sovereignty or jurisdiction in accordance with reasonable criteria, having regard to their geographical, geological and biological situation and their socio-economic needs and responsibilities;

That the dangers and damage resulting from indiscriminate and abusive practices in the extraction of marine resources, among other reasons, have led an important group of coastal States to extend the limits of their sovereignty or jurisdiction over the sea, with due respect for freedom of navigation and flight in transit for ships and aircraft, without distinction as to flag;

That certain forms of utilization of the marine environment have likewise been giving rise to grave dangers of contamination of the waters and disturbance of the ecological balance, to combat which it is necessary that the coastal States should take steps to protect the health and interests of their populations;

That the development of scientific research in the marine environment requires the widest possible co-operation among States, so that all may contribute and share in its benefits, without prejudice to the authorization, supervision and participation of the coastal State when such research is carried out within the limits of its sovereignty or jurisdiction;

That in declarations, resolutions and treaties, especially inter-American instruments, and also in unilateral declarations and in agreements signed between Latin American States legal principles are embodied which justify the aforementioned rights;

That the sovereign right of States over their natural resources has been recognized and reaffirmed in numerous resolutions of the General Assembly and other United Nations bodies;

That in the exercise of these rights the respective rights of other neighbouring coastal States on the same sea must be mutually respected; and

That it is desirable to assemble and reaffirm the foregoing concepts in a joint declaration which will take into account the plurality of existing legal regimes on maritime sovereignty or jurisdiction in Latin American countries.

DECLARES as common principles of the Law of the Sea:

1. The inherent right of the coastal State to explore, conserve and exploit the natural resources of the sea adjacent to its coasts and the soil and subsoil thereof, likewise of the Continental Shelf and its subsoil, in order to promote the maximum development of its economy and to raise the level of living of its people;

2. The right of the coastal State to establish the limits of its maritime sovereignty or jurisdiction in accordance with reasonable criteria, having regard to its geographical, geological and biological characteristics, and the need to make rational use of its resources;

3. The right of the coastal State to take regulatory measures for the aforementioned purposes, applicable in the areas of its maritime sovereignty or jurisdiction, without prejudice to freedom of navigation and flight in transit of ships and aircraft, without distinction as to flag;

4. The right of the coastal State to prevent contamination of the waters and other dangerous and harmful effects that may result from the use, exploration or exploitation of the area adjacent to its coasts;

5. The right of the coastal State to authorize, supervize and participate in all scientific research activities which may be carried out in the maritime zones subject to its sovereignty or jurisdiction, and to be informed of the findings and the results of such research.

This declaration shall be known as the "Declaration of the Latin American States on the Law of the Sea."

5. THE DECLARATION OF SANTO DOMINGO 1972

THE SPECIALIZED CONFERENCE OF THE CARIBBEAN COUNTRIES ON PROBLEMS OF THE SEA

Recalling:

That the International American Conferences held in Bogotá in 1948, and in Caracas in 1954, recognized that the peoples of the Americas depend on the natural resources as a means of subsistence, and proclaimed the right to protect, conserve and develop those resources, as well as the right to ensure their use and utilization.

That the "Principles of Mexico on the Legal Regime of the Sea" which were adopted in 1956 and which were recognized "as the expression of the juridical conscience of the Continent and as applicable, by the American States," established the basis for the evolution of the Law of the Sea which culminated, that year, with the anunciation by the Specialized Conference in the Capital of the Dominican Republic of concepts which deserved endorsement by the United Nations Conference on the Law of the Sea, Geneva, 1958.

Considering:

That the General Assembly of the United Nations, in its Resolution 2750 (XXV) decided to convoke in 1973 a Conference on the Law of the Sea, and recognized "the need for early and progressive development of the law of the sea";

That it is desirable to define, through universal norms, the nature and scope of the rights of States, as well as their obligations and responsibilities relating to the various oceanic zones, without prejudice to regional or sub-regional agreements, based on the said norms;

That the Caribbean countries, on account of their peculiar conditions, require special criteria for the application of the Law of the Sea, while at the same time the co-ordination of Latin America is necessary for the purpose of joint action in the future;

That the economic and social development of all the peoples and the assurance of equal opportunities for all human beings are essential conditions for peace;

That the renewable and non-renewable resources of the sea contribute to improve the standard of living of the developing countries and to stimulate and accelerate their progress;

That such resources are not inexhaustible since even the living species may be depleted or extinguished as a consequence of irrational exploitation or pollution;

That the law of the sea should harmonize the needs and interests of States and those of the International Community;

That international co-operation is indispensable to ensure the protection of the marine environment and its better utilization;

That as Santo Domingo is the point of departure of the American civilization, as well as the site of the First Conference of the Law of the Sea in Latin America in 1956, it is historically significant that the new principles to advance the progressive development of the Law of the Sea be proclaimed in this city;

Formulate the following Declaration of Principles:

TERRITORIAL SEA

1. The sovereignty of a State extends, beyond its land territory and its internal waters, to an area of the sea adjacent to its coast, designated as the territorial sea, including the superjacent air space as well as the subjacent sea-bed and subsoil.

2. The breadth of the territorial sea and the manner of its delimitation should be the subject of an international agreement, preferably of a worldwide scope. In the meantime, each State has the right to establish the breadth of its territorial

sea up to a limit of 12 nautical miles to be measured from the applicable baseline.

3. Ships of all States, whether coastal or not, should enjoy the right of innocent passage through the territorial sea, in accordance with International Law.

PATRIMONIAL SEA

1. The coastal State has sovereign rights over the renewable and non-renewable natural resources, which are found in the waters, in the seabed and in the subsoil of an area adjacent to the territorial sea called the patrimonial sea.

2. The coastal State has the duty to promote and the right to regulate the conduct of scientific research within the patrimonial sea, as well as the right to adopt the necessary measures to prevent marine pollution and to ensure its sovereignty over the resources of the area.

3. The breadth of this zone should be the subject of an international agreement, preferably of a worldwide scope. The whole of the area of both the territorial sea and the patrimonial sea, taking into account geographic circumstances, should not exceed a maximum of 200 nautical miles.

4. The delimitation of this zone between two or more States should be carried out in accordance with the peaceful procedures stipulated in the Charter of the United Nations.

5. In this zone ships and aircraft of all States, whether coastal or not, should enjoy the right of freedom of navigation and overflight with no restrictions other than those resulting from the exercise by the Coastal State of its rights within the area. Subject only to these limitations, there will also be freedom for the laying of submarine cables and pipelines.

CONTINENTAL SHELF

1. The coastal State exercises over the continental shelf sovereign rights for the purpose of exploring it and exploiting its natural resources.

2. The continental shelf includes the sea-bed and subsoil of the submarine areas adjacent to the coast, but outside the area of the territorial sea, to a depth of 200 metres or, beyond that limit, to where the depth of the superjacent waters admits the exploitation of the natural resources of the said areas.

3. In addition, the States participating in this Conference consider that the Latin American Delegations in the Committee on the Sea-bed and Ocean Floor of the United Nations should promote a study concerning the advisability and timing for the establishment of precise outer limits of the continental shelf taking into account the outer limits of the continental rise.

4. In that part of the continental shelf covered by the patrimonial sea the legal regime provided for this area shall apply. With respect to the part beyond the patrimonial sea, the regime established for the continental shelf by International Law shall apply.

INTERNATIONAL SEA-BED

1. The sea-bed and its resources, beyond the patrimonial sea and beyond the continental shelf not covered by the former, are the common heritage of man-

kind, in accordance with the Declaration adopted by the General Assembly of the United Nations in Resolution 2749 (XXV) of December 17, 1970.

2. This area shall be subject to the regime to be established by international agreement, which should create an international authority empowered to undertake all activities in the area, particularly the exploration, exploitation, protection of the marine environment and scientific research, either on its own, or through third parties, in the manner and under the conditions that may be established by common agreement.

HIGH SEAS

The waters situated beyond the outer limits of the patrimonial sea constitute an international area designated as high seas, in which there exists freedom of navigation, of overflight and of laying submarine cables and pipelines. Fishing in this zone should be neither unrestricted nor indiscriminate and should be the subject of adequate international regulation, preferably of worldwide scope and general acceptance.

MARINE POLLUTION

1. It is the duty of every State to refrain from performing acts which may pollute the sea and its seabed, either inside or outside its respective jurisdictions.
2. The international responsibility of physical or juridical persons damaging the marine environment is recognized. With regard to this matter the drawing up of an international agreement, preferably of a worldwide scope, is desirable.

REGIONAL CO-OPERATION

1. Recognizing the need for the countries in the area to unite their efforts and adopt a common policy vis-à-vis the problems peculiar to the Caribbean Sea relating mainly to scientific research, the pollution of the marine environment, conservation, exploration, safeguarding and exploitation of the resources of the sea;
2. Decides to hold periodic meetings, if possible once a year, of senior governmental officials, for the purpose of co-ordinating and harmonizing national efforts and policies in all aspects of oceanic space with a view to ensuring maximum utilization of resources by all the peoples of the region.
The first meeting may be convoked by any of the States participating in this Conference.

Finally, the feelings of peace and respect for international law which have always inspired the Latin American countries are hereby reaffirmed. It is within this spirit of harmony and solidarity, and for the strengthening of the norms of the inter-american system, that the principles of this document shall be realized.
The present Declaration shall be called: *"Declaration of Santo Domingo."*
Done in Santo Domingo de Guzmán, Dominican Republic, this ninth day of June one thousand nine hundred and seventy-two (1972), in a single copy in the English, French and Spanish languages, each text being equally authentic.

ANNEX III

BILATERAL INSTRUMENTS AND DECLARATIONS

1. AGREEMENT ON FISHING BETWEEN BRAZIL AND ARGENTINA, SIGNED AT BUENOS AIRES ON 29 DECEMBER 1967

Article 1

Each of the High Contracting Parties shall authorize nationals of the other Party to fish, free of any tax or charge, in waters beyond a limit of six miles from the baselines for measuring the breadth of the respective territorial sea. Such right may be exercised subject only to the lawful use of the flag flown and authorization, in the country of that flag, to engage in fishing.

Sole paragraph. Within a period of 60 days from the entry into force of this Agreement, a Joint Commission shall be set up to study and to recommend to the respective Governments the requisite measures for standardizing the registration requirements for fishing vessels.

Article 2

Pending the entry into force of the Convention provided for in the Agreement on Conservation of the Natural Resources of the South Atlantic, signed between the High Contracting Parties on today's date, fishing vessels of either Party shall comply with the laws of the coastal State concerned in respect of conservation of the natural resources of the area covered by this Agreement. They shall do so especially in respect of the types of fishing gear to be used, the method of use thereof, the authorized fishing seasons and areas, and any other measure designed to protect the fish species or preserve the ecological conditions and biological balance.

Article 3

Each High Contracting Party undertakes to respect the jurisdiction of the other within the limits established in article 1, as the area covered by this Agreement.

No provision of this Agreement shall be interpreted as affecting the rights or claims of the Contracting Parties within the aforementioned limits, including the right to verify compliance with the Agreement.

Article 4

This Agreement shall remain open for accession by any other South American State of the South Atlantic which grants the same fishing facilities as do the signatories.

2. AGREEMENT ON FISHING AND CONSERVATION OF LIVING RESOURCES BETWEEN BRAZIL AND URUGUAY, SIGNED AT MONTEVIDEO ON 12 DECEMBER 1968

The President of the Federative Republic of Brazil and the President of the Eastern Republic of Uruguay,

Considering the need to safeguard the living resources both of the sea waters adjacent to their respective countries and of the internal boundary waters against wasteful forms of exploitation which render difficult the renewal of such resources;

Considering the desirability, in the spirit underlying the friendly relations that exist between Brazil and Uruguay, of promoting the development and expansion of forms of co-operation, both as regards fishing engaged in by nationals of the two countries and as concerns improvement of the techniques and equipment of the respective fishing industries;

Considering that such co-operation could make a substantial contribution to the conservation of the species and the better economic utilization of the fishery resources available to the respective countries;

Having decided to conclude this Agreement on Fishing and Conservation of Living Resources. . . .

Article I

The High Contracting Parties declare that they regard the fishing and conservation of the living resources in the sea adjacent to their coasts and in the internal boundary waters as a matter of special importance and high priority.

Article II

In accordance with the provisions of the preceding article, the High Contracting Parties decide to establish, on a permanent basis, a Joint Brazilian-Uruguayan Commission on Fishing and Conservation of the Living Resources of the Sea and the Internal Boundary Waters.

Article III

The Joint Commission provided for in article II of this Agreement shall study and formulate conclusions with regard to matters of common interest relating to the fishing and conservation of the living resources in the waters of the sea adjacent to the coasts of the two countries and in the internal boundary waters and also draw up, as soon as possible, a Convention designed to promote, by means of appropriate technical regulations, the conservation of the species, so as to ensure an optimum sustainable yield. The said Convention shall prescribe measures for ensuring compliance with existing or future regulations in accordance with its provisions.

Article IV

In drafting the Convention referred to in article III of this Agreement, the High Contracting Parties shall, where possible, take due account of the provisions agreed upon in similar instruments to which they are parties and shall also endeavour to co-ordinate their action with similar action in the area, so as to promote the adoption of uniform multinational solutions.

Article V

The Joint Commission provided for in article II above shall be formally established within a period of 90 (ninety) days from the entry into force of this Agreement and may meet at any time by joint decision of the respective national delegations, transmitted through the Ministries of Foreign Affairs of the High Contracting Parties, or on the initiative of those Ministries.

Article VI

Each of the national delegations to the Joint Commission established under this Agreement shall consist of four representatives; the Chairman of the meetings shall be the representative of the country in whose territory they are held.

Article VII

Nothing in this Agreement shall be construed as affecting the rights and claims of the High Contracting Parties with respect to the sea adjacent to their coasts.

3. AGREEMENT BETWEEN THE UNITED STATES OF AMERICA AND THE UNITED MEXICAN STATES ON TRADITIONAL FISHING IN THE EXCLUSIVE FISHERY ZONES CONTIGUOUS TO THE TERRITORIAL SEAS OF BOTH COUNTRIES. EFFECTED BY EXCHANGE OF NOTES SIGNED AT WASHINGTON ON 27 OCTOBER 1967

Considering

I. That the Government of the United States of America, pursuant to Public Law 89-658, approved 14 October 1966, established an exclusive fishery zone contiguous to the territorial sea of the United States in which it will exercise the same exclusive rights in respect to fisheries as it has in its territorial sea, subject to the continuation of traditional fishing by the foreign States within this zone as may be recognized by the Government of the United States;

II. That the Government of Mexico, pursuant to the law of 9 December 1966, promulgated by the Mexican Congress, established the exclusive jurisdiction of Mexico, for fishing purposes, in a zone of 12 nautical miles (22,224 metres) in breadth, measured from the base line used to measure the breadth of the territorial sea, and provided that the legal regime for the exploitation of the living resources of the sea within the territorial sea extends to the entire exclusive fishery zone of the nation and that nothing contained in this law modifies in any way the legal provisions which determine the breadth of the territorial sea, and finally that Mexico's Federal Executive will determine the conditions and terms under which nationals of countries which traditionally have exploited the living resources of the sea within the three nautical mile zone beyond the territorial sea may be authorized to continue their activities for a period not to exceed five years, beginning on 1 January 1968;

III. That both Governments consider it necessary and convenient to establish the terms and conditions under which, without any modification of and in total accord with the laws cited in previous paragraphs I and II, fishing vessels of the United States and those of Mexico may, beginning 1 January 1968, continue their activities during five years in the waters within the exclusive fishery zone of the other country in which vessels of the same flag fished in a sustained manner during the five years immediately preceding 1 January 1968; and

IV. That both Governments state that the establishment of said terms and conditions does not imply a change of position or an abandonment of the positions maintained by each Government regarding the breadth of the territorial sea, this matter not being the object of this agreement, nor does it limit their freedom to continue defending them in the international forum or in any of the ways recognized by international law;

The Government of the United States of America and the Government of the United Mexican States

Agree to establish the following terms and conditions under which American and Mexican fishermen will continue to operate in the above-mentioned waters during the established period of five years:

1. Fishing vessels of the United States will be permitted to continue their activities in the exclusive fishery zone of the United Mexican States in the Gulf of Mexico:

(a) In the waters between 9 and 12 nautical miles off the coast of the mainland and around the islands of Mexico, measured from the baseline from which the breadth of the territorial sea is measured, bounded on the north by a line to be constructed by the International Boundary and Water Commission, United States and Mexico, as the maritime boundary between both countries, extended to the 12-nautical-mile limit, and bounded on the south by a straight line connecting the geographic co-ordinates of 21°20'00" north latitude, 86°38'00" west longitude, and 21°20'00" north latitude, 86°35'00" west longitude (north-east of Isla Mujeres), where fishing vessels of the United States have traditionally carried on shrimp fishing, they will be permitted to continue to take shrimp and such species of fish as are taken incidentally;

(b) United States fishing vessels will be permitted to continue to fish for snappers (genera *Lutjanus, Rhomboplites, Ocyurus, Etelis, Holocentrus,* and *Pristipomoides*), groupers (genera *Epinephelus* and *Mycteroperca*), and other genera that are captured incidentally, such as *Seriola, Calamus, Stenotomus, Balistes, Paralichthys, Ancyclopsetta,* and *Cyclopsetta,* in waters between 9 and 12 nautical miles around Cayo Arcas, Arrecifes Triangulos, Cayo Arenas, and Arrecifes Alacran;

(c) The fishing referred to in subparagraphs (a) and (b) above will continue during the five years beginning 1 January 1968, at levels such that the total catch by United States vessels will not exceed the total in the five years immediately preceding that date.

2. In the maritime waters off the Mexican coast in the Pacific Ocean:

(a) In the waters between 9 and 12 nautical miles measured from the baseline from which the breadth of the territorial sea is measured, off the mainland and around the islands of Mexico, bounded on the north by a line to be constructed by the International Boundary and Water Commission, United States and Mexico, as the maritime boundary between both countries, extended to the 12-nautical-mile limit and bounded on the south by a straight line connecting the geographical co-ordinates of 14°32'42" north latitude, 92°27'00" west longitude, and 14°30'36" north latitude, 92°29'18" west longitude, where fishing vessels of the United States have traditionally carried on fishing, they will be permitted to fish for albacore *(Thunnus alalunga)*, yellowfin tuna *(Thunnus albacares)*, bluefin tuna *(Thunnus thynnus)*, skipjack *(Euthynnus (Katsuwonus) pelamis)*, bonito *(Sarda chiliensis)*, thread herring *(Opisthonema* spp.), white sea bass *(Cynoscion nobilis)*, giant sea bass *(Stereolepis gigas)*, rockfishes *(Sebastodes* spp.), California halibut *(Paralichthys californicus)*, yellowtail *(Seriola dorsalis)*, barracuda *(Sphyraena argentea)*, groupers *(Mycteroperca* spp.), and such other species as are commonly taken incidentally in fishing for the above-mentioned species, and for anchoveta *(Cetengraulis mysticetus)*, northern anchovy *(Engraulis mordax)* and Pacific sardine *(Sardinops caerulea)* exclusively as tuna bait fish;

(b) The fishing referred to in subparagraph (a) above will continue during five years beginning on 1 January 1968, up to a total volume that will not exceed the total catch taken by United States vessels in the five years immediately preceding that date; and

(c) United States fishing vessels will be permitted, during the same term of five years, to continue sport or recreational fishing in the waters indicated.

3. Mexican fishermen will be permitted to continue their activities within the exclusive fishery zone of the United States, in regards to the Gulf of Mexico:

(a) In the waters between 9 and 12 nautical miles measured from the baseline from which the breadth of the territorial sea is measured, off the mainland and around the islands of the United States, from the maritime boundary indicated in paragraph 1 (a) above to a line on the 26th parallel of north latitude connecting points 9 and 12 miles from the said baseline on the West Coast of Florida where fishing vessels of Mexico have carried on fishing traditionally and in a sustained manner, they will be permitted to fish for shrimp and other genera that are captured incidentally, as well as to fish for snappers (genera *Lutjanus, Rhomboplites, Ocyurus, Etelis, Holocentrus* and *Pristipomoides*); and

(b) The fishing referred to in subparagraph (a) above will continue during five years beginning on 1 January 1968, up to a total volume that will not exceed the total catch taken by Mexican vessels in the five years immediately preceding that date.

4. In the maritime waters off the United States coast on the Pacific Ocean:

(a) In the waters between 9 and 12 nautical miles measured from the baseline from which the breadth of the territorial sea is measured, off the mainland and around the islands of the United States, from the maritime boundary indicated in paragraph 2 (a) above, to a western extension of the California-Oregon border (42° north latitude) where fishing vessels of Mexico have carried on fishing traditionally and in a sustained manner, they will be permitted to fish for Pacific mackerel *(Pneumatophorus* ssp.), yellowfin tuna *(Thunnus albacares)*, bluefin tuna *(Thunnus thynnus)*, albacore *(Thunnus alalunga)*, yellowtail *(Seriola dorsalis)*, hake *(Merluccius* ssp.), giant sea bass *(Stereolepis gigas)*, rockfishes *(Sebastodes* spp.), and such other species as are commonly taken incidentally in fishing for tuna, as well as anchoveta *(Cetengraulis mysticetus)*, northern anchovy *(Engraulis mordax)* and Pacific sardine *(Sardinops caerulea),* these last ones exclusively as tuna bait fish; and

(b) The fishing referred to in subparagraph (a) above will continue during five years beginning on 1 January 1968, up to a total volume that will not exceed the total catch taken by Mexican vessels in the five years immediately preceding that date.

5. In the event that the International Boundary and Water Commission, United States and Mexico, is unable to complete the lines referred to in paragraphs 1 (a), 2 (a), 3 (a) and 4 (a) prior to 1 January 1968, it will, prior to that date, for the purposes of this agreement, prepare lines to be used as provisional boundaries until the two countries are able to agree on permanent boundaries of their exclusive fishery zones.

6. In view of the fact that the catch by United States vessels within the exclusive fishery zone of Mexico and the catch by Mexican vessels within the exclusive fishery zone of the United States have not substantially increased during recent years, both Governments agree that said catches should not increase, and because of this they do not consider it necessary to establish during the five years beginning 1 Januaiy 1968 specific control measures, other than the following:

(a) The Government of the United States of America will submit to the Government of Mexico, and the latter will submit to the former, before 1 January 1968, or, at the latest, 30 days after that date, a report designating the areas now included within the exclusive fishery zone of the other country where its fishermen have operated in a sustained manner during the years 1963 to 1966 inclusive, indicating the species caught and the volume of each species, and the two Governments will submit to each other similar reports for the year 1967 no later than 30 June 1968;

(b) The two Governments will report to each other before 1 January 1968, or, at the latest, 30 days after that date, the number of vessels and the types and net tonnage of said vessels as well as the types of fishing gear used during the previous years by their respective nationals;

(c) The two Governments will exchange, no later than 31 January of each year, and at such other times as it may become necessary owing to special circumstances, lists of vessels that will operate under the terms of the present agreement;

(d) Representatives of the two Governments will meet annually on mutually agreeable dates to review the operation of this agreement and to determine the need for any additional arrangements. To facilitate this review, the Government of the United States will submit to the Government of Mexico, and the latter will submit to the former, as soon as practicable after 1 January, but not later than 1 April, each year a report on the fishing activities of its nationals in the exclusive fishery zone of the other country, indicating the volume of catch of each species authorized to be taken and the areas in which such catches were made.

7. The United States and Mexican fishermen may continue to use, within the exclusive fishery zone of the other country, only vessels and fishing gear not prohibited by the laws of the respective country and of the same types as those employed during the five years prior to 1 January 1968, except that technologi-

cal improvements to existing types of vessels and gear are not precluded, provided they are not inconsistent with the legislation of the respective country.

8. Notwithstanding the limitations on fishing indicated in paragraphs 1, 2, 3, 4, and 7 of this agreement, each Government may establish additional limitations when, in its judgement, they become indispensable in order to protect the living resources of the sea in the exclusive fishery zone under its jurisdiction, or when each Government or both Governments must establish extraordinary restrictions pursuant to resolutions or recommendations of international organizations of which they are members. In any of these eventualities, the interested Government will consult with the other Government before establishing the new limitations and will notify the other Government 60 days in advance of their application in order to reasonably allow the fishermen of the other country to adjust their activities accordingly.

9. The United States of America and the United Mexican States, in accordance with their respective laws on the exclusive fishery zone, will exercise within their respective zones the same exclusive rights with respect to fisheries as they exercise in their territorial sea. Nevertheless, without renouncing their sovereign powers and in order to respect the traditional fisheries by their respective nationals in the zone of the other country during the period indicated in this agreement, both Governments state that it is their intention neither to impose duties or taxes nor to impose other fiscal obligations, nor to propose to their respective Congresses the establishment of financial burdens upon the fishermen of the other country, who, within the terms of this agreement, will continue to operate in the waters within their respective exclusive fishery zones during the five years beginning 1 January 1968.

10. Notwithstanding the provisions of the previous paragraph, if either of the two Governments, due to circumstances which may arise during the life of this agreement, should deem it necessary or convenient to establish and collect such taxes, duties or fiscal obligations from the fishermen of the other country, it will first grant the other Government the opportunity to express its point of view. If, finally, such taxes, duties or obligations are established, the other Government, in strict reciprocity, will have the right to impose identical or similar fiscal measures, within its exclusive fishery zone, upon the fishermen of the country that first applied them.

11. For purposes of this agreement, the Government of Mexico will permit only vessels flying the flag of the United States of America to continue to operate within its exclusive fishery zone. For purposes of this agreement, only vessels flying the Mexican flag will be permitted to operate within the exclusive fishery zone of the United States of America.

12. Any fishing vessel of either country operating under the present agreement which acts contrary to the provisions of the agreement will not have the protection of the agreement in the particular case and will be subject exclusively to the legal regime, penal and administrative, of the country having jurisdiction over the exclusive fisheries zone.

13. The Government of the United States understands that neither the enact-

ment of the Mexican law on the exclusive fishery zone of the nation nor the provisions of the present agreement imply *ipso facto* and of themselves any change regarding the legal regime on the exploitation of the living resources of the Mexican territorial sea, including the provisions of Mexico's law relating to the imposition of fees and taxes on foreign fishermen who fish within Mexico's territorial sea, since the law on the fishery zone of the nation, in accordance with its article 2 (transitory), only repeals previous provisions contrary to it, and this agreement, as was expressed in the points of initial consideration, is based on said law.

14. The Government of the United States of America will co-operate with the Government of Mexico in the formulation and execution of a programme of scientific research and conservation of the stocks of shrimp and fish of common concern off the coast of Mexico, consistent with the Convention on Fishing and Conservation of Living Resources of the High Seas, opened for signature at Geneva on 29 April 1958, to which both Governments are parties. The two Governments at an appropriate time will meet to make the special arrangements necessary to formulate and execute such a programme.

15. The provisions of this agreement will be enforced by the Government of the United States of America and by the Government of Mexico in their respective exclusive fishing zones.

16. This agreement shall be in effect for a period of five years beginning on 1 January 1968, provided that either Party may denounce the agreement at any time after one year from that date if in its judgement the agreement is not operating satisfactorily. Such denunciation shall have the effect of terminating the agreement six months from the date of the formal notice of denunciation.

4. AGREEMENT BETWEEN THE GOVERNMENT OF THE UNITED STATES OF AMERICA AND THE GOVERNMENT OF CANADA ON RECIPROCAL FISHING PRIVILEGES IN CERTAIN AREAS OFF THEIR COASTS SIGNED AT OTTAWA ON 24 APRIL 1970

The Government of *the United States of America* and the Government of *Canada,*

CONSIDERING that both Governments have established exclusive fishery zones,

RECOGNIZING that fishermen of the two countries have traditionally fished for the same species in certain areas now encompassed within the exclusive fishery zones,

DEEMING it desirable to establish the terms and conditions under which nationals and vessels of each of the two countries may conduct, on a reciprocal basis, commercial fishing operations within certain areas off their coasts, and

HAVING in mind the mutuality of interest on the part of the two countries in the conservation and rational exploitation of certain living marine resources off their coasts,

Have agreed as follows:

264

1. For the purposes of this agreement,

(a) the reciprocal fishing area of the United States of America shall be the fishing zone established in 1966 south of 63° north latitude;
(b) the reciprocal fishing area of Canada shall be as follows:

(i) in those "Areas" listed in Order-in-Council P.C. 1967-2025 and Order-in-Council P.C. 1969-1109, issued by the Government of Canada on 8 November 1967, and 11 June 1969, respectively, those waters extending 9 miles seaward of the territorial sea of Canada as it existed in 1966;

(ii) in those areas not listed in the Orders-in-Council cited above, those waters south of 63° north latitude which are contiguous to and extend from three to twelve miles from the coast of Canada, with the exception of bays where they cease to exceed 24 miles in breadth.

Nothing in this agreement shall affect waters other than those referred to in this paragraph.

2. Nationals and vessels of each country may continue to fish within the reciprocal fishing area of the other country, except that there shall be no such fishing for the following:

(a) any species of clam, scallop, crab, shrimp, lobster or herring;
(b) any salmon other than salmon taken by trolling off the Pacific coast northward from a line projected due west from the Cape Disappointment Light (46° 18' N) and southward from a line projected due west from the Cape Scott Light (50° 46.9' N).

Subject to its domestic legislation, each Government will continue to permit transfers of herring between nationals and vessels of the two countries within the reciprocal fishing areas west and north of a line drawn between Cape Sable, Nova Scotia, and Race Point, Massachusetts. The Governments agree that the principal purpose of this provision is to enable the continuation of transfers of herring intended for purposes other than reduction and, further, that they will meet within one year to assess the status of the herring stocks of the Bay of Fundy and the Gulf of Maine to determine whether restrictions on fishing or fish use are necessary.

3. Nationals and vessels of either country will not initiate fisheries within the reciprocal fishing area of the other country for species which are fully utilized by fishermen of the latter country. If fishermen of either country wish to initiate a fishery within any part of the reciprocal fishing area of the other country for species not fully utilized, their Government will first consult with the other Government and reach an understanding concerning conditions for such a fishery.

4. Regulations established by one country pertaining to the taking or possession of fish within its reciprocal fishing area shall apply equally to the nationals and vessels of both countries operating within such area. Such regulations shall be enforced by the Government which issued them. Should either Government consider it necessary to alter such fishery regulations, that Government shall notify the other Government of such proposed changes 60 days in advance of their application. Should such changes in fishery regulations require

265

major changes in fishing gear an adequate period of time, up to one year, will be afforded the nationals and vessels of the other country to adapt to such changes prior to their application.

5. The two Governments recognize the importance of maintaining the fishery resources in their reciprocal fishing areas at appropriate levels. Both Governments agree to continue and expand co-operation in both national and joint research programmes on species of common interest off their coasts. The appropriate agencies of the two Governments will arrange for exchanges and periodic joint reviews of scientific information.

6. Nothing in this agreement shall prejudice the claims or views of either of the parties concerning internal waters, territorial waters, or jurisdiction over fisheries or the resources of the continental shelf; further, nothing in this agreement shall affect either bilateral or multilateral agreements to which either Government is a party.

7. This agreement shall remain in force for a period of two years. Representatives of the two Governments will meet annually or as mutually deemed necessary, but in any event prior to the expiration of the period of validity of this agreement, to review its operation and decide on future arrangements.

The two Governments further agree, in connexion with the provisions of paragraph 2 (b) of this agreement, to consult within one year regarding all matters of mutual concern related to the fisheries for Pacific salmon.

5. AGREEMENT BETWEEN THE GOVERNMENT OF THE FEDERATIVE REPUBLIC OF BRAZIL AND THE GOVERNMENT OF THE UNITED STATES OF AMERICA CONCERNING SHRIMP. DONE AT BRASILIA MAY 9, 1972

The Parties to this Agreement,

Note the position of the Government of the Federative Republic of Brazil,

that it considers its territorial sea to extend to a distance of 200 nautical miles from Brazil's coast,

that the exploitation of crustaceans and other living resources, which are closely dependent on the seabed under the Brazilian territorial sea, is reserved to Brazilian fishing vessels, and

that exceptions to this provision can only be granted through international agreements,

Note also the position of the Government of the United States of America that it does not consider itself obligated under international law to recognize territorial sea claims of more than 3 nautical miles nor fisheries jurisdiction of more than 12 nautical miles, beyond which zone of jurisdiction all nations have the right to fish freely, and that it does not consider that all crustaceans are living organisms belonging to sedentary species as defined in the 1958 Geneva Convention on the Continental Shelf, and further

Recognizing that the difference in the respective juridical positions of the Parties has given rise to certain problems relating to the conduct of shrimp fisheries,

Considering the tradition of both Parties for resolving international differences by having recourse to negotiation,

Believing it is desirable to arrive at an interim solution for the conduct of shrimp fisheries without prejudice to either Party's juridical position concerning the extent of territorial seas or fisheries jurisdiction under international law,

266

Concluding that, while general international solutions to issues of maritime jurisdiction are being sought and until more adequate information regarding the shrimp fisheries is available, it is desirable to conclude an interim agreement which takes into account their mutual interest in the conservation of the shrimp resources of the area of this Agreement,

Have Agreed as Follows:

Article 1

This Agreement shall apply to the fishery for shrimp *(Penaeus* (M.) *duorarum notialis, Penaeus braziliensis* and *Penaeus* (M.) *aztecus subtilis)* in an area of the broader region in which the shrimp fisheries of the Parties are conducted, hereinafter referred to as the "area of agreement" and defined as follows: the waters off the coast of Brazil having the isobath of thirty (30) meters as the south-west limit and the latitude 1° north as the southern limit and 47°30' west longitude as the eastern limit.

Article II

1. Taking into account their common concern with preventing the depletion of the shrimp stocks in the area of agreement and the substantial difference in the stages of development of their respective fishing fleets, which results correspondingly in different kinds of impact on the resources, the two Parties agree that, during the term of this Agreement, the Government of the Federative Republic of Brazil is to apply the measures set forth in Annex I to this Agreement and the Government of the United States of America is to apply the measures set forth in Annex II to this Agreement.

2. The measures set forth in Annexes may be changed by agreement of the Parties through consultation pursuant to Article X.

Article III

1. Information on catch and effort and biological data relating to shrimp fisheries in the area of agreement shall be collected and exchanged, as appropriate, by the Parties. Unless the Parties decide otherwise, such exchange of information shall be made in accordance with the procedure described in this Article.

2. Each vessel fishing under this Agreement shall maintain a fishing log, according to a commonly agreed model. Such fishing logs shall be delivered quarterly to the appropriate Party which shall use the data therein contained, and other information it obtains about the area of agreement, to prepare reports on the fishing conditions in that area, which shall be transmitted periodically to the other Party as appropriate.

3. Duly appointed organizations from both Parties shall meet in due time to exchange scientific data, publications and knowledge acquired on the shrimp fisheries in the area of agreement.

Article IV

1. The Party which under Article V has the responsibility for enforcing

observance of the terms of the Agreement by vessels of the other Party's flag shall receive from the latter Party the information necessary for identification and other enforcement functions, including name, port of registry, port where operations are usually based, general description with photograph in profile, radio-frequencies by which communications may be established, main engine horsepower and speed, length, and fishing method and gear employed.

2. Such information shall be assembled and organized by the flag Government and communications relating to such information shall be carried out each year between the appropriate authorities of the Parties.

3. The Party which receives such information shall verify whether it is complete and in good order, and shall inform the other Party about the vessels found to comply with the requirements of paragraph 1 of this Article, as well as about those which would, for some reason, require further consultation among the Parties.

4. Each of those vessels found in order shall receive and display an identification sign, agreed between the Parties.

Article V

1. In view of the fact that Brazilian authorities can carry out an effective enforcement presence in the area of Agreement, it shall be incumbent on the Government of Brazil to ensure that the conduct of shrimp fisheries conforms with the provisions of this Agreement.

2. A duly authorized official of Brazil, in exercising the responsibility described in paragraph 1 of this Article may, if he has reasonable cause to believe that any provision of this Agreement has been violated, board and search a shrimp fishing vessel. Such action shall not unduly hinder fishing operations. When, after boarding or boarding and searching a vessel, the official continues to have reasonable cause to believe that any provision of this Agreement has been violated, he may seize and detain such vessel. In the case of a boarding or seizure and detention of a United States vessel, the Government of Brazil shall promptly inform the Government of the United States of its action.

3. After satisfaction of the terms of Article VI as referred to in paragraph 4 of this Article, a United States vessel seized and detained under the terms of this Agreement shall, as soon as practicable, be delivered to an authorized official of the United States at the nearest port to the place of seizure, or any other place which is mutually acceptable to the competent authorities of both Parties. The Government of Brazil shall, after delivering such vessel to an authorized official of the United States, provide a certified copy of the full report of the violation and the circumstances of the seizure and detention.

4. If the reason for seizure and detention falls within the terms of Article II or Article IV, paragraph 4 of this Agreement, a United States vessel seized and detained shall be delivered to an authorized official of the United States, after satisfaction of the terms of Article VI relating to unusual expenses.

5. If the nature of the violation warrants it, and after carrying out the provision of Article X, vessels may also suffer forfeiture of that part of the catch determined to be taken illegally and forfeiture of the fishing gear.

6. In the case of vessels delivered to an authorized official of the United States under paragraphs 3 or 4 of this Article, the Government of Brazil will be informed of the institution and disposition of any case by the United States.

Article VI

In connection with the enforcement arrangements specified in Article V, including in particular any unusual expenses incurred in carrying out the seizure and detention of a United States vessel under the terms of paragraph 4 of Article V, and taking into account Brazil's regulation of its flag vessels in the area of agreement, the Government of Brazil will be compensated in an amount determined and confirmed in an exchange of notes between the Parties. The amount of compensation shall be related to the level of fishing by United States nationals in the area of agreement and to the total enforcement activities to be undertaken by the Government of Brazil pursuant to the terms of this Agreement.

Article VII

The implementation of this Agreement may be reviewed at the request of either Party six months after the date on which this Agreement becomes effective, in order to deal with administrative issues arising in connection with this Agreement.

Article VIII

The Parties shall examine the possibilities of cooperating in the development of their fishing industries; the expansion of the international trade of fishery products; the improvement of storage, transportation and marketing of fishery products; and the encouragement of joint ventures between the fishing industries of the two Parties.

Article IX

Nothing contained in this Agreement shall be interpreted as prejudicing the position of either Party regarding the matter of territorial seas or fisheries jurisdiction under international law.

Article X

Problems concerning the interpretation and implementation of this Agreement shall be resolved through diplomatic channels.

Article XI

This Agreement shall enter into force on a date to be mutually agreed by exchange of notes, upon completion of the internal procedures of both parties and shall remain in force until January 1, 1974, unless the Parties agree to extend it.

In witness whereof the undersigned representatives have signed the present agreement and affixed thereto their seals.

Done in duplicate this 9th day of May, 1972, in the English and Portuguese languages both texts being equally authoritative.

6. TREATY BETWEEN THE UNITED KINGDOM AND VENEZUELA RELATING TO THE SUBMARINE AREAS OF THE GULF OF PARIA, FEBRUARY 26, 1942

"His Majesty The King of Great Britain, Ireland and the British Dominions beyond the Seas, Emperor of India, and the President of the United States of Venezuela.

"Desiring in a spirit of goodwill to make provision for and to define as between themselves their respective interests in the submarine areas of the Gulf of Paria,

"Have decided to conclude a treaty for that purpose and, to that end, have named as their Plenipotentiaries: ...

"Who, having communicated to each other their full powers, found in good and due form, have agreed as follows:

"Article 1.

"In this treaty the term 'submarine areas of the Gulf of Paria' denotes the sea-bed and sub-soil outside of the territorial waters of the High Contracting Parties to one of the other side of the lines A-B, B-Y and Y-X.

"Article 2.

"(1) His Majesty The King declares that he for his part will not assert any claim to sovereignty or control over those parts of the submarine areas of the Gulf of Paria which lie westerly of the line A-B, or southerly of the lines B-Y and Y-X respectively described in article 3 of the present treaty, and that he will recognize any rights of sovereignty or control which have been or may hereafter be lawfully acquired by the United States of Venezuela over the said parts of the submarine areas of the Gulf of Paria.

"(2) The President of the United States of Venezuela declares that he for his part will not assert any claim to sovereignty or control over those parts of the submarine areas of the Gulf of Paria which lie easterly of the line A-B or northerly of the lines B-Y and Y-X respectively, described in article 3 of the present treaty, and that he will recognize any rights of sovereignty or control which have been or may hereafter be lawfully acquired by His Majesty The King over the said parts of the submarine areas of the Gulf of Paria.

"Article 3.

"The lines A-B, B-Y and Y-X mentioned in the preceding article are drawn on the annexed map [not here reproduced] and are defined as follows:

"Line A-B runs from point A, which is the intersection of the central meridian of the island of Patos with the southern limit of the territorial waters of the island, the approximate co-ordinates of which are: latitude 10°35'04" N., longitude 61°51'53" W. From there the line runs straight to point B which is situated at the limit of the territorial waters of Venezuela at the point of their intersection with the meridian of 62°05'08" W., the approximate latitude of which is 10°02'24" N.

"Line B-Y runs from point B, already established, and follows the limits of the territorial waters of Venezuela to point Y, where the said limits intersect the parallel of 9°57'30" N., the approximate longitude of which is 61°56'40" W.

"Line Y-X runs from point Y, already established, and follows the said parallel of 9°57'30" N. to point X, situated on the meridian of 61°30'00" W.

"The longitude of the central meridian of the island of Patos to which this article refers shall be determined by taking the mathematical half of the most eastern and the most western longitudes of the said island.

"Should the straight lines A-B or Y-X described in this article intersect in their course the outside limit of the territorial waters of either of the two high contracting parties, the dividing line shall follow along the said limit until it reaches again the intersecting straight line in conformity with the stipulations in articles 1 and 5 of this treaty, which exclude the bed of the sea and the sub-soil of territorial waters.

"The co-ordinates of points A, B and Y which are here given approximately shall be determined with exactness by the Commission provided for in article 4 of this treaty.

"Article 4.

"(1) The high contracting parties shall, as soon as practicable after the coming into force of this treaty, appoint a mixed Commission to take all necessary steps to demarcate the lines A-B, B-Y and Y-X by means of buoys or other visible methods on the surface of the sea or on the land as the case may be. Any buoys or other means employed shall, however, conform in all respects to the provisions of article 6 of this treaty.

"(2) The manner in which this mixed Commission shall be constituted and the instructions to which it shall be subject for the fulfilment of its duties shall be laid down in a special protocol or by an exchange of notes.

"Article 5.

"This treaty refers solely to the submarine areas of the Gulf of Paria, and nothing herein shall be held to affect in any way the status of the islands, islets or rocks above the surface of the sea together with the territorial waters thereof.

"Article 6.

"Nothing in this treaty shall be held to affect in any way the status of the waters of the Gulf of Paria or any rights of passage or navigation on the surface of the seas outside the territorial waters of the contracting parties. In particular passage or navigation shall not be closed or be impeded by any works or installations which may be erected, which shall be of such a nature and shall be so constructed, placed, marked, buoyed and lighted, as not to constitute a danger or obstruction to shipping.

"Article 7.

"Each of the high contracting parties shall take all practical measures to prevent the exploitation of any submarine areas claimed or occupied by him in the Gulf from causing the pollution of the territorial waters of the other by oil, mud or any other fluid or substance liable to contaminate the navigable waters

271

or the foreshore and shall concert with the other to make the said measures as effective as possible.

"Article 8.

"Each of the high contracting parties shall cause to be inserted in any concession which may be granted for the exploitation of submarine areas in the Gulf of Paria stipulations for securing the effective observance of the two preceding articles, including a requirement for the use by the concessionaire of modern equipment, and shall cause the operation of any such concession to be supervised in order to ensure that the provisions of the present treaty are complied with.

"Article 9.

"All differences between the high contracting parties relating to the interpretation or execution of this treaty shall be settled by such peaceful means as are recognized in international law."